Business Valuation

An Integrated Theory
Second Edition

Z. CHRISTOPHER MERCER,
ASA, CFA
TRAVIS W. HARMS,
CPA/ABV, CFA

John Wiley & Sons, Inc.

For general information on our other products and services or for technical support, please contact our Customer Care Department within the United States at (800) 762-2974, outside the United States at (317) 572-3993 or fax (317) 572-4002.

Wiley also publishes its books in a variety of electronic formats. Some content that appears in print may not be available in electronic books.

For more information about Wiley products, visit our Web site at www.wiley.com.

Library of Congress Cataloging-in-Publication Data:

Mercer, Z. Christopher.
   Business valuation : an integrated theory / Z. Christopher Mercer,
Travis W. Harms,.–2nd ed.
     p. cm.
   Rev. ed. of: Valuing enterprise and shareholder cash flows. Memphis :
Peabody Pub., 2004.
    ISBN-13: 978-0-470-14816-7 (cloth)
  1. Business enterprises–Valuation. 2. Corporations–Valuation. I.
 Harms, Travis W. II. Mercer, Z. Christopher. Valuing enterprise and
shareholder cash flows. III. Title.
HG4028.V3M47 2008
658.15'5–dc22

                                           2007008850

Printed in the United States of America.

10 9 8 7 6 5 4 3 2 1

Contents

CHAPTER 4
Adjustments to Income Statements: Normalizing and Control Adjustments

CHAPTER 5
Fundamental Adjustments to Market Capitalization Rates

Introduction

Simply put, this book helps the reader understand the *why* of business valuation. Most business valuation texts deal with the *how* by focusing on an interesting amalgamation of seemingly unrelated financial concepts. These concepts appear as pieces of a puzzle. The reader implicitly knows that the pieces somehow relate to each other and should fit together; however, the puzzle seems impossible to put together, because there is no picture on the front of the box to guide you. This book is the picture on the front of the box because once the *why* of business valuation is understood, the *how* becomes much more straightforward and, instead of dealing with disjointed pieces, the completed puzzle emerges.

Business Valuation: An Integrated Theory assembles these various valuation concepts into a theoretically and practically consistent whole. The reader views financial concepts not as unrelated, but as part of a complete and clear picture of business valuation.

THE INTEGRATED THEORY OF BUSINESS VALUATION DEFINED

The Integrated Theory of Business Valuation is a theoretical discussion of financial and valuation concepts designed to explain the behavior of real-world market participants in the context of financial theory. We examine the broad range of observed behavior of real-world market participants in the context of the cash flows of business enterprises—and the derivative cash flows attributable to specific interests in those enterprises.

The Integrated Theory accomplishes a number of important objectives by:

- Presenting certain organizing principles of business valuation in the context of what we term the "GRAPES of Value" (Growth, Risk and Reward, Alternative Investments, Present Value, Expectations, and Sanity).
- Examining the relationships between the Gordon Dividend Discount (or Growth) Model, or the Gordon Model, and the discounted cash flow model of valuation.

- Defining the various "levels of value," ranging from strategic enterprise concepts to the level of nonmarketable, minority interests in those enterprises.
- Defining relevant valuation premiums and discounts (e.g., control premiums, minority interest discounts, and marketability discounts) in the context of financial and valuation theory.
- Placing business acquisition pricing decisions into practical and theoretical perspective.
- Accounting for all the cash flows from the enterprise level to the derivative cash flows of the shareholder level.

The Integrated Theory is grounded in the real world of market participants. The Integrated Theory is fully developed in Chapter 3 and elaborated upon in numerous other chapters. The Integrated Theory illustrates the normal behavior of the market participants buying and selling business enterprises and interests in them, whether in the public or private markets. Many aspects of less normal behavior can also be explained in the context of the Integrated Theory.

While grounded in the real world of market participants, it is logical to ask what the Integrated Theory says about fair market value because this is the standard under which a majority of appraisals are rendered. The hypothetical participants in the world of fair market value look at the real-world transactional data, including rational and irrational data points, in their determinations of price. But the definition of fair market value refines the behavior of hypothetical market participants (relative to real-world participants) in several specific ways by eliminating elements of compulsion found in the real world; eliminating knowledge disparities that may exist when real-world market participants engage in transactions; and equating the financial capacities of hypothetical buyers and sellers.

In addition, one of the most important insights of the Integrated Theory is the relationship between enterprise valuation concepts and the valuation of shareholder interests in enterprises. The value of enterprises is based on the expectation of future cash flows from the enterprise. The value of interests in enterprises, particularly minority interests, is based on the portion of expected enterprise cash flows attributable to those interests.

In other words, the valuation of minority interests of enterprises is a derivative process. It begins with the valuation of the enterprise, then follows (projects) the derivative cash flows to minority interests for the duration of the expected holding periods of the investments, and then discounts the derivative, shareholder cash flows to the present at a discount rate appropriate for the risk of the interests (in relationship to the risk of the enterprises).

THE INTEGRATED THEORY PROVIDES ANSWERS

A series of questions that have been the subject of debate in the business appraisal profession are presented at the beginning of each chapter. We have structured the content of each chapter to provide answers to these questions. Keep in mind that it will not be uncommon to see certain questions repeated in other chapters because naturally some of the information provided overlaps chapters. These questions will be answered using the Integrated Theory, which provides the framework within which we can address these seemingly unrelated topics.

WHO SHOULD READ THIS BOOK?

A variety of business, finance, business valuation, legal, and accounting professionals should read *Business Valuation: An Integrated Theory*.

Corporate Finance and M&A Professionals

Business Valuation: An Integrated Theory is designed to be helpful for corporate finance and M&A professionals in a variety of ways. We are targeting corporate finance and M&A professionals first in this introduction because most valuation books do not address their conceptual and practical needs to understand valuation.

- Chapter 1 on the discounted cash flow (DCF) model provides helpful perspective for users of the DCF method. The discussion of the interrelationships between the Gordon Model and the DCF method provides important perspective for finance practitioners.
- This book provides thoughtful assistance in principal areas of concern to all those in the corporate finance arena, including corporate finance staffs, CFOs, legal counsel, accountants, and boards of directors when examining acquisitions, investment projects, and joint ventures.
  - The analysis of the difference between the long-term growth rate used in DCF models to estimate terminal values and the earnings growth rates that are the focus of securities analysts will help avoid overvaluation of acquisitions. The discussion of the impact of expected growth on valuation should provide thoughtful guidance in this area.

- ○ The overall presentation of the Integrated Theory and the insights it provides regarding the appropriate discount rates for valuing acquisition subjects can also help in analyzing acquisitions.
- ○ The discussion of the "GRAPES of Value," or organizing principles of business valuation (Chapter 2).
- ○ Many joint ventures, partnerships, and subsidiaries of major corporations have buy-sell agreements or other repurchase or cross-purchase agreements where the valuation mechanism is set to be fair market value. An understanding of the meaning of fair market value is critical for all existing and future partnership and joint ventures.[1]
- ○ Importantly, the book provides a means of articulating valuation concepts for internal use and in negotiations with outside parties.

Business Appraisers

The Integrated Theory pulls the many seemingly unrelated financial concepts employed by business appraisers into a unified system. These multiple concepts call for a deeper understanding of their interrelationships. A few examples of the valuation concepts that will be "integrated" include:

- The discounted cash flow model
- The Gordon Model
- Levels of value concepts
  - ○ Marketable minority level of value
  - ○ Marketability discounts
  - ○ Nonmarketable minority level of value
  - ○ Financial control level of value
  - ○ Financial control premiums
  - ○ Minority interest discounts
  - ○ Strategic control level of value
  - ○ Strategic control premiums
- Normalizing adjustments to the income statement
- Controlling interest adjustments to the income statement available to financial buyers or strategic buyers of particular subject interests

---

[1]For a further discussion of buy-sell agreements from business and valuation perspectives, and the relationship of the Integrated Theory to buy-sell agreement pricing, see Z. Christopher Mercer, *Buy-Sell Agreements: Ticking Time Bomb or Reasonable Resolutions?* (Memphis, Peabody Publishing, L.P., 2007). See in particular Chapter 17, "Defining Element #2: The Level of Value," and the Addendum to Chapter 17, "The Levels of Value and the Integrated Theory of Business Valuation." Available at www.mercercapital.com or 1-800-769-0967.

- Discount rates—required rates of return
  - ○ Applicable to net income or net cash flow at the level of the enterprise?
  - ○ Differences at the enterprise and shareholder levels
  - ○ Models and key assumptions for development
- Capitalization rates and expected growth
- Control premium studies
- The so-called "prerogatives of control"
- Restricted stock and pre-IPO studies
- Fair market value
- Investment value
- Transactional databases
- Guideline public company information and fundamental adjustments
- S corporations vs. C corporations
- And so on. . . .

The Integrated Theory provides the foundation for a deeper understanding business valuation concepts. These insights will be helpful for beginning and experienced appraisers alike. In addition, the Integrated Theory raises (and answers) a number of questions about "standard" valuation practices employed by many appraisers, for example, the application of control premiums, minority interest discounts, and marketability discounts.

Auditors and Financial Statement Users Considering Fair Value Measurements

With the implementation of numerous accounting pronouncements mandating the measurement of more assets and liabilities at their fair values, it is becoming exceedingly important for CPAs charged with auditing financial statements to understand valuation concepts.

While the Integrated Theory does not attempt to define fair value in the context of recent accounting statements or regulations, it does provide assistance to CPAs and appraisers as they both attempt to translate interpretations of the concept from the FASB, the SEC, or elsewhere into reliable valuation techniques. In other words, the Integrated Theory allows any discussion of enterprise cash flows to be situated within a reasonable and consistent framework.

Users of Business Appraisal Reports

The Integrated Theory will also be helpful for users of appraisal reports, including accountants, financial planners, and attorneys. The basic concepts of the Integrated Theory are not difficult, and the limited use of symbolic math is fairly easy to follow (we hope!). Informed users of business appraisals (and related products and services) are best able to benefit reading (and paying for) them. We have advised clients for many years: "If you don't understand it, then don't stand for it." Reading the Integrated Theory, particularly on a specific-topic basis when questions arise, can help readers develop a better understanding of business appraisal reports.

The Integrated Theory of Business Valuation takes the seemingly disjointed pieces of the business valuation puzzle and assembles them together for the first time in a complete picture.

THE QUANTITATIVE MARKETABILITY DISCOUNT MODEL

We describe the Quantitative Marketability Discount Model (the QMDM), a shareholder level discounted cashflow model, in detail in Chapters 7 (Introduction to the QMDM), 8 (The QMDM Assumptions in Detail), and 9 (Applying the QMDM). The *QMDM Companion*, or the model itself, is referenced in Chapter 8. To obtain a copy of the *QMDM Companion*, visit Mercer Capital's Web site at www.mercercapital.com or ValuSource's Web site at www.valusourcesoftware.com/qmdm.

Discounted Cash Flow and the Gordon Model: *The Very Basics of Value*

INTRODUCTION

We begin by focusing on "The Very Basics of Value." This subtitle is intentional because our purpose here is to explore the foundation of both the discounted cash flow model and the Gordon Model to enhance our understanding of these basic tools of valuation and finance. As will be shown, the discounted cash flow model and the Gordon Model can be used to develop the Integrated Theory of Business Valuation.

COMMON QUESTIONS

In order to move the reader from theory to practice, we begin each chapter with a series of often vexing questions. We have structured the content of each chapter to provide answers to these questions. Keep in mind that it will not be uncommon to see certain questions repeated in other chapters.

- What are the necessary conditions for use of the Gordon Model?
- Where does the generalized valuation model, Value = Earnings × Multiple, come from?
- What are the conditions that define g, the long-term growth rate of core earnings used in the Gordon Model?
- What is the relationship between the net income and the net cash flow of business enterprises?
- When applying the DCF method, is the appropriate measure of benefits for discounting net income or net cash flow?
- What is the difference between the expected growth rate in the core *earnings* of a business and its expected growth rate in *value*?

- Are the DCF and single-period income capitalization methods intrinsically different?
- How fast can the earnings of an enterprise reasonably be expected to grow?
- When capitalizing net income rather than net cash flow, should adjustment factors to r, the discount rate, be applied?

Keep these questions in mind as we begin with a discussion of the discounted cash flow model.

THE BASIC TOOLS OF VALUATION

The Discounted Cash Flow Model

The value of a business enterprise can be described as:

- The value today (i.e., in *cash-equivalent terms*)
- of all expected future cash flows (or benefits) of the business
- forecasted or estimated over an indefinite time period (i.e., *into perpetuity*)
- that have been *discounted to the present* (expressed in terms of *present value* dollars) at an appropriate *discount rate* (which takes into consideration the riskiness of the projected cash flows of the business relative to alternative investments).

The valuation and finance literature consistently confirm this conceptual definition of the value of a business enterprise. In order to value a business, therefore, we need the following:

- A forecast of all expected future cash flows or benefits to be derived from ownership of the business; and,
- An appropriate discount rate with which to discount the cash flows to the present.

This conceptual definition of business value can be defined symbolically in Equation 1.1:

$$\text{Value} = V_0 = \left(\frac{CF_1}{(1+r)^1} + \frac{CF_2}{(1+r)^2} + \frac{CF_3}{(1+r)^3} + \frac{CF_4}{(1+r)^4} + \cdots + \frac{CF_n}{(1+r)^n} \right)$$

$$(1.1)$$

Where:

V_0 is the value of the equity of a business today.

CF_1 to CF_n represent the expected cash flows (or benefits) to be derived for periods 1 to n.[1]

r is the discount rate that converts future dollars of CF into present dollars of value.

Equation 1.1 is the basic discounted cash flow (DCF) model. To employ the model in this form, however, the analyst must make a forecast of *all* the relevant cash flows into the indefinite future. For clarity, the cash flows or earnings discussed in this chapter are the net earnings and net cash flows of the enterprise or the business as a whole. V_0 is the value of the equity of the enterprise, or the present value of the expected cash flows to the owners of the equity of the enterprise.[2] Expanding the analysis to correspond to the total capital (equity plus debt) of an enterprise is beyond the scope of this chapter.

The Gordon Model

In his 1962 finance text, Myron J. Gordon showed that under the appropriate assumptions, Equation 1.1 is equivalent to the simplified equation represented by Equation 1.2:[3]

$$V_0 = \frac{CF_1}{r - g} \qquad (1.2)$$

The Gordon Model initially dealt with dividends, hence it has been called the Gordon Dividend Model, or the Gordon Growth Model.[4]

---

[1]The discounted cash flow model is based on time periods of equal length. Because forecasts are often made on an annual basis in practice, we use the terms "periods" and "years" almost interchangeably for purposes of this theoretical discussion.

[2]For purposes of this book, we are discussing enterprises where there is little risk of imminent bankruptcy.

[3]Myron J. Gordon, *The Investment, Financing, and Valuation of the Corporation* (Homewood, IL: Richard D. Irwin, 1962).

[4]Equation 1.2 has become so generalized that it reflects what can be called the generalized valuation model. In practice, CF_1 often represents the estimate of earnings for the next period so we can generalize and refer to the cash flow measure as *Earnings*. The expression $(r - g)$ is known as the capitalization rate (see "Glossary," *ASA Business Valuation Standards* [Washington, DC: American Society of Appraisers, 2005], p. 21). And the expression $(1 / (r - g))$ is a multiple of earnings. So the Gordon Model is consistent with the general valuation model:

$$\boxed{\text{Value} = \text{Earnings} \times \text{Multiple}}$$

For Equations 1.1 and 1.2 to be equivalent, the following conditions must hold:

- CF_1 is the measure of *expected cash flow* for the next period (sometimes derived as $(CF_0 x\ 1 + g)$ or otherwise derived specifically).
- Cash flows must grow at the constant rate of g into perpetuity.
- All cash flows must be: 1) distributed to owners; or, 2) reinvested in the enterprise at the discount rate, r.
- The discount rate, r, must be the appropriate discount rate for the selected measure of cash flow, CF.[5]

By comparing Equations 1.1 and 1.2, we see two ways to estimate the value of an enterprise. Equation 1.3 restates Equation 1.1 to reflect constant growth and relates it to Equation 1.2.

- The left portion of Equation 1.3 illustrates a forecast of cash flows growing at a constant rate into perpetuity, discounted to the present.
- With appropriate algebraic manipulation, the left portion of Equation 1.3 reduces to the Gordon Model.

$$V_0 = \left(\frac{CF_0(1+g)}{(1+r)^1} + \frac{CF_0(1+g)^2}{(1+r)^2} + \cdots + \frac{CF_0(1+g)^n}{(1+r)^n} \right) = \frac{CF_1}{r-g}$$

$$(1.3)$$

Two-Stage DCF Model

Recall the conditions that must hold for Equations 1.1 and 1.2 to be equivalent expressions. In practice, these conditions may limit the strict application of either expression.

- Application of Equation 1.1 requires a discrete forecast to time period n, or effectively into perpetuity. Few forecasts extend reliably beyond five or ten years in practice.

These factors are so familiar that appraisers sometimes forget their source. Earnings in the generalized valuation model must be clearly defined and the "multiple" must be appropriate for the defined measure of earnings. These comments could be based on common sense, and they are. However, as will be shown, they are also theoretically sound.

[5] In the real world, businesses make reinvestments and accept the returns of these investments, some of which will exceed r and some of which may be less than r. This model assumes that all reinvestments will achieve a return of r.

- Application of Equation 1.2 requires that the estimate of next year's cash flow grow into perpetuity at a constant rate of *g*. This condition may not be consistent with an analyst's expectations regarding near-term cash flow growth, which may be significantly different from longer-term expectations for growth.

In practice, these two limitations are overcome by use of a "two-stage" DCF model that combines elements of Equations 1.1 and 1.2. The two-stage DCF model is presented in Equation 1.4, and consists of the following two sets of forecast cash flows:

- *Interim Cash Flows (for finite period ending in Year f).* While accurate predictions regarding the future are certainly elusive, diligent analysts can often prepare reasonable forecasts of near-term financial results for many businesses. The left side of Equation 1.4 depicts the Present Value of Interim Cash Flows (PVICF).
- *Terminal Value (all remaining cash flows after Year f).* Following the discrete forecast period, the two-stage DCF model reverts to the Gordon Model, as the accuracy of the analyst's discrete financial forecast wanes, and violation of the constant-growth condition becomes less significant. When discounted to the present from the end of Year *f*, the Present Value of the Terminal Value (PVTV) is obtained.

$$V_0 = \left(\frac{CF_1}{(1+r)^1} + \frac{CF_2}{(1+r)^2} + \frac{CF_3}{(1+r)^3} + \cdots + \frac{CF_f}{(1+r)^f}\right) + \left(\frac{CF_{f+1}/(r-g)}{(1+r)^f}\right)$$

Present Value of Interim Cash Flows (PVICF) Using this portion of the basic DCF model, the analyst is not constrained by the requirement of constantly growing cash flows during the finite forecast period ending with Year *f*. This part of the equation is the present value of interim cash flows through the finite forecast period ending with Year *f*, or PVICF.

Present Value of the Terminal Value (PVTV) Using the Gordon Model, all cash flows are capitalized after Year *f*, assuming cash flows are growing from that point at the constant rate of g. This portion of the equation therefore represents the present value of $CF_{f+1} = CF_f \times (1+g)$.

(1.4)

Appraisers using the two-stage DCF model typically employ discrete forecast periods ranging from about three to ten years or so, followed by application of the Gordon Model as shown in Equation 1.4.[6]

---

[6]Alternatively, in practice, many appraisers and market participants use a market-based method that applies current market multiples to the forecasted cash

We can use the two-stage DCF model to illustrate the equivalency between the DCF method and the Gordon Model under the conditions previously specified. In this case, the "proof" of equivalency will be practical rather than algebraic.

Practical Proof: DCF = Gordon Model

Consider a business enterprise that is expected to generate earnings of $1.0 million next year, followed by growth of 10% per year into the indefinite future.[7] Further, assume that the appropriate discount rate is 20%. Given these assumptions, we can value the enterprise using the Gordon Model (Equation 1.2). We can also value the enterprise using the DCF methodology from Equation 1.4.

Exhibit 1.1 depicts the Gordon Model valuation.

The indicated value for the enterprise using the Gordon Model is $10.0 million. The capitalization rate, $(r - g)$, is 10% (20% – 10%), and the multiple of cash flow is 10.0x (1/10%). Recall the conditions for use of the Gordon Model: *Cash flows are growing at the constant rate of g, and all cash flows are either distributed or reinvested in the enterprise at the discount rate, r.* An additional condition is that the cash flows are distributed (or reinvested) at the end of each year of the forecast. This will be clear in the DCF method shown next.

EXHIBIT 1.1   Application of the Gordon Model

Gordon Model Value Indication	
Next Year's Expected Cash Flow (CF$_1$) ($000's)	**$1,000**
Constant Growth Rate of CF (g)	**10.0%**
Discount Rate *(r)*	**20.0%**
Capitalization Rate $(r - g)$	**10.0%**
Multiple of CF (1 / $(r - g)$)	**10.0x**
Value of Enterprise	**$10,000**

flow for Year *f* or Year *f*-plus-1. This alternative practice, if employed with reasonable multiples from the public marketplace, should not be considered unusual or incorrect. For a further discussion on this point, see "Practical Observations" at the conclusion of this chapter.

[7] In the "Practical Observations" section at the end of this chapter, we suggest that a long-term *g* of 10% may be on the high side for many discounted cash flow applications. For purposes of this example we ask the reader's indulgence. A 10% growth rate is convenient for calculations and therefore facilitates this discussion.

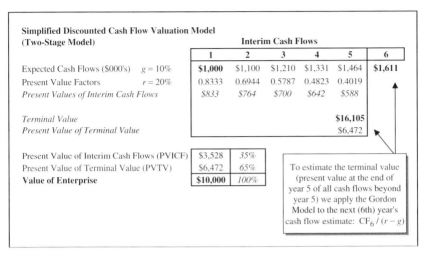

EXHIBIT 1.2   Application of Two-Stage DCF Model

We can now develop a parallel valuation using the DCF methodology. In doing so, we employ Equation 1.4 in Exhibit 1.2. First, we calculate the present value of cash flows for the finite period (PVICF). At the end of the finite forecast period, we use the Gordon Model to derive the value of all remaining cash flows (from year 6 into perpetuity). We discount this Terminal Value to the present at the discount rate, r, to derive the Present Value of the Terminal Value (PVTV). Recall that in this example, it is assumed that cash flows are growing at the constant rate of g, or 10%, during the finite forecast period as well as in the perpetuity calculation.

The DCF valuation conclusion is $10.0 million, or precisely the same as the conclusion of the Gordon Model in Exhibit 1.1. In this example, the conditions for use of the Gordon Model are consistent with the explicit assumptions of the DCF model. Value is the sum of the present values of the five interim cash flows ($3.5 million), and the terminal value ($6.5 million). Note the following about this example:

- We assume receipt of each of the interim cash flows by the owners of the enterprise.
- The Present Value of Interim Cash Flows (PVICF) represents $3.5 million, or 35%, of the concluded value of $10 million.
- The Present Value of the Terminal Value (PVTV) represents $6.5 million, or 65% of the total value. This analysis should alert readers to the importance of the terminal value estimation in DCF valuations. For example, with 10% compound growth in cash flow for five years, the

terminal value accounts for almost two-thirds of the total value. If cash flow growth were faster or there were losses during the finite forecast period, the influence of the terminal value on the conclusion would be amplified.

■ The starting point for the model is the valuation date (denoted as year 0, or the day prior to the start of year 1). The cash flows are received at the end of each year of the forecast, such that the present value factors for years 1 and 2 are calculated as follows:

Year 1: $(1/(1 + 20\%)^1 = 0.8333$
Year 2: $(1/(1 + 20\%)^2 = 0.6944$

These calculations illustrate discounting in Exhibit 1.2 for the whole periods, i.e., one full year, two full years, and so on. Assessing the merit of this assumption is beyond "the very basics of value."[8] The purpose at this point is simply to focus on the assumptions of the model.

DIVIDENDS, REINVESTMENT, & GROWTH

Owners of the example enterprise expect to receive a total return equal to the discount rate of 20%. How does this happen? There are two components of the expected return: the current return from expected distributions and the expected growth in the value of the enterprise. The first is the expected return from interim cash flows, which can be described as the yield on current value. For the first period in Exhibit 1.2, cash flow is $1.0 million, which reflects a 10% yield on the current value of $10.0 million. We can also calculate the expected value at the end of each period and see that the yield on current value for each subsequent year is also 10%.[9]

The expected growth rate in value is also 10%, as can be confirmed by the growth of value from $10.0 million today to $16.1 million at the end of

---

[8]Sensitivity to changes in assumptions is a fact of life in valuation. For example, changing the assumption to reflect receipt of cash flows at mid-year into perpetuity would raise value in this example from $10 million to $10.95 million, or increase it by 9.5%. The sensitivity of the Gordon Model and the DCF model to changes in assumptions is beyond the scope of this chapter.

[9]For example, projected value at the end of year 2 is equal to $12.1 million (year 3 cash flow of $1,210 capitalized by $r - g$ of 10%). Expected cash flow for Year 3 divided by value at the end of year 2 is 10% ($1.210 million / $12.1 million). Under the assumptions of Exhibit 1.2, this expected current return, or current yield, will be 10% for every year.

Year 5 (($10.0 \times (1 + 10\%)^5) = \$16.1$). Therefore, the total expected return for the owners of the enterprise in Exhibit 1.2 is 20%, or the discount rate. This is comprised of the yield on current value of 10%, plus the expected growth in value of 10%. The total return of 20% is achieved with full distribution of all interim cash flows.

Intuitive Impact of Reinvesting Cash Flows

Each period, the owners of a business make one of three decisions:

- Distribute (through dividend or share repurchase) all cash flows; or,
- Retain all cash flows in the business for reinvestment; or,
- Distribute a portion of the cash flows and retain the remainder for reinvestment.

Intuitively, the value of a business whose cash flows are reinvested should grow more rapidly than an otherwise similar but fully distributing business. This makes sense because retained cash flows increase the asset base on which the company generates a return. Said another way, the business that retains a greater portion of its earnings can experience more rapid growth in expected future earnings (upon which expected future value is based).[10]

Reinvestment and the Gordon Model

As presented in Equation 1.2, the Gordon Model calculates the present value of a cash flow stream growing at a constant rate into perpetuity. The g in Equation 1.2 reflects the expected growth rate in the cash flows (or earnings) of the enterprise. Assuming equality of cash flow and earnings, Equation 1.2 can be rewritten in generalized form as Equation 1.5 to show this relationship specifically:

$$V_0 = \frac{\text{Earnings}}{r - g_e} \tag{1.5}$$

In this case, g_e is the expected constant growth rate in earnings (consistent with the distribution of all earnings to shareholders).

---

[10]However, retention of earnings does not necessarily imply optimal returns to shareholders. This will become clear when we focus on the importance of the expected reinvestment rate for nondistributing or partially distributing enterprises.

We stated earlier that the Gordon Model expresses the value of a security today as the present value of its expected dividends growing at a constant rate into perpetuity (g_d).

$$P_0 = \frac{D_1}{r - g_d} \qquad (1.6)$$

Where:

P_0 is the expected price of the security

D_1 is the expected dividend for the security at the end of period 1

g_d is the expected growth rate of the dividend, D_1

D_1 represents the portion of earnings to be distributed. To relate Equations 1.5 and 1.6, we can express D_1 as follows:

D_1 = Earnings × DPO

DPO = Dividend Payout Ratio ((dividends as a percentage of earnings))

Equation 1.6 can be rewritten as Equation 1.7:

$$P_0 = \frac{\text{Earnings} * \text{DPO}}{r - g_d} \qquad (1.7)$$

If all earnings are distributed (DPO = 100%), Equation 1.7 is equal to Equation 1.6, and the expected growth rate of the dividend (g_d) is equal to the expected growth rate of earnings (g_e). Further, if we hold constant the discount rate (r), the price of the security (P_0), and the expected earnings, the expected growth rate in the dividend (g_d) must vary inversely with the dividend payout ratio.[11]

In Exhibit 1.3, the expected growth in dividends (g_d) is shown to equal the expected growth in the value of the enterprise, which we denote as g_v.

EXHIBIT 1.3 Relationship between Growth in Value and Dividends

$$\frac{D_1}{r - g_d} \times (1 + g_v) = \frac{D_2}{r - g_d}$$

$$1 + g_v = \frac{D_2}{r - g_d} \times \frac{r - g_d}{D_1}$$

$$1 + g_v = D_2 / D_1 = 1 + g_d$$

$$g_v = g_d$$

---

[11]This insight is not particularly new; however, its implications for business valuation are not yet generally recognized. We will explore these implications in the remainder of this chapter.

Substituting g_v for g_d in Equation 1.6 yields the following:

$$P_0 = \frac{D_1}{r - g_v}$$

$$(1.8)$$

$$g_v = r - D_1/P_0$$

In other words, the expected growth in value is equal to the discount rate less the expected dividend yield (Equation 1.8). If the dividend payout percentage is 100%, the expected growth in value is equal to the discount rate less the earnings yield. If the dividend payout percentage is 0% (and all earnings are retained), the expected growth in value is equal to the discount rate. This analysis confirms the intuitive logic that reinvestment accelerates the expected growth in value over the base level of earnings growth without reinvestment. With reinvestment at r, the expected g_v increases to offset the diminution in dividend yield such that the expected reinvestment at r will generate the required return of r for the enterprise.

The Core Business vs. Reinvestment Decisions

We have demonstrated that, under the conditions of the Gordon Model, the value of a business enterprise is unaffected by the level of reinvestment, although the level of reinvestment does affect the components—dividend yield and capital appreciation—of total return.

In order to understand the effect of reinvestment decisions, it is helpful to think conceptually (and somewhat artificially in terms of the way we look at businesses) of all business enterprises as having two components—a core business and a series of incremental investments:

- *The core business.* The core business is the existing enterprise. The core level of earnings is normally expected to grow at a rate consistent with the company's market position and management capabilities (in the context of the relevant economy). When business appraisers discuss the expected (long-term) growth rate of earnings, they should be referring to the growth of this core level of earnings, or g_e.

  What is the expected growth in core earnings? This very important concept needs explanation. We define g_e as the level of (constant) long-term growth available to a business assuming that all the net earnings of the business are distributed (i.e., DPO = 100%). This assumption has several important implications, including:
  - Inflationary price increases are achieved (to the extent reasonably available over time).
  - Productivity enhancements are also captured (to the extent reasonably available over time).

⊃ Positive net present value capital investments may be available.[12] In other words, the core business operates under the constraint of no earnings retention.[13] Under this constraint, value can be estimated using Equation 1.7 as follows:

$$V_0 = \frac{E_1 \times \text{DPO}}{r - g_d} = \frac{E_1 \times 100\%}{r - g_d} = \frac{\text{Earnings}}{r - g_d} \qquad (1.9)$$

The long-term level of expected core earnings growth for private companies will seldom exceed 10%. In fact, the *long-term* level of expected core earnings growth for larger public companies seldom exceeds 10%, in spite of the fact that earnings for the next one, three, or five years might be expected to grow at rates of 15%, 25%, or more.[14]

- *Incremental investments.* Healthy business enterprises are earnings (cash flow) machines. They are designed to engage in economic activities and to generate earnings and cash flow. When earnings are retained in a business, such earnings should be viewed as being *reinvested* in the business. Over time, the bulk of all value growth in a business tends to result from reinvestment decisions, rather than to the growth in core earnings.

While the distinction between the core business and incremental investments, or the cumulative impact of reinvestment decisions, may seem artificial, it is essential to understanding the nature of value creation. The DCF model can be used to examine both the core business and reinvestment decisions to facilitate this understanding. To do so, we will now focus on *future values*, rather than the *present values* that are the result of the DCF model as presented in Exhibit 1.2. This inversion does not pose any conceptual problems. After all, without the expectation of future value, there is no present value. We use the same valuation example as that in Exhibit 1.2.

---

[12]The prospect for positive NPV capital investment (i.e., that which earns a return in excess of r) frees companies from the straitjacket imposed by some analysts suggesting that g_e can never exceed the level of inflation. Such an artificial constraint ignores expectations for future value creation and is inconsistent with observed capitalization ratios in the public and guideline transaction markets.

[13]Note that, in the short term, the conditions of no earnings retention can also be satisfied if "excess" capital expenditures and working capital investments are funded with borrowings. The long-term ramifications of such a decision are beyond the scope of this chapter.

[14]Bear in mind that typical public company EPS growth estimates of 10%–20% almost always include the effect of substantial near term reinvestment of earnings.

		Today	1	2	3	4	5	6
Enterprise Discount Rate	20%				**Future Cash Flows and Values**			
Expected Growth in Earnings (G_e)	10%							
Expected Growth in Value (G_v) of Enterprise		$10,000	$11,000	$12,100	$13,310	$14,641	**$16,105**	
Projected Cash Flows (Core Earnings = G_e)		$909	$1,000	$1,100	$1,210	$1,331	$1,464	*$1,611*
Earnings on Reinvested Cash Flows @ R	20%			$200	$460	$794	$1,219	*$1,756*
Accumulated Reinvested Cash Flows			$1,000	$2,300	$3,970	$6,095	**$8,778**	
Present Value of Reinvested Cash Flows	35.3%	$3,528						
Present Value of Terminal Value	64.7%	$6,472					**$16,105**	
Value Indication Today	100.0%	$10,000						
							FV	% of FV
Expected Future Value of Core Business			$11,000	$12,100	$13,310	$14,641	$16,105	64.7%
Expected Future Value of Reinvestments			$1,000	$2,300	$3,970	$6,095	$8,778	35.3%
			$12,000	$14,400	$17,280	$20,736	$24,883	100.0%
Expected Appreciation in Value			10.0%	10.0%	10.0%	10.0%	10.0%	
Earnings "Yield"			10.0%	10.0%	10.0%	10.0%	10.0%	
Total Expected Return (by Year)			20.0%	20.0%	20.0%	20.0%	20.0%	

EXHIBIT 1.4 Illustration of Core Business and Cumulative Reinvestments

Exhibit 1.4 adapts the DCF model of Exhibit 1.2 to focus on expected future values, consistent with the two components of the enterprise. Note the primary difference between Exhibit 1.4 and Exhibit 1.2. In Exhibit 1.2, all cash flows were *distributed* and investors achieved a return equal to the discount rate. In Exhibit 1.4, the cash flows are *reinvested* in the business at the discount rate of 20%. The future value of the core business is determined as of the end of each year, given the next year's cash flow expectations, the discount rate of 20%, and expected growth rate in (core) earnings of 10%, or g_e.

Several observations about the future value analysis of Exhibit 1.4 help our understanding of the value creation process:

- The expected future value of the core business is $16.1 million, which is identical to the terminal value calculation in the DCF model in Exhibit 1.2. The terminal value comprises 65% of expected future value, just as the present value of the terminal value provided 65% of present value.
- The expected future value of cumulative reinvestments of cash flow is $8.8 million, or 35% of expected future value at the end of five years. The present value of the expected future value of reinvestments is the present value of expected interim cash flows, or $3.5 million (from Exhibit 1.2).
- All reinvestments are assumed to provide a return equal to the discount rate of 20%. If this assumption is violated, the present value of the cash flows to be received by the shareholders will differ from the value of the business enterprise calculated using the Gordon Model. For example, if this company could grow core earnings at 10% and reinvested all cash flows at a net rate of 5% in cash and liquid securities for the first five years, rather than 20%, the present value of the expected cash

flows would fall to $9.2 million from $10 million. This result holds true even if the terminal value is calculated based on the assumption that reinvestments after the terminal year earn the discount rate. We will investigate the impact of this issue on the value of enterprises and minority interests in those enterprises in later chapters.

- The expected return from an investment in this company is 20% per year over the five-year forecast period. The expected return has two sources, the expected growth in value of the core business (10% per year based on g_e) and the incremental capital appreciation attributable to reinvestment, which is equivalent to 10% in this case (or r of 20% minus g_e of 10%). Note in Exhibit 1.4 that the forecasted cash flows for Year 6 are $1.611 million and that the earnings on reinvested cash flows are $1.756 million.

In Chart 1.1, we can see the increasing importance of reinvestment in terms of expected future value for a ten-year forecast. Chart 1.1 continues to use the base example valuation but carries the discrete forecast period to ten years:

Chart 1.1 illustrates the magic of compound interest in the form of expected future values of a business. The expected growth in value of the core business, the bottom area of the chart, is based on the expected growth of core earnings, or 10%. As a result, this base value grows from $10 million

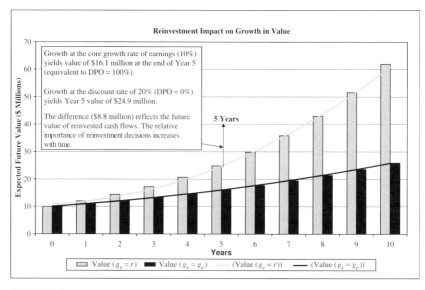

CHART 1.1 Reinvestment Impact on Growth in Value

today to $16.1 million in five years. The compounding effect of reinvestment decisions is shown in the upper area of the chart. The upper boundary of the chart provides the cumulative effect of the growth of the core business and reinvestment decisions. Expected future value grows to $24.9 million after five years, aided by $8.8 million of future value of reinvested cash flows. The relative importance of reinvestment decisions is magnified with the passage of time, as can be seen as the forecast is extended to ten years in Chart 1.1.

It should be clear from the preceding discussion that the expected growth rate of core earnings is one driver in the determination of expected future value (and therefore, present value). In the present case, g_e is 10%. If all reinvested earnings are invested to yield r, the discount rate of 20%, then the total realized return in the example is 20%. The cumulative impact of reinvestment of cash flows raises the total return from 10% (based on g_e) to 20%, or r.[15]

The (present) value of the business in the example is $10 million. The (future) value of the business at the end of five years will be $24.9 million, which is the sum of the value of the core business growing at g_e and the accumulated value of all reinvestments, which have been made at r. Accordingly, the expected growth in value (g_v) is equal to r, the discount rate of 20%.

At this point, it should be clear that g_e and g_v are different concepts. The inherent growth potential of the core business (g_e) is unaffected by the level of reinvestment.[16] The impact of reinvestment decisions is, however, manifest in the expected growth in value. Exhibit 1.5 summarizes the relationship between g_e, g_v, and the dividend payout ratio.

EXHIBIT 1.5   Range of Potential Reinvestment Decisions

No cash flows are retained DPO = 100% $g_v = g_e$ No reinvestment

All cash flows are retained DPO = 0% $g_v = r$ All earning reinvested at r

---

[15] Of course, the same return would be earned by shareholders if all earnings were distributed to them and the business did not grow beyond its core earnings.

[16] The potential for positive NPV projects does suggest, however, that g_e can be affected by the quality of available investments.

In other words, g_v will equal or exceed g_e and be less than or equal to r, depending upon the expectations regarding the dividend payout ratio.

Two important observations have been made thus far:

- The Gordon Model is equivalent to a discounted cash flow model with certain restrictive conditions, namely, (a) earnings grow at a constant rate into perpetuity and (b) all earnings are either distributed to shareholders or reinvested by the company at the discount rate.

- The expected growth in core earnings of an enterprise (g_e from Equation 1.5) is a distinct concept from the expected growth in value of an enterprise, or g_v. The expected growth in core earnings is a function of the markets in which a company operates, the quality of its management, the strength of the economy, inflation, long-term productivity enhancements, and other variables. The expected growth in value is a function of the expected dividend and reinvestment policy of the enterprise and the risk of the enterprise (as manifest in the required return), in addition to the expected growth in core earnings.

We can view the Gordon Model as a summary formulation for the valuation of public and private securities. It is a shorthand way of expressing key relationships between expected earnings (or cash flow), expected growth of those earnings, and risk. Reinvested earnings, if successfully deployed at the discount rate, accelerate the growth in value, g_v, toward the discount rate, r. If all earnings are retained, and successfully reinvested at the discount rate, then the expected growth rate in value will equal the discount rate.

Core Earnings Growth (g_e) vs. Analysts' Expected Earnings Growth (g^*)

In this section, we focus specifically on the relationship between expected growth in core earnings and the expected growth in reported earnings in the public securities markets that we call *analysts' g*, or g^*.

The Gordon Model calculates the present value of a growing perpetuity. In other words, it is a mathematical relationship akin to the formula for determining the present value of an annuity. In the context of a publicly traded stock, we can specify the Gordon Model as follows:

$$P_0 = \frac{D_1}{r - g_d} \tag{1.10}$$

The price of a publicly traded stock today reflects the present value of all expected future dividends. Ignoring for a moment the possibility of share repurchases by the company, the receipt of dividends represents the only return to shareholders from ownership of the stock—other than a sale of stock in the public market, where all expected future dividends are continuously capitalized in the market price. We derive the price/earnings multiple by dividing both sides of the equation by earnings for the coming year (E_1).

$$P_0/E_1 = \frac{D_1/E_1}{r - g_d} \tag{1.11}$$

Recognize that the expression (D_1/E_1) is the dividend payout ratio, or DPO.

$$P_0/E_1 = \frac{\text{DPO}}{r - g_d} \tag{1.12}$$

Now, assume that DPO equals 100%. Therefore, the *P/E* of Equation 1.12 is ($1/(r - g)$). This should clarify that valuation analysts, who typically derive earnings multiples as ($1/(r - g)$), are making an implied assumption that all earnings of the company will be distributed, i.e., that the DPO = 100%.

We know it is a rare public company that distributes all of its earnings to shareholders. Therefore, it is important to understand the relationship between the expected earnings growth rates discussed by public securities analysts, the dividend payout ratios of public companies, and the expected earnings growth rates that analysts apply in the derivation of valuation multiples for closely held companies.

Assume the hypothetical company described in Exhibit 1.1 is publicly traded. As shown in Exhibit 1.1, an earnings multiple of 10.0x is appropriate, given the discount rate and core earnings growth assumptions. Assume further that the consensus estimate of analysts is that the company's reported earnings will grow at an annual rate of 17.5%. Does this imply that the company is undervalued with an earnings multiple of 10.0x? Not necessarily.

Why? Assume the company is expected to distribute approximately 25% of earnings as dividends. As shown in Exhibit 1.3, the retention (and subsequent reinvestment) of earnings fuels incremental earnings growth beyond that of the core earnings stream. The public securities analyst is concerned with growth in reported earnings, which includes both core earnings and those attributable to prior reinvestment. According to the dividend discount model described in Equations 1.10 through 1.12, the estimated 17.5% growth in reported earnings is consistent with the earnings multiple of 10.0x and the dividend payout ratio of 25%. Note that the g_d in Equation 1.12 is g^*, or 17.5%. In Exhibit 1.6, these values are substituted into Equation 1.12.

EXHIBIT 1.6 Illustration of the Price/Earnings Ratio

$$10.0 = \frac{25\%}{20\% - 17.5\%}$$

EXHIBIT 1.7 Overstatement of the Price/Earnings Ratio

$$40.0 = \frac{1}{20\% - 17.5\%}$$

Note that if there is a constant DPO, then $g_d = g^*$. If the valuation analyst had relied upon the $(1/(r - g))$ framework for determining the earnings multiple, consideration of the growth in reported earnings rather than core earnings would result in a price/earnings multiple of 40.0x and a material overvaluation of the company (Exhibit 1.7).

We can see then that an important and predictable relationship exists among the growth in core earnings, the dividend payout ratio, and the expected growth in reported earnings. This analysis assumes a constant dividend payout ratio (or its complement, a constant earnings retention ratio), so the growth in reported earnings will be equal to the growth rate of the dividend.

We can now work with the Gordon Model equation to develop the following relationship between the expected growth rate of core earnings and the expected growth rate in dividends, or assuming a constant payout ratio, earnings in the series of equations labeled Equation 1.13.

$$P_0 = \frac{D_1}{r - g_d} = \frac{E_1}{r - g_e}$$

$$D_1(r - g_e) = E_1(r - g_d)$$

$$g_d = \frac{E_1 - D_1}{E_1} + \frac{D_1}{E_1}(g_e)$$

$$g_d = RR \times (r) + DPO \times (g_e) \tag{1.13}$$

The derived relationship is intuitively appealing. RR signifies the earnings retention rate. Reinvested earnings contribute to growth at the discount rate. The portion distributed contributes only the core earnings growth rate. The overall reported earnings growth rate is the weighted average of the two components.

The table in Exhibit 1.8 illustrates these relationships.

EXHIBIT 1.8   Relationship between Reinvestment and Reported Earnings Growth

(A)	(B)	(C)	(D)	(E)	(F)	(G)
					(D−E)	(C+F)
				g_e		g^*
				Core		Reported
Retention	Discount		Payout	Earnings		Earnings
Ratio	Rate	Product	Ratio	Growth	Product	Growth
0%	20%	0%	100%	10%	10%	10%
20%	20%	4%	80%	10%	8%	12%
40%	20%	8%	60%	10%	6%	14%
60%	20%	12%	40%	10%	4%	16%
80%	20%	16%	20%	10%	2%	18%
100%	20%	20%	0%	10%	0%	20%

As Exhibit 1.8 illustrates, the expected growth in core earnings (g_e) is equal to that of reported earnings (g^*) only when the dividend payout ratio is 100%, or when there are no expected earnings from reinvested cash flows. Exhibit 1.8 also indicates that, for a given level of core earnings growth, reported earnings growth is inversely related to the dividend payout ratio.

We have seen that the growth in reported earnings estimated by public securities analysts is conceptually distinct from the core earnings growth rate. As our example has illustrated, failure to understand the relationship between these growth rates can result in significant overvaluation of a business. Put more simply, investors do not pay for earnings both as they are created (core earnings) and as the earnings subsequently generate returns after being reinvested by the company (earnings on reinvestment). Investors will only pay for a given dollar of earnings once. If an analyst relies on an estimate of growth in reported earnings, the valuation analysis should be based on cash flows actually received by the investor (a dividend discount model, rather than a single-period income capitalization model based on earnings).[17]

NET INCOME VS. NET CASH FLOW

In the preceding section, we made what might appear to be an artificial distinction between the core growth in core earnings and the growth in

---

[17]If a single-period income capitalization model is used, it should be appropriately adjusted for the dividend payout ratio (which would be complicated if the DPO is not expected to be constant over time).

reported earnings. However, the distinction is critical to properly using the Gordon Model and the discounted cash flow model.

Multiple *g*'s and One *r* for the Gordon Model

Equation 1.14 illustrates four equalities using the algebraic framework of the Gordon Model. Three critical insights should be drawn from these equations.

$$V_0 = \frac{\text{Earnings}}{r - g_e} = \frac{D_1}{r - g_d} = \frac{\text{Earnings} * \text{DPO}}{r - g_d} = \frac{\text{CF}_1}{r - g_{cf}} \qquad (1.14)$$

Recall that Earnings are net of depreciation and taxes, with no reinvestment into the business. Earnings are derived from the core, or existing, business.

V_0 is constant. We show multiple expressions that indicate the same value for an enterprise. Now consider the following:

- *Insight 1.* Differences between Earnings and expected cash flow (CF_1) are the result of differences in dividend payout policies.
- *Insight 2.* The expected growth rate, *g*, *varies* with the earnings measure employed (i.e., with DPO changes). This should be apparent, because earnings paid out cannot be retained to finance future growth.
- *Insight 3.* *r*, the discount rate *remains unchanged* with the degree of earnings retention or distribution.

We have shown that there are multiple g's involved in single-period capitalization models:

- g_e is the growth in core earnings. It is associated with the first identity, which capitalizes Earnings.
- g_d is the expected growth rate associated with a particular dividend, D_1.
- And g_{cf} is the expected growth rate associated with a particular dividend payout policy, which is to say, with a particular earnings retention or reinvestment policy.

In other words, as the portion of net earnings that is capitalized changes, *g* must change to retain the equality of V_0.

Now focus on the fact that *r* did not change in any of the equations. In other words, *r* is the discount rate applicable to expected Earnings, to the expected dividend next period, and to the expected net cash flow of the enterprise. We have a symbolic answer to the frequently asked question: "Does *r* relate to net income or to net cash flow?" Clearly the answer is yes. We now explore the implications of this observation.

Focus Again on g_e — the Long-Term Expected Growth Rate in Earnings

Although they were just stated, the assumptions defining g_e bear repeating. g_e is the constant, long-term growth in earnings achievable by a business that distributes all reported earnings each year. In other words, this level of growth occurs within the following constraints:

- Inflationary price increases are achieved over time.
- Productivity enhancements are also captured over time.
- Incremental working capital requirements are negligible, with incremental assets being financed by incremental liabilities.
- There may be potential for positive NPV capital investments.

g_e is the long-term expected growth rate of the core earnings of a business. Otherwise, there would be some "automatic" level of reinvestment for which there would be no incremental return. Recall that the owners of businesses make one of three decisions each period:

1. Distribute all cash flows or earnings (through dividends or share repurchase) to the owners; or,
2. Retain all cash flows or earnings in the business and reinvest them; or,
3. Distribute a portion of cash flows and retain the rest for reinvestment.

There is no reason to retain earnings if there are no reinvestment opportunities. Reinvestment implies incremental return, or an acceleration of growth from the level of g_e toward r, the discount rate. Investors always demand returns equal to the discount rate, r. That return can come in the form of current return (yield) or capital appreciation, which is fueled by reinvestment of net earnings.

Focus Again on g^* — the Long-Term Growth Rate in Cash Flow

If g_e is the long-term growth in the net earnings of an enterprise, what is g^*? In Equation 1.14, we note that the g of the Gordon Model framework changes with dividend payout policy. This is to be expected, because funds that are distributed provide current returns and are not available to finance future growth. In Exhibit 1.8, we showed that g^*, which was characterized as the growth in reported earnings, was different than g_e because of differences in the dividend payout ratio.

We use g^* to represent the expected growth in both reported earnings and net cash flow (assuming a constant dividend payout ratio). Consider the typical definition of net cash flow, which is defined as:

Net Income (after taxes)
+ Noncash Charges (depreciation and amortization and, possibly, deferred taxes)
− Net Capital Expenditures (new purchases of fixed assets less disposals)
+/− Incremental Changes in Working Capital
+/− Net Changes in Interest-Bearing Debt
= Net Cash Flow

It is not necessarily obvious from examining this definition, but the reconciling factor between Net Income (*Earnings* from Equation 1.14) and Net Cash Flow (CF_1 from Equation 1.14) is the firm's dividend policy. For a firm with attractive growth prospects, net cash flow is usually less than net income as at least a portion of earnings are reinvested to exploit those growth opportunities. The net cash flow (CF_1) is distributed, while the difference between net income and net cash flow, the net reinvestment, is retained in the firm to finance growth.[18]

We now see that g^*, which was developed in the previous section "Core Earnings Growth vs. Analysts' Expected Earnings Growth," as the *analysts'* g, or the expected growth in reported earnings, is also the expected growth rate in net cash flow under the assumption of a constant dividend payout policy.

The Relationship between Net Income and Net Cash Flow

Exhibit 1.8 presented one way of illustrating the relationship between net income and net cash flow in terms of expected growth rates. Exhibit 1.8 demonstrates that the expected growth rate in reported earnings (net cash flow) increases as the retention rate increases. However, a picture is often worth the proverbial thousand words.

Chart 1.2 shows the long-term relationship between net income (*Earnings*) and net cash flow (CF_1) in graphical form as two "strategies" are illustrated. The first strategy distributes 100% of earnings and the second distributes only 75%, retaining 25% to finance future growth. Investors are

---

[18] Astute readers may object that for private companies, net cash flow is not always distributed on a pro rata basis, and undistributed earnings are not always reinvested efficiently. These objections are valid, and are addressed in detail in Chapter 7.

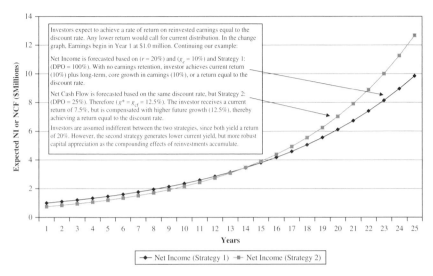

The chart contains the following boxed text:

Investors expect to achieve a rate of return on reinvested earnings equal to the discount rate. Any lower return would call for current distribution. In the change graph, Earnings begin in Year 1 at $1.0 million. Continuing our example:

Net Income is forecasted based on ($r = 20\%$) and ($g_e = 10\%$) and Strategy 1: (DPO = 100%). With no earnings retention, investor achieves current return (10%) plus long-term, core growth in earnings (10%), or a return equal to the discount rate.

Net Cash Flow is forecasted based on the same discount rate, but Strategy 2: (DPO = 25%). Therefore ($g^* = g_{cf} = 12.5\%$). The investor receives a current return of 7.5%, but is compensated with higher future growth (12.5%), thereby achieving a return equal to the discount rate.

Investors are assumed indifferent between the two strategies, since both yield a return of 20%. However, the second strategy generates lower current yield, but more robust capital appreciation as the compounding effects of reinvestments accumulate.

CHART 1.2 Expected Net Income vs. Expected Net Cash Flow

assumed to be indifferent to the two strategies. The first provides a higher current return and lower expected growth. The second provides a lower current yield, but higher expected capital appreciation.

Does *r* Relate to Net Income or to Net Cash Flow?

In 1989, Mercer wrote an article introducing the Adjusted Capital Asset Pricing Model (ACAPM), which presented a methodology for building up discount rates based on the Capital Asset Pricing Model(CAPM).[19] While some appraisers had been using similar techniques for some time, to the best of our knowledge, the 1989 article was the first published presentation of the build-up method using the CAPM. Appraisers were (and remain) somewhat divided regarding whether build-up method discount rates are properly applied to the net income or the net cash flow of enterprises.

From a practical viewpoint, analysts at Mercer Capital did (and still do) capitalize net income estimates, rather than net cash flow estimates, because

---

[19]Z. Christopher Mercer, "The Adjusted Capital Asset Pricing Model for Developing Capitalization Rates: An Extension of Previous 'Build-Up' Methodologies Based Upon the Capital Asset Pricing Model," *Business Valuation Review*, Vol. 8, No. 4 (1989): pp. 147–156. The concepts in this 1989 article form the foundation for the discussion of discount rates in Chapter 6.

we have consistently achieved reasonable results doing so. Other appraisers, in making the case that net cash flow is the appropriate measure for capitalization, have argued the following (with our comments in brackets):

- For companies with attractive growth prospects, net cash flow is generally less than net income. This point was made based on the definition of net cash flow that we examined earlier:

  Net Income (after taxes)
  +   Noncash Charges (depreciation and amortization and, possibly, deferred taxes)
  −   Net Capital Expenditures (new purchases of fixed assets less disposals)
  +/−   Incremental Changes in Working Capital
  +/−   Net Changes in Interest-Bearing Debt
  =   Net Cash Flow

  [Recall that if Net Cash Flow is less than Net Income, a portion of earnings is being retained (i.e., DPO < 100%).]
- If the same discount rate and growth rate are developed and used to capitalize both net income and an estimate of net cash flow, capitalized net income will exceed capitalized net cash flow. [We have demonstrated that differences between net income and net cash flow are directly related to differences in growth rates. There is no conceptual or practical link to differences in discount rates.]
- Because the returns used in the Ibbotson data series are derived from *net cash flow to investors* (i.e., dividends plus capital appreciation), the appropriate income measure to capitalize (or to discount) is therefore *the net cash flow of enterprises*. [This conclusion is inconsistent with the analysis in this chapter.]

Given these premises, it would follow that if the ACAPM (build-up) discount rate is used to capitalize net income rather than net cash flow, an *adjustment factor* must be employed to convert the net cash flow discount rate to one applicable to net income. But no one could determine what it should be, except in a general range of 2% to 6% or so. In light of these comments, Mercer wrote an article in 1990 with the title "Adjusting Capitalization Rates for Differences Between Net Income and Net Free Cash Flow."[20] While the title of the article mentions adjusting *capitalization rates*, the article actually developed an adjustment factor to adjust *discount rates*.

---

[20]Z. Christopher Mercer, "Adjusting Capitalization Rates for Differences Between Net Income and Net Free Cash Flow," *Business Valuation Review*, Vol. 11, No. 4 (1992): p. 201.

The adjustment factor was then evaluated over a range of expected growth assumptions to determine the impact on capitalization rates.

The article showed that under relevant ranges of assumptions regarding earnings retention (dividend payout) policies, the factor would be fairly small. It further concluded that the magnitude of any adjustment factor applicable to *r* was within the range of judgments routinely made by appraisers regarding discount rates and capitalization rates. These judgments include the choice of Treasury rates, the selection of arithmetically or geometrically derived equity risk premiums (or something in between), and the estimation of size premiums and other company-specific risk premiums.

The analysis in this chapter, however, suggests that the appropriate focus is on different growth rates attributable to net income and net cash flow, rather than different discount rates. There is no adjustment factor for *r*, but rather to *g*, to reflect the effect of earnings retention and reinvestment. In Equation 1.13 (and repeated in Equation 1.15), we developed the means to convert an estimate of g_e into g^*, or the expected growth rate in net cash flow given a particular *r* and retention policy:

$$G^* = \text{RR} \times (r) + \text{DPO} \times (g_e) \tag{1.15}$$

Further Analysis Regarding Net Income vs. Net Cash Flow

At least two of the most prominent business valuation texts suggest that discount rates (derived using a variety of methods) are applicable to net cash flow rather than net income. For example, consider the following treatment of this topic:

> 501.10 Both of the methods mentioned above [either guideline company or build-up] result in a discount rate for *net cash flow*, which is the benefit stream used in the discounted cash flow method. However, another common benefit stream that may be appropriate is *net earnings*. This benefit stream is used in the capitalized net earnings method. Whatever benefit stream is selected (net cash flow or net earnings), the corresponding discount rate or cap rate must be stated in that same manner. For example, a net cash flow discount rate should not be used to discount net earnings. Instead, a separate net earnings discount rate must be developed, or the benefit stream should be adjusted to net cash flow.[21] [emphasis in original]

---

[21]Jay E. Fishman, Shannon P. Pratt, and J. Clifford Griffith, *Guide to Business Valuations* 17th ed. (Fort Worth, TX: Practitioners Publishing Company, 2007), pp. 5–6. For convenience, we refer to this as the Fishman text.

The Fishman text then discusses two methods to convert net cash flow discount rates to net income discount rates (at pages 5–8 to 5–10). The first method is based on judgmental comparisons to a rule of thumb range of 3% to 6%. The second method is based on the procedures outlined in the 1990 article quoted earlier. The Fishman text outlines the procedure from the 1990 article for converting a net cash flow discount rate (using the build-up method or the ACAPM method) to one applicable to net income. The discussion in the Fishman text relates specifically to single-period income capitalization methods. The same methodology is discussed in the fourth edition of Pratt's *Valuing a Business*.[22]

It should be clear from the discussion in this chapter, however, that the market's discount rate does not change as a result of changes in dividend policy or with changes in earnings retention decisions. Market-derived discount rates apply to enterprise cash flows. This is true whether they are derived directly from guideline company analysis or indirectly using build-up methods (a more detailed treatment is presented in Chapter 6).

A practical example will illustrate. Exhibit 1.9 displays a two-stage valuation model to value the net cash flows of a hypothetical public

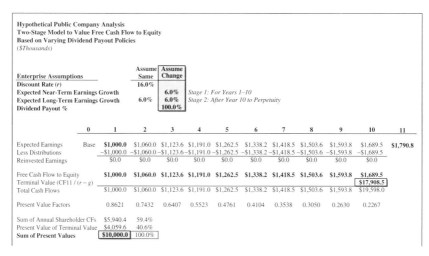

EXHIBIT 1.9 Application of Two-Stage DCF Model to Public Company

---

[22] Shannon P. Pratt, Robert F. Reilly, and Robert P. Schweihs, *Valuing a Business: The Analysis and Appraisal of Closely Held Companies*, 4th ed. (New York, NY: McGraw-Hill, 2000), pp. 151–201.

Summary of Free Cash Flow to Equity Model for Four Different Assumptions re Dividend Payout Policy ($Thousands)					
Assumptions/Results	DPO #1	DPO #2	DPO #3	DPO #4	
Discount Rate	16.0%	16.0%	16.0%	16.0%	Only difference is DPO policy – otherwise companies exactly identical
Expected Near-Term Earnings Growth	6.0%	11.0%	13.5%	16.0%	Increasing reinvestment fuels near-term growth of earnings
Expected Long-Term Earnings Growth	6.0%	6.0%	6.0%	6.0%	The second stage calls for 6% long-term growth in all cases
Dividend Payout %	100.0%	50.0%	25.0%	0.0%	Assume four different levels of constant free cash flow to equity holders
Year 1 Expected Net Income	$1,000.0	$1,000.0	$1,000.0	$1,000.0	
Indicated Value	$10,000.0	$10,000.0	$10,000.0	$10,000.0	Dividend policy should not impact enterprise value
Year 11 Net Income	$1,790.8	$2,839.4	$3,547.8	$4,411.4	The "cost" of a current, higher payout is lower expected future
Terminal Value	$17,908.0	$28,394.0	$35,478.0	$44,114.0	earnings and lower expected terminal values
Present Value of Dividends	$5,940.4	$3,563.5	$1,957.7	$0.0	As the DPO % decreases, the shareholder returns are shifted to
Present Value of Terminal Value	$4,059.6	$6,436.5	$8,042.3	$10,000.0	the future
Portion of Expected Value as Terminal Value	40.6%	64.4%	80.4%	100.0%	
		Model Discounts/Capitalizes			
	Net Income	FCF	FCF	Nothing	Near-Term (Years 1–10)
	Net Income	Net Income	Net Income	Net Income	Terminal Value
	The Gordon Model	As the DPO % varies (the ratio of Net Cash Flow to Net Income), the model discounts Free Cash Flow during the interim periods and Net Income for the Terminal Value. The discount rate does not change.			

EXHIBIT 1.10   Influence of Dividend Policy on Components of Two-Stage DCF Model

company. The discrete forecast period is ten years. The discount rate is 16.0%, and the expected growth rate in core earnings is 6.0%.

The value of the enterprise is $10.0 million. Note that application of the Gordon Model ($1,000/(6% – 6%)) yields the same conclusion. The purpose of this illustration is to show clearly that because all earnings are distributed, growth in reported earnings is equal to expected growth in core earnings at 6.0%.

In Exhibit 1.10, the model is run under three other assumptions regarding dividend payout: 50%, 25%, and 0%. This confirms our prior analysis as summarized in Exhibit 1.8.

In the two-stage model, there is a relationship between the dividend payout policy and the ability of the enterprise to grow during the discrete forecast period. If DPO = 100%, the enterprise can grow at its expected growth in core earnings (g_e) of 6.0%. At the other extreme, if DPO = 0%, and all earnings are reinvested, the business can grow earnings (and value) at 16.0%, or at r, the discount rate (assuming reinvestment at the discount rate). And with dividend payouts in between, near-term earnings growth is accelerated from the core rate of 6.0% toward the discount rate (again, assuming reinvestment at r).

This analysis illustrates again that the discount rate *relates both to the net income and the net cash flow* of business enterprises. Distribution policy does not change the discount rate, but rather, distribution policy (and the implied reinvestment policy) affects growth in reported earnings and cash flows, and capital appreciation.

In practical application, these observations suggest at least the following:

- When applying single-period income capitalization methods, it is entirely appropriate to estimate ongoing earning power based on the net income of an enterprise, and then to capitalize that earning power using a build-up discount rate and expected growth in core earnings (g_e).
- When using the discounted cash flow model, the appropriate measure to discount during a discrete forecast period is the net cash flow of the business. This net cash flow would be that level of cash flow distributed to shareholders after all capital expenditures, working capital requirements, debt service, and the like. When developing the terminal value, it is then appropriate to capitalize the expected net income of the enterprise, using the expected growth rate in core earnings at the end of the forecast period.

PRACTICAL OBSERVATIONS

In this chapter, we have analyzed and reconciled the discounted cash flow model with the Gordon Model. Hopefully, readers will have gained fresh perspective into both models. At this point it is helpful to place our discussion of the DCF and the Gordon Model into the context of everyday valuation practice.

There are three basic approaches to valuation. Within the basic approaches, there are numerous valuation methods, and within various methods, appraisers apply appropriate valuation procedures. Definitions for each of the three valuation approaches can be found in the most current *Business Valuation Standards* of the American Society of Appraisers, but they can be described generally as follows:

- *Cost Approach, or Asset-Based Approach.* The cost approach considers the cost to reproduce or replace the service capability of assets. In business valuation, methods under the cost approach are usually asset-based methods.
- *Income Approach.* Under the income approach, measures of income are discounted to the present or capitalized.[23] The discounted cash flow method is a method under the income approach, as is the single-period

---

[23]As demonstrated in this chapter, valuation methods that capitalize a measure of current income are a subset of methods that discount projections of future income to the present.

income capitalization method represented by the Gordon Model. The two-stage DCF model represented by Equation 1.4 incorporates both the DCF method (for the PVICF) and the single-period income capitalization (for the PVTV).

■ *Market Approach.* The market approach compares financial measures for a subject company with valuation metrics taken from the markets—either the public securities markets, the market for similar companies, or even the market for the securities of the subject (public or private) company. Typical valuation methods under the market approach are the guideline (public) company method and the guideline transactions method.

This book outlines the Integrated Theory of Business Valuation. However, theory must be applied in everyday practice. At this point, it will be helpful to make several observations about the discounted cash flow method. An examination of Equation 1.4 and experience lead to a number of important observations about the discounted cash flow method:

■ *The projected earnings are important.* While this observation may seem obvious, the projected earnings must be reasonable for the subject company. What does this mean? It means that the projection for the interim period must make sense in the context of a company's past (if it has one), the market within which the company operates, the performance of similar companies, the capabilities of management, other logical benchmarks, and common sense. A spreadsheet will forecast anything, depending on the inputs. It is up to the appraiser to make logical and reasonable assumptions when forecasting earnings and cash flow.

■ *The interim period of the forecast is a matter of appraiser judgment.* If income is stable and growing at a fairly constant rate, a single-period income capitalization method may be appropriate. The DCF method is most helpful when the expected cash flows over the next year or two (or three or four or more) are significantly different from those that may be expected after a finite period of growth, decline, recovery, or stabilization. Appraisers may forecast for any relevant period, although most forecasts are in the range of three to ten years, with five years being the most common.

■ *The discount rate, r, should be appropriate to the measure of cash flow selected.* This chapter on the very basics of valuation is conceptual and does not address the practical development of the discount rate, which is treated in Chapter 6. But note that the measure of cash flow can vary from Net Earnings (DPO $= 100\%$) to Net Cash Flow (DPO $< 100\%$), while the discount rate does not change. All cash flows considered thus far have been net (after-tax) cash flows. If pre-tax cash flows are considered, the discount rate should be adjusted appropriately.[24]

■ *The terminal value estimation is critical.* In a typical five-year DCF forecast, the terminal value will account for 60% to 80% or more of the total present value for the method. Obviously, the development of the terminal value is important.

 ○ Other things being equal, the higher the discount rate, r, the lower will be the terminal value (and the indication of value for the method), and the terminal value will account for a lower portion of the total present value.

 ○ Other things being equal, the higher the expected growth rate, g (i.e., the long-term expected growth in core earnings, or g_e), used in the terminal value calculation, the higher will be the terminal value, and it will account for a larger portion of the total present value.

 ○ In theory, the g_e in the terminal value should not be very high—and most appraisers use long-term g's in the range of 3% or 4% up to 8% or 10% on the high side. Double-digit long-term g's are typically considered unusual, because the implied earnings become astounding over time. Further, higher g's almost certainly include the effect of reinvestment on reported earnings rather than simply growth in core earnings.

 ○ While this book will scarcely address the r to be used in a DCF forecast based on the total capital of an enterprise, i.e., the weighted average cost of capital (WACC), the terminal value determination is even more sensitive to the selection of g in such scenarios than for forecasts of cash flows to equity holders.

■ *Not all appraisers use the Gordon Model to develop the terminal value.* In practice, many appraisers (and market participants) use market-based methods to develop the terminal value multiple. Current market multiples (of net income, pre-tax income, EBITDA, debt-free net income, or others, as appropriate to the selected cash flow measure) are often applied to the forecasted cash flow in Year f, the last year of the discrete forecast, or to the year $f + 1$. Some appraisers have suggested that this method is "wrong" because it mixes an income

---

[24]In our opinion, it is generally preferable to adjust the cash flows rather than the discount rate. Alternatively, analysts need to be keenly aware of whether the projected cash flows are applicable to equity only, or to all capital providers. The Integrated Theory presented in this book deals with cash flows applicable to equity. If the projected cash flows are applicable to all capital providers, the appropriate discount rate is the weighted average cost of capital (WACC), rather than the cost of equity.

approach method (DCF for the finite forecast) and a market approach method (usually guideline company methods for the terminal value). It is unclear why such a mixing is necessarily wrong. Given this procedure's usefulness and widespread use in developing reasonable indications of value using the DCF method, it should not be considered unusual or incorrect—provided that reasonable multiples from the public market-place (or the market for transactions) are selected.[25] But "reasonable multiples" from the public marketplace today may not be reasonable for application five to ten years from now, particularly if the industry is in a very rapid growth phase and growth is expected to slow in a few years.

■ What projections should be used? This observation is the corollary to the statement that the cash flow forecast is important. In many cases, the management of a subject enterprise will provide a forecast (or forecasts) of expected future performance. Appraisers using such forecasts are obligated to test their reasonableness and to develop discount rates that reasonably reflect of the risks of achieving the forecasted results. In the absence of management forecasts, appraisers must take care to develop forecasts that make sense in the context of the relevant market and industry, the company's history, its outlook, and the capabilities of its management.

The discounted cash flow method is an excellent tool for appraisers. However, its use is neither appropriate nor necessary in every appraisal. Some appraisers seem to believe that the DCF method provides "ultimate valuation truth." It does not. It can be used directly to provide reasonable valuation indications and, like other valuation methods, it can be misused. The DCF method can also be used effectively to test the reasonableness of other valuation methods or conclusions.

---

[25]This point about the reliability of "mixing" approaches is further substantiated by common practice. If the Gordon Model is used to develop a terminal multiple, the very first test of the reasonableness of the derived multiple is to test it in the context of current public market multiples. For example, an appraiser used $1 / (r-g)$ to develop a terminal multiple of 20.0x debt-free net income in a subject company's DCF method. The credibility of that multiple will be supported if the median debt-free net income multiple for his guideline public group is in the range of 18x to 22x or so. However, its credibility might be questioned if the range of similar multiples in his guideline group was from 10x to 14x.

CONCLUSION

The "very basics of value" are not so basic. This chapter has analyzed the discounted cash flow model and the Gordon Model in considerable detail. Hopefully, we have provided fresh insights and a growing understanding of these two tools that appraisers often use without fully appreciating their implications.

The "very basics of value" form the foundation for the Integrated Theory of Business Valuation introduced in Chapter 3. Before proceeding to the Integrated Theory, however, we examine certain fundamental principles of valuation that are important to applying the "very basics of value" to investing and financial decision-making in the real world, as well as in the hypothetical world of fair market value.

CHAPTER 2

The GRAPES of Value

INTRODUCTION[1]

During the formative years of my business valuation career, I gradually became aware that six underlying financial, economic, logical, and psychological principles provide a solid basis for looking at what we can call the "world of value." Let us refer to these as the *organizing principles of business valuation*, because the integration of the principles provides a logical and consistent framework within which to examine business valuation questions and issues. These principles also provide the qualitative framework within which to discuss the Integrated Theory of Business Valuation. This chapter reflects my continuing journey to understand the world of value and is written in a more personal tone than the other chapters in the book.

COMMON QUESTIONS

1. Where does the generalized valuation model, Value = Earnings × Multiple, come from?
2. How can business appraisers test the reasonableness of their valuation assumptions and conclusions?

THE WORLD OF VALUE

The "world of value" consists of all the various markets in which valuation and investment decisions are made by real investors, whether individuals, companies, institutions, or governments. This world includes, but is certainly not limited to, the public stock and bond markets, the private placement markets for debt and equity securities, and the market participation reflected by the investment decisions of individuals, corporations, institutions, and governments.

---

[1]This chapter reflects the personal and professional experiences of Z. Christopher Mercer, ASA, CFA.

The world of value is the real world. If appraisers develop a solid understanding of the world of value, they are more likely to be able to develop reasonable valuation conclusions under the standards of value appropriate for specific valuation assignments, including fair market value, fair value, investment value, and others. So we begin with a general discussion of the world of value.

GRAPES OF VALUE

I have identified six organizing principles of the world of value, and the six give rise to a seventh. The acronym, GRAPES, provides a convenient way to help arrange and remember the first six organizing principles. So, with a tribute to John Steinbeck, we refer to the "GRAPES of Value."

G   Growth
R   Risk/Reward
A   Alternative Investments
P   Present Value
E   Expectational
S   Sane, Rational, and Consistent

The seventh principle embodies the characteristics of the six elements of GRAPES—*knowledge*. The element of knowledge is the proverbial basket that holds the GRAPES of Value.

The world of value is fascinating. The organizing principles lay the groundwork for the Integrated Theory of Business Valuation, which will be introduced in Chapter 3. In the meantime, the organizing principles provide a basis for addressing nearly every business valuation issue. They describe the underlying behavior of public securities markets, which form the (direct or indirect) comparative basis for the valuation of most businesses and business interests.

The principles also provide a framework for testing the rationality or reasonableness of valuation positions advanced by appraisers. I have used these principles actively for many years, both as an organizing tool for valuation thinking and as a review tool for work performed by Mercer Capital and other firms.

CLARITY COMES SLOWLY

The following section relates to my first valuation client and a business relationship that lasted almost fifteen years. It represents an element of self-indulgence, although I do believe it highlights the process of grappling with valuation issues and growing in the process. Readers can skip it or read it without loss of continuity.

Lessons Learned from First Valuation Client

My business valuation career began officially in late 1978, when I was hired as the bank stock analyst by Morgan Keegan & Company, Inc., then, a small New York Stock Exchange member investment banking firm. No one there was doing appraisals, so I volunteered to take over that small segment of the firm's business, as well as the bank research function. As luck would have it, I sold a business valuation engagement within a few days of being hired, and then had to provide the service. I searched everywhere at the firm for a book on business valuation—to no avail.

Fortunately, my former boss, the CFO at First Tennessee National Corporation, gave me the only book he had. It was written by two partners of what was then Price Waterhouse & Co., and had been published in 1971.[2]

Unfortunately, after reading the book in its entirety, I did not have the foggiest idea of what a business valuation was or how to perform one. In fairness to the authors, the book was filled with useful information about the public markets, securities regulation, and accounting issues. However, it did little to solve my immediate problem, which was to provide the annual appraisal for Plumley Rubber Company.[3]

So I did what any rational person would do under the circumstances. I located every written appraisal report I could find, read them all, and played a game of "monkey see, monkey do." The first two reports I wrote on Plumley Rubber Company ("Plumley") have been lost. However, I have file copies beginning with 1980, the third year of Morgan Keegan's assignment with the company. Plumley obtained an annual appraisal in connection with a non-qualified Employee Retirement and Savings Plan. The appraisals

---

[2]George D. McCarthy and Robert E Healy, *Valuing a Company: Practices and Procedures* (New York: The Roland Press Company, 1971).

[3]As a matter of policy, Mercer Capital does not disclose client names without specific permission. Mr. Harold Plumley was my first business appraisal client. When I left Morgan Keegan in 1982 and formed Mercer Capital, Morgan Keegan declined to continue to provide Mr. Plumley's annual appraisal, so he became one of Mercer Capital's first clients. We valued the company every year until 1995, the year in which it was sold. Mr. Mike Plumley, son of the founder, and then chairman of Plumley Companies, made a presentation at the Advanced Business Valuation Conference of the American Society of Appraisers in 1996. During that presentation, he discussed, among other things, the value to the Plumley family and to the company of having an annual appraisal over a period of nearly 20 years.

were used as the basis for employee stock purchases and for repurchases of shares from departing employees, so they provided the basis for the pricing of transactions each year. The company and its employees took these appraisals seriously.

A brief walk down memory lane may be instructive. In fairness to myself and to Morgan Keegan, my comments about the Plumley reports are made from today's perspective and with today's experience. The quality of the reports at the time exceeded that of the best appraisals I was aware of in the late 1970s and early 1980s. So we walk:

- *Fiscal 1978.* Somehow, I wrote a valuation report and valued Plumley Rubber Company. As it turns out, Morgan Keegan's appraisal was the second appraisal of Plumley that year—Mr. Plumley had been having another firm provide an annual appraisal for several years. When I called to discuss a reappraisal for fiscal 1979, Mr. Plumley told me that Morgan Keegan had the job going forward. I was, of course, ecstatic, and thanked him for the business. Mr. Plumley asked me if I wanted to know why we had gotten the business exclusively for future years. Then he said something I have never forgotten, "Chris, when I read your report, I recognized my company." May we all remember the advice embodied in Mr. Plumley's comment!
- *Fiscal 1980.* The report consisted of 12 pages of text and four pages of exhibits. The financial analysis was decent and on point. The comparable company analysis reflected a reasonable understanding of public markets and the need to make relevant comparisons between the subject company and the guideline group. However, it is apparent that I had little concept of what a marketability discount was, and little objective information to support one. The report reads: "In addition, we have considered the lack of marketability of the minority interests being valued. In each of the previous reports we have arrived at a discount to the average price/earnings multiple, considering all factors, of between 20–25 percent." That was the conclusion, and that was the extent of the discussion of the marketability discount. However, it is apparent from the surrounding text that the 20% to 25% discount also related to fundamental differences between Plumley Rubber Company and the comparable public companies. The conclusion seems reasonable based on a reading of the report and the information included in it. However, the report lacked clarity with regard to several important issues.
- *Fiscal 1981.* The report grew to 15 pages of text and five pages of exhibits, and the financial analysis was lengthened. We added a statement of independence, and information on the qualifications of the firm and the appraisers. We also added an appendix listing contingent and limiting conditions. The fundamental/marketability

discount remained nebulously specified in the 20% to 25% range. Still not so good on these important issues.

■ *Fiscal 1982.* The business relationship shifted to Mercer Capital in early calendar 1983, when the annual appraisal for fiscal year 1982 was prepared. The guideline company analysis was more thorough, and we (I) developed the appropriate multiple by focusing on specific companies in a broader group. In effect, without using the term, we applied a *fundamental discount* to the group's median and average multiples.[4] For the first time, there is a section entitled *Minority Discount.* In that section, we actually discussed the concept of lack of marketability and applied a 20% *discount for lack of marketability.* So it was late 1982 or early 1983 before I focused specifically and solely on the issue of the marketability discount. There is no reference to benchmark pre-IPO or restricted studies, but the brief discussion indicates that the selected discount was mitigated by the company's long-standing policy of repurchasing shares (at appraised values) from departing or terminated employees who had obtained stock under the employee savings and investment program. Some progress. We distinguished between fundamental issues relating to the value of the enterprise and issues related to the value of the shareholders' minority interests.

■ *Fiscal 1984.* This report was issued in February 1985, and demonstrates considerable evolution in report structure and content. The report consisted of 25 pages of text and eight pages of exhibits. The fiscal 1984 report contained three features that remain, to this date, part of "the way things are done" at Mercer Capital. More progress:

○ *Fundamental Adjustments.* In a section labeled *Adjustments to the Base Capitalization Rate*, we developed a 15% fundamental discount based primarily on differences in leverage and growth between Plumley and the comparable public companies. That was pretty good. However, we confused this concept with an additional 10% discount relating to the fact that our subject paid no dividends and all but one of the comparables paid regular dividends. This clearly (now) should have been considered as an element influencing the marketability discount. So clarity began to come only slowly.

○ *Marketability Discount.* There is a section entitled *Adjustments for Lack of Marketability.* Because this book discusses the concept of the marketability discount at great length in future chapters, I thought it

---

[4]We now refer to fundamental *adjustments* relative to public guideline groups because subsequent experience has proven that such adjustments can be positive or negative (see Chapter 5).

would be instructive to quote this early discussion of the marketability discount in its entirety:

> *The valuation of shares in stock in closely held corporations typically warrants large discounts (up to 50%) for lack of marketability and control. An interest in a public company can readily be sold at or near its quoted price. Shares in closely held corporations are not easily sold due to the lack of a public market.*

> *In our opinion, a valuation discount of approximately 10% is necessary to reflect the net impact of the lack of marketability and control for the minority interest nature of the Company's shares under the definition of fair market value cited above.*

> *The marketability discount considers the Company's recent "market making" activities will continue for the near future. The assumption is made based upon specific conversations with management about plans to continue purchasing stock at currently appraised values. Apart from these considerations, the marketability discount would be higher. The 10% discount is the same as used in our valuation report for the fiscal year ending October 31, 1983.*

Except for the confusion between marketability and (lack of) control, we were on the right track with the marketability discount. We likely had Shannon Pratt's first edition of *Valuing a Business* by 1984, therefore the reference to marketability discounts of up to 50%.[5] And it

---

[5]Pratt, *Valuing a Business*, 1st ed. I met a former librarian for Willamette Management Associates at a CFA review course in May 1984. I cannot remember if we already had a copy of Shannon Pratt's first edition (1981) of *Valuing a Business*, but if we did not, I am sure that we purchased it shortly thereafter. We exchanged information on the valuation of bank core deposits (which we knew something about), and I was introduced to Shannon Pratt on the telephone. In the summer of 1985, I had dinner with Shannon and Millie Pratt for the first time. They were attending the ASA International Conference in Orlando, and I drove from a client location in Florida to meet them.

Shannon shared a good deal of his knowledge about business valuation and the business of business valuation with me that night. At that time, Mercer Capital's business was split about evenly between business appraisal and bank consulting. By late 1985, Ken Patton, my friend and business partner since 1984, and I decided

was refreshing to see that I did not *always* fall into the trap of thinking that all marketability discounts had to be around 35%, plus or minus a bit (not to suggest that we did not frequently fall into that trap in the early years).

■ *Test of Reasonableness and Reconciliation of Value Conclusions.* The fiscal 1984 report provided a brief discussion of the reasonableness of its conclusion in light of relative comparisons with the guideline group of public companies. And because this was a recurring client, the report provided a table that compared the key components of the 1984 valuation with those of the 1983 appraisal. For example, the table included adjusted earnings, the base price/earnings multiples, the selected fundamental discounts, the adjusted price/earnings multiples, the initial valuation conclusions, the number of shares outstanding, the initial per-share valuations, the marketability discount, and the conclusions of value. The concluded fair market value per share rose 17.5%, and the table showed, and the text discussed, the components of the net change.

The appraisal reports for Plumley Companies continued to reflect the growth of our knowledge and understanding of business valuation until 1995, when the company was sold. The point of the memory walk through fiscal 1984 (early 1985) is to show that we were grappling with the key valuation issues from the start. As our understanding of the organizing principles evolved, that understanding has been reflected in Mercer Capital's valuation analysis and in our writing and speaking.

Let me recommend that you take a similar walk down the memory lane of your valuation career. As I said in a short article in *Business Valuation Review* in 1988 (reproduced as Appendix 2-B of this chapter) "Make it a regular practice to go back and reread your older appraisals if you need an object lesson in humility."

THE ORGANIZING PRINCIPLES

Others have surely discussed the meaning and implications of the organizing principles. I make no claim of originality here, other than in using them

---

that the future of our company would be in business appraisal and not bank consulting. By 1987, we were out of the bank consulting business and had become a business appraisal shop with perhaps eight employees. I credit Shannon with helping us see the potential for the business of business appraisal. I recall that I bought dinner that night. The advice has definitely been worth the price of dinner, even inflation-adjusted since 1985! Thankfully, there have been many more conference meetings and dinners with Shannon over the past 20 plus years.

as a means of describing and discussing the world of value. In the following sections, we will discuss each of the organizing principles. At the conclusion of the chapter we will see that, while each principle is separate, it is their integration that provides for solid understanding of valuation issues.

G—the Principle of GROWTH and Time

We live in a growing world. Change and growth are an integral part of nature, economies, and business. Investors look at the world, the economy, and individual businesses with an underlying assumption that growth will occur. Implicitly, growth occurs over time, so we call this the Principle of Growth and Time. There can, of course, be negative aspects to economic, industrial, or business growth. But we live in an economic world where growth is viewed, on balance, as good.

The national and world economies have grown steadily for hundreds of years. All valuation of businesses is considered in the context of population and productivity, growth, and inflation. Equity securities are purchased for their growth prospects.

Other things being equal, a growing business is more valuable than a similar business that is not growing. Other things being equal, a business that is growing more rapidly than another similar business is more valuable than the slower-growing entity. The Growth Principle suggests, in nonmathematical terms, that there is an underlying relationship over time between growth and value. That relationship is indirectly reflected in Chart 2.1, which tracks the Dow Jones and S&P 500 for the past 50-plus years. Both indices have shown substantial growth in value over the charted period, as well as for longer periods not shown.

As appraisers address valuation questions, we need to focus on relevant aspects of growth, ranging from the world economy, to the national economy, to the regional economy, to a local economy, to a particular industry, to a particular company, or to the facts and circumstances influencing the ownership of a particular business interest. As Chart 2.1 illustrates, while the long-term trend in market valuation is rising, the rise is punctuated by reversals, or decreases in valuation. This is significant because we value companies at particular points in time. The level and direction of movement of relevant markets will influence valuation decisions at any particular date.

The Principle of Growth and Time is often linked, as we will see, to the Principle of Expectation and to the Present Value Principle. But they are not distinct principles.

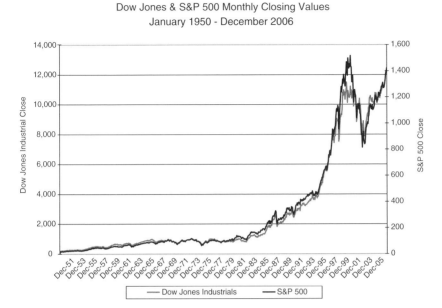

CHART 2.1 DJIA and S&P 500 Monthly Closing Values

R—the Principle of RISK and REWARD

Life is full of risks and rewards. The relationship between risk and reward that has been known for many centuries—long before the development of modern financial and valuation theory.

This relationship is illustrated by the biblical "Parable of the Talents" (Matthew 25:14–30). In this New Testament parable, there are three servants who, upon the departure of their master, are given stewardship responsibility for resources. One steward receives five talents (currency units), another two talents, and the third, one talent.

The first servant invests the five talents and grows the master's stake. The second servant invests the two talents and similarly grows the master's stake. The third steward is fearful of loss and buries his talent until the master's return.

When the master returns, the first servant renders his report and tells the master of his gain. The second servant reports similarly. And the third steward gives the original talent back to the master. The master is pleased with the work of the first two servants. But the third servant, who was not a good steward, is rebuked. The master takes away the talent and gives it to the first steward, who had handled his responsibilities well.

The "Parable of the Talents" is summarized here, not to make a theological statement (if, indeed I could), but to illustrate that the concept of the relationship between risk and reward has been in existence for thousands of years.

The Principle of Risk and Reward can be summed up in the words of an immortal unknown: "No risk, no blue chips!" This principle is integrated with the Present Value Principle via the factor known as the discount rate, or required rate of return. It is also manifest when we employ the Principle of Alternative Investments.

The Principle of Risk and Reward suggests that an investor considering two possible investments, with one clearly riskier than the other, will require a greater expected reward for the riskier investment. Otherwise, there would be no incentive to purchase the riskier investment.

The bottom line of the Principle of Risk and Reward is that the markets require higher expected returns from riskier investments. This principle is related to the Principle of Expectations.

A—the Principle of ALTERNATIVE Investments

We live in an alternative investment world. The Principle of Alternative Investments suggests that investments are made in the context of choices between or among competing alternatives. When investors make investment decisions, there are almost always choices that must be made.

The Principle of Alternative Investments lies at the heart of business valuation theory and practice. For example, many valuations of private companies begin with the development of a valuation indication at the marketable minority interest level of value, which is also called "as-if-freely-traded." In other words, appraisers develop hypothetical indications of value in the process of appraising private companies.[6] From the derived marketable minority interest values, appraisers may adjust their initial conclusions by the application of control premiums (if appropriate to achieve a controlling interest value) or marketability discounts (to achieve a nonmarketable minority interest value).

When Revenue Ruling 59-60 directs appraisers to make comparisons of a subject enterprise with the securities of similar companies with active public markets, the Principle of Alternative Investments is being invoked.

---

[6]Note that this is completely different from rendering a hypothetical appraisal, which is made based on "assumed conditions which are contrary to fact or which are improbable of realization or consummation." See *Principles of Appraisal Practice and Code of Ethics*, Section 6.5 (Washington, D.C.: The American Society of Appraisers, 1994). The overlap of terms is unfortunate.

The public securities markets are massive and active and provide liquid investment alternatives to investments in many privately owned businesses. Business appraisers need to have a thorough, working knowledge of these markets in order to provide realistic appraisals of private business interests.

By combining the organizing principles, we can begin to describe the workings of the world of value. For example, by combining aspects of the Principle of Risk and Reward and the Principle of Alternative Investments, investors make asset allocation decisions regarding their investments. In the public securities markets investors ask questions like: "Should we buy FedEx or UPS stock? Should we buy large cap or small cap stocks? Should we buy stocks or bonds or real estate?"

The Principle of Alternative Investments suggests that there are many competing, alternative investments. The mirror suggestion is that there are many alternative investors, who may look at investments in different ways. This realization is causing appraisers to focus more frequently on who the typical buyers are for particular assets. For example, appraisers now generally recognize that there are different types of buyers for companies, including financial buyers and strategic or synergistic buyers. Strategic or synergistic buyers can often pay more for companies than financial buyers who may be substantially dependent upon a company's existing cash flows for returns. Decisions by appraisers regarding who constitutes the "typical buyer" for an asset can have a significant impact on their conclusions of value.

The Principle of Alternative Investments also suggests the concept of opportunity costs. When resources are deployed to acquire one asset, they are not available to purchase another. When business assets are lost, destroyed, or diminished in value, appraisers and economic experts employ the organizing principles to estimate the magnitude of alleged damages.

The point of this discussion of the Principle of Alternative Investments is that the principle requires (or assumes) that business appraisers be familiar with the public securities markets and capable of making objective comparisons between the public and private markets and drawing reasonable valuation inferences.

P — the PRESENT Value Principle

Stated in its simplest form, the Present Value Principle says that a dollar today is worth more than a dollar tomorrow. Alternatively, a dollar tomorrow is worth less than a dollar today. Present value is really an intuitive concept that even children understand. Ask any child whether it is better to get a toy today or to get the same toy next week! Or to have a piece of candy now or after finishing his or her dinner!

When we talk about present value, we really talk about four aspects of investments:

- *Investments (in equities) are expected to grow in value.* Recall the Principle of Growth.
- *Investments have cash flow characteristics that must be understood.* Appraisers must understand the nature of the cash flows of a business over time, and the fact that the cash flows of the business may differ materially from the cash flows available to its (minority) shareholders.
- *Investments have an expected duration.* They exist over time. We forego consumption today (or make a choice among competing alternatives) in order to gain the benefit of the investment over its expected duration.
- *Investments have different risk characteristics.* Risk is the great leveling force in the world of present value via investors' required rates of return, or discount rates.

The Present Value Principle enables us to compare investments of differing durations, growth expectations, cash flows, and risks. We use present value calculations to express the value of different investments in terms of dollars today and, therefore, to provide a means to make investment or valuation decisions. Alternatively, we sometimes compare investments based on their expected values at dates in the future.

The generalized valuation model based on the Gordon Model was developed and discussed in Chapter 1. The generalized model is summarized as:

$$\text{Value} = \text{Earnings}/(r - g) = \text{Earnings} \times \text{Multiple}$$

This generalized model reflects a single-period income capitalization valuation method commonly employed by business appraisers. The appropriate earnings (cash flow) might be the net income, the pre-tax earnings, or some measure of cash flow expected to be achieved and from which income can grow. The discount rate is developed by comparisons with relevant alternative investments, and the expected growth rate of the cash flow is estimated by the appraiser. Value in the preceding equation represents the present value of all expected future cash flows of an enterprise, which are assumed to be growing at a constant rate (g). Present value is determined by discounting all those future cash flows to the present at the appropriate discount rate (r). This method yields an identical conclusion of value to a discounted cash flow method under the same assumptions.

Normally, we use the Gordon Model (or the DCF method) to solve for the value of a business. However, the Principle of Present Value can also be used to facilitate comparing alternative investments. If we can estimate the future cash flows from a business (or a business strategy or investment), and we know what that business or strategy or investment costs today, we can solve for the implied internal rate of return. If we calculate the implied internal rates of return from similar investments with comparable durations and hold other risk factors constant, the investment with the higher internal rate of return is the preferable investment.

Whether an appraiser solves the DCF equation for its value conclusions, or the CFO of a company makes comparisons of investments based on their relative expected internal rates of return, different aspects of the same principle are being considered.

Business appraisers must be fluent with present value concepts and be able to articulate valuation facts and circumstances in a present value context.

E — the Principle of EXPECTATIONS

Today's value is a function of tomorrow's expected cash flows, not yesterday's performance. This is a simple but often overlooked aspect of valuation.

Appraisers routinely examine a company's historical performance and develop estimates of earning power based on that history. The earnings that are capitalized may be a simple average of recent years' earnings, or a weighted average of those earnings. In the alternative, an appraiser might capitalize the current year's earnings or the annualization of a partial year of earnings, or a specific forecast of expected earnings for next year might be made. The purpose of all historical analysis, however, is to develop reasonable expectations for the future of a business.

History is the window through which appraisers look at the future. We should never forget, however, that visibility is not the same through all windows. Some windows have been cleaned recently and provide a good picture; others are shaded, tinted, or dirty. And the view through some windows is just blocked. Appraisers must make reasonable judgments about the expected future performance of subject companies. And those judgments can often be tested or evaluated in light of a company's recent history.

The Gordon Model underscores the expectational nature of valuation. Nevertheless, the Principle of Expectations is one of the most difficult for beginning (and even experienced) appraisers to embrace in practice.

The efficient market hypothesis suggests that, in general, the markets incorporate information that is known about a company (that forms the basis for future expectations regarding its performance) into its stock price today. This information is considered, of course, in the context of expectations regarding the company's industry and economic conditions. In other words, the market evaluates the expected future performance in light of the consensus estimate of riskiness for a security and moves the price of a

A sidebar to this brief discussion of the role of expectations in valuation relates to the use of *unrealistic* expectations. One of the most frequent problems seen in appraisal reports today is the use of projected earnings that bear little or no resemblance to those of the past. These projections often lack any explanation of how the rose-colored glasses, through which they view a business, reflect realistic expectations for the future of a business. The projection phenomenon just described is so common that it has been given a name—"hockey-stick projections."

In a deposition a number of years ago, I was asked how a bank with currently low earnings could possibly meet the projections found in bank management's own current capital plan for the next five years. The deposing attorney accused me of unrealistically relying on the capital plan, which was prepared by his client for regulatory review in the normal course of business. How could any bank possibly achieve the results of such a "hockey-stick" set of projections?

I referred the attorney to the exhibit in our report that compared the previous five years' performance with the earnings and returns of the capital plan. There, it was clear that the projected returns (on assets and equity) were within the levels achieved by the bank in the previous few years, and below the current level of the bank's peer group. The Principle of Expectation says that value today is a function of expectations for future performance—and the expectations we used were in line with past performance, management's stated plans, management's business plan, and the performance of similar banks.

Appraisers should remember that every going-concern business appraisal reflects, implicitly or explicitly, a projection of expected future performance. If the expectations embedded in the appraisal are not realistic, the appraisal's conclusions will be flawed.

stock to the level that equates that expected performance with its expected riskiness.

The Principle of Expectations suggests that participants in the world of value must deal with uncertainty. After all, we cannot know the future until it happens, and then it is no longer the future.

Sometimes expectations are binary. Either A will occur or B will occur. If A occurs, one level of pricing for a company is suggested. If B occurs, an entirely different level of pricing is indicated. Investors deal with the potential for binary (or multiple) future outcomes using various forms of probability analysis. In appropriate circumstances, appraisers may need to use probability analysis, as well.

Consider the following example: a real-world investor plans to invest in a company that expects to engage in an initial public offering (IPO) within a year or so. The stock is currently illiquid and is burdened by a right of first refusal flowing to the shareholders and the company. If the IPO does occur as expected, there will likely be a substantial boost in the overall value of the company. The shares under consideration would be marketable in that case, so there would be potential for a significant gain.

However, if the IPO does not occur, growth prospects will be significantly lower than if it had (because the expected capital infusion will not occur). And the investor knows that one of the reasons that companies do not go public is because their emerging performance does not meet expectations. If the company does not have the IPO, the investor faces a potentially lengthy holding period before other opportunities for liquidity arise. In this case, the stock would be worth much less than if the IPO had occurred.

What does the investor do in this world of value we live in? He or she makes an informed judgment ("best guess") about the probabilities of the favorable and unfavorable outcomes. A decision is made at a value above the no-IPO scenario level, but considerably below the IPO scenario. Why? *Because investors tend to be risk-averse, and, according to the Principle of Risk and Reward, may charge a high, even a very high, price for uncertainty.*

The investor in our hypothetical example makes a decision based on his probability-adjusted expected return, writes a check, and moves on. Either A (the IPO) or B (getting stuck) will occur, and the ultimate return on the investment will be determined over time.

Unlike the investor just described, who will take his licks or count his rewards based on the negotiated price, the business appraiser must write a report. In situations like this, the report's conclusion is almost certain to be wrong at a point in the future with the benefit of hindsight. If the company goes public, the conclusion of value may appear low in relationship to the ultimate IPO price. If the IPO is unsuccessful, the report's conclusion, which considered favorable aspects related to that potential, will appear to have been too high.[7]

Business appraisers facing similar valuation situations must attempt to mirror the thinking of investors in the world of value and must reach conclusions and document them. We must solve valuation problems with reference to the appropriate organizing principles if our conclusions are to

---

[7]Note that these observations are true even if the earlier report provided both favorable and unfavorable scenarios and probability weighted them.

have credibility and the potential to withstand critical scrutiny after the uncertainties about the future have been resolved by the passage of time.

S — the Principle of SANITY (and Rationality and Consistency)

The Principle of Sanity might have been that of Rationality had another "R" fit into the acronym of GRAPES. But sanity will do.

When I speak to appraisers about the nature of the public securities markets, many are quick to explain to me the many (apparent or real) exceptions to sane, rational, or consistent investment behavior. However, while the exceptions are always interesting, what we are discussing is the underlying rationality of the markets operating as a whole.

Many an unthinking investor has been taken to the proverbial cleaners by the investment pitch that "seemed almost too good to be true." It probably was too good to be true. Lying beneath the surface of this comment are implicit comparisons with alternative investments that are sane, rational, or consistent with normal expectations.

Other appraisers are quick to point out that the markets sometimes behave abnormally or, seemingly, irrationally. I am using the comments of appraisers to illustrate that too many of us get caught up in the exceptions and miss the big picture that is played out in the public securities markets. If we can understand the underlying rationality or sanity of the markets, we then have a basis to explain or to try to understand the apparent exceptions.

The Principle of Sanity should be applied to appraisers as well as markets. Revenue Ruling 59–60, in the paragraph prior to the enumeration of the eight factors that are listed in nearly every appraisal report, suggests that appraisers employ three additional factors—common sense, informed judgment, and reasonableness. We call the eight factors the "Basic Eight" factors of valuation. We call the less well-known factors from Revenue Ruling 59–60 the "Critical Three" factors of valuation.

The Principle of Sanity suggests that appraisers need to study the markets they use as valuation reference points (comparables or guidelines). It also suggests that valuation conclusions should be sane, rational, consistent, and reasonable.

We employ tests of reasonableness in Mercer Capital valuation reports to compare our conclusions with relevant alternative investments or to explain why we believe our conclusions are reasonable. Other appraisers call the same process that of using sanity checks. Readers of appraisal reports should expect such "proof" of the sanity of the conclusions found in those reports as well as at key steps along the way as critical valuation decisions are made.

THE BASKET FOR GRAPES: THE PRINCIPLE OF KNOWLEDGE

The organizing principles provide an excellent framework within which to think about the world of value. Business value is determined by investors "out there" who either have or are seeking information about their potential investments. The various bits of information that are gathered are part of a mosaic. When the pieces are put together in an organized fashion, they form the knowledge that is necessary for decision-making about investments and their future performance in the face of uncertainty.

From the viewpoint of business appraisers, the GRAPES of Value provide a number of avenues along which to seek and obtain the knowledge necessary to develop and support, and later to defend, valuation conclusions.

Knowledge is gained by employing one or more or all of the GRAPES of Value. The objective of every business valuation should be to provide well-developed, well-reasoned, and well-written conclusions of value upon which clients and other intended users can rely for their intended purposes. If meeting that objective can be likened to creating a fine wine, then the GRAPES of Value are the ingredients: If employed in the right proportions for the right amount of time, a fine wine can develop; if not employed properly, vinegar may be the result.

To carry this analogy to its logical conclusion, knowledge is the full basket of GRAPES that enables the business appraiser to turn facts, circumstances, and bits of information that may seem disjointed and unrelated into appropriate valuation judgments and reasonable valuation conclusions.

CONCLUDING COMMENTS

The importance of these organizing principles of business valuation, summarized by GRAPES, lies in their integrated consideration by appraisers. We offer a few thoughts in conclusion:

G-rowth. Examine the outlook for the future of the business, i.e., for its earnings and cash flows.

R-isk/Reward. Examine the history and nature of a business to discern its particular risk characteristics. These characteristics are used in the overall assessment of riskiness, which affects value through the discount rate (r) selected.

A-lternative Investments. Compare subject private companies to publicly traded securities or other similar investments because they represent realistic alternative investments for hypothetical buyers of private companies or to the valuation metrics from change of control transactions.

P-resent Value. The common denominator for comparing alternative or competing investments is found in present value analysis. Value for a *business* today is, conceptually, the present value of the expected future cash flows of the enterprise discounted to the present at an appropriate discount rate. Value for an *illiquid interest in a business* is, conceptually, the expected future cash flows attributable to the interest (in the context of an overall enterprise valuation) discounted to the present at an appropriate discount rate.

E-xpectations. The market price for securities in companies is based on expected future benefits. The baseline valuation question is not: "What have you done for me in the past?" Nor is it even: "What can I expect that you will do for me today?" Valuation is forward-looking or expectational. "What can I expect for you to do for me tomorrow?"

S-anity. There is an underlying sanity, rationality, and consistency to the public markets that is sometimes difficult to discern. Appraisers who focus on exceptions in the marketplace rather than on underlying logic and rationality are prone to major swings of overvaluation or undervaluation.

And, **Knowledge.** It should be clear that decisions in the world of value are made based on knowledge available about various investments.

Appraisers who have a grasp on the organizing principles, or the GRAPES of Value, have a leg up in the process of developing reasonable valuation conclusions. Attorneys and other advisors to business owners who use the GRAPES of Value as a framework in which to discuss valuation questions can get to bottom-line issues more rapidly and effectively.

The importance of understanding the organizing principles of business valuation and being able to employ them in appraisal assignments should become clearer as this book progresses. The Integrated Theory of Business Valuation presented in the next chapter relies heavily on these principles.

As noted at the outset of this chapter, we have been discussing the world of value thus far. We have made only passing references to fair market value and no mention of any other standards of value. The world of value is where value is created. The investment decision-making processes of many thousands of businesses and millions of investors are observed everyday in the securities markets.

The Principles Crystallize

Z. Christopher Mercer, ASA, CFA

I did not consciously articulate the organizing principles during the 1980s, but they were firmly established in my thinking by the time my earliest articles on business valuation were published in 1988 and 1989:

- "Not So Random Thoughts Regarding the Business of Business Appraisal," *Business Valuation Review*, June 1988, pp. 62–63. This article was written in response to an earlier article by John Emory, ASA (who prepares the Emory Restricted Stock Studies). It was quoted in a speech shortly thereafter marking me as a "friend" of using the public markets as benchmarks in the valuation of private companies. Guilty as charged.[8] It was also in this article that I suggested that appraisers review their historical work to provide a benchmark for comparison regarding the extent of their work's improvement over time. This article is reproduced as Appendix 2-B to this chapter.[9]
- "Issues in Recurring Valuations: Methodological Comparisons from Year-to-Year," A Letter to the Editor to the *Business Valuation Review*, December 1988, pp. 171–173. In this article, I suggested that appraisers need to be consistent and rational in valuing companies from year to year, and that significant changes in methodologies need to be explained. We realized the importance of this procedure as a result of clients like

---

[8]The label works if we consider both direct and indirect comparisons to the public markets. Reasonable groups of guideline companies simply cannot be developed as a basis for valuing many private companies.

[9]I was asked to update the "not so random thoughts" for the American Society of Appraisers in early 2004. The current comments are also reproduced as part of Appendix 2-B.

Plumley Rubber Company and our growing list of ESOP and planning clients, all of whom had to be valued each year (or so).

- "The Adjusted Capital Asset Pricing Model for Developing Capitalization Rates: An Extension of Previous 'Build-Up' Methodologies Based Upon the Capital Asset Pricing Model," *Business Valuation Review*, December 1989, pp. 147–156. This last article, which we call the ACAPM article, provided the first clear, published articulation of the use of the Capital Asset Pricing Model to develop capitalization rates for valuing private companies. This article introduced the concept of the *fundamental adjustment* and provided an analytical method for estimating its magnitude based on differences in risk and expected growth between subject enterprises and guideline companies. All of the organizing principles were present in the ACAPM article, either implicitly or explicitly.

Not So Random Thoughts Regarding the Business of Business Appraisal[10]

Z. Christopher Mercer, ASA, CFA

- There is no such thing as a "simple" valuation.
- Business Rule No. 1: Prepare an engagement letter for client acceptance for every valuation assignment specifying what is being valued, the as of date, the purpose of the appraisal, and the fee arrangement.
- Business Rule No. 2: Reread Business Rule No. 1 until it is second nature.
- There is no such thing as "the value" of anything. Valuation is a "range" concept tied to another concept, that of "reasonableness." Experience will probably tend to narrow your personal concept of "reasonable range."
- If you start with reasonable facts and make reasonable assumptions or assertions along the way, chances are your conclusions will be perceived as reasonable.
- The public marketplace provides many objective "markers" as reference points for appraisals of closely held companies. A well-crafted valuation conclusion will sit reasonably in relationship to one, or preferably, several of these markers.
- Summarize your valuation conclusions for related businesses over time. As your business grows, your internal data base will become

---

[10]Z. Christopher Mercer, "Not So Random Thoughts Regarding the Business of Business Appraisal," *Business Valuation Review*, Vol. 7, No. 7 (1988): pp. 62–63.

your "conscience" and an automatic test of reasonableness for many situations.

■ When you draft any appraisal report, keep in mind that in a litigation situation, every word you write is fodder for cross examination.

■ Caveat. Do not play the "compromise" game by preparing an opinion that is higher or lower than you can reasonably justify. Courts are increasingly getting out of the "averaging" game and are selecting the more convincing appraisal conclusion. The average of two unreasonable opinions will not necessarily yield a reasonable result.

■ Corollary. Beware of walking too far out on a limb. If it doesn't break of its own accord, someone will invariably saw it off at the trunk.

■ The more complex your valuation rationale, the less likely those who count (judges, juries, clients, IRS agents, etc.) will understand, and the more likely you will be challenged and unable to successfully support your conclusions.

■ Most trial attorneys do not stop cross examination soon enough. Use this flaw to your advantage by being well prepared and ready to establish and reestablish the overall reasonableness of your conclusions at every opportunity.

■ Never be intimidated by a cross-examination attorney. Most good attorneys will craft their questions to require "yes" or "no" answers that will seemingly damage your case. You always have the right to explain your answer. Don't worry about the uncomfortable "yes" or "no" response. Make your points with a clearly stated and reasonable explanation.

■ ESOP appraisals are far more complex than many appraisers seem to believe. Be sure you understand the complete situation, the entire transaction, and its implications before issuing a valuation opinion.

■ When dealing with controlling shareholders who are selling to an ESOP, remember the difference between a minority appraisal and a control appraisal and know which one is appropriate for the circumstance.

■ Remember, when you value a company for an ESOP the first time, you will have to value it the next year and the next year and the next year. It is a professional challenge to maintain reasonableness, consistency, objectivity, and clients over time.

■ Beware of the appraiser who boasts of how many tax-related appraisals he has defended. The objective in a tax appraisal should be quiet acceptance by the IRS.

■ In spite of admonitions to the contrary, clients almost always tell you what they want the answer to be. Sometimes they are overt, and other times they are subtle. Sometimes they are reasonable. In spite of this, your valuation conclusions must be your own. You cannot satisfy every client and retain your independence. How you deal with the issue, and the reasonableness of your approach, will determine if you retain your independence, the client, or both.

- The best definition of "independence" is having many clients, no one of which accounts for a significant portion of your business.
- Re-read Revenue Ruling 59–60 from time to time. You may be surprised at what it says.
- When valuing financial institutions, never confuse the bank and the bank holding company.
- Make it a regular practice to go back and re-read your older appraisals if you need occasional object lesson in humility.

Not So Random Thoughts on the Business of Business Appraisal 2004 Edition[11]

Z. Christopher Mercer, ASA, CFA

J ohn Emory and I captured our "not so random thoughts" on the business of business valuation in 1988. For those who have entered the field in the last few years, picture our world in 1988:

- The use of personal computers was in its infancy. We had them, but they were not very robust. Mercer Capital had one computer with a hard drive—a Compaq luggable machine with a 5 MB hard drive, which we thought was huge!
- Networks in most appraisal shops were of the "tennis shoe" kind—save onto a floppy disk and take it to another machine—you know, the really floppy, floppy disks!
- Fax machines were not omnipresent. This was the year of Federal Express' big failure with ZapMail, a same-day service using facsimile transmission between FedEx locations and the delivery capabilities in local markets. So the proliferation of "fax it to me" was just beginning.
- The Internet did not exist, at least commercially, and neither did e-mail.
- The Business Valuation Standards of the ASA did not exist, and USPAP had little, if any, impact on business appraisal.
- The "levels of value" chart had not yet been published although the concepts were generally known.

---

[11]Z. Christopher Mercer, "Not So Random Thoughts on the Business of Business Appraisal," *ASA BV E-Letter*, Issue 8.15, April 14, 2004.

- There was great confusion regarding how to develop capitalization rates using so-called build-up methods or the Adjusted Capital Asset Pricing Model.

It is now 2004, nearly 16 years later, and things have certainly changed. Let's discuss a few current "not so random thoughts" through the lens of over 25 years of experience.

- Professional standards are here to stay. Maintain your personal, current copies of the Uniform Standards of Professional Appraisal Practice and the Business Valuation Standards and Principles of Appraisal Practice and Code of Ethics of the American Society of Appraisers. Remember to:
  - Read these documents frequently.
  - Evaluate your personal work and the relevant work products of your firm in light of these standards.
  - Prepare in advance for the day that your work is subjected to detailed examination based on its compliance with these standards.
- Remember that everything you do (or do not do) in your professional career builds your professional reputation over time. There are no shortcuts on the road to professional success.
- Professional growth is all about learning and that cannot be accomplished when you are in your comfort zone doing things the same way "because that's the way we've always done them."
- Computers are wonderful; however, they will never do your thinking for you.
- Begin every valuation assignment with a detailed spreadsheet analysis of the company's historical performance. As a former boss instilled in me long ago: "You have to talk to the numbers until the numbers talk to you." Ask questions raised by the changes you see. Do not stop until you understand how things have worked. Your appraisals are forecasts of how things will or may work in the future. A company's past provides a window into the present that enables appraisers to anticipate its future. If the window is dirty, or worse yet, broken, the future may be cloudy indeed.
- Some appraisers love litigation and others hate it. Others love to hate it and still others hate to love it. Regardless, if you stay in the business for some length of time you will likely end up testifying in deposition and/or trial related to your work, the reports of others, or on valuation or damages issues. Always be in the process of getting ready.
- Nearly every valuation conclusion is highly sensitive to one or more of the assumptions made in its determination. *This is a fact of life.*

Appraisers need to be keenly aware of these sensitivities and may need to alert readers of their reports at appropriate points. Tests of the sensitivity of conclusions to changes in assumptions can be helpful as can proving the reasonableness of assumptions in light of available economic and valuation evidence.

- Differences in appraisal conclusions almost always relate to differences in one or more of a limited number of assumptions. When you are making those key assumptions in your appraisals, be sure of your facts and rationale at each point along the way.
- Never bury a calculating number in a cell. Always show all calculating numbers so they can be checked.
- In 1988, I wrote that courts are getting out of the business of "splitting the baby," or averaging the conclusions of opposing experts. I think I was wrong.
- Judging from what has been written about appraisers in many court decisions, I believe that many judges hold our profession in low regard. The job of the expert in a valuation matter is to provide his or her independent rationale and conclusions. It often seems that judges assume at the outset that the appraisers are advancing the positions of their respective sides. Maybe that is why there are so many "split babies."
- Benchmark analysis based on using the averages of restricted stock studies or pre-IPO studies is dead in the Tax Court—as it should be. Comparisons to the average of a study or attempts to use a very limited database of restricted stock transactions stretching over many years will yield appropriate marketability discounts only by chance and that is simply not good enough.
- Appraisers need to place similar effort, energy, and intellect into valuing illiquid *interests* of enterprises as they do with valuing the enterprises themselves.
- Post-valuation date information is often misused by appraisers and by courts. Given a valuation date, the "future" becomes clearer and clearer with the passage of time. Mercer's Law states: "If post-valuation date information will corroborate my valuation conclusions, it will not be admitted into evidence; however, if is not corroborative, it will be admitted!" That makes it all the more important to provide well-reasoned, well-written, and reasonable valuation opinions every time based on what is known or reasonably knowable at the valuation date.
- E-mail is wonderful. However, here is a good rule to follow: Never write anything in an e-mail that you do not mind explaining under hostile circumstances at a future date.

- One of the toughest things we have to deal with in the business appraisal arena is *ambiguity*. Things are seldom as certain as many would like them to be. How we deal with this ambiguity reflects on the credibility of our work.
- If your assignment calls for rendering an independent opinion of value, then do just that. Clients have problems, and that is why they hire us. But the moment you lose your independence in a matter, you make the client's problem your own and lose the credibility to help resolve it.

The business of business appraisal has been intellectually stimulating, challenging, and rewarding over the last 25-plus years. I have high expectations for an even brighter future.

CHAPTER 3

The Integrated Theory of Business Valuation

INTRODUCTION

In this chapter, we introduce the Integrated Theory of Business Valuation. Simply stated, the Integrated Theory allows business appraisers to account for all the cash flows of an enterprise, whether in the aggregate or the portions of enterprise cash flows attributable to specific ownership interests. It does this by harmonizing the Gordon Model (and implicitly, the discounted cash flow model) with the familiar levels of value concept.

More specifically, the Integrated Theory uses the Gordon Model to explain each level of value in the context of financial and valuation theory, as well as why value might differ from level to level. In addition, the Integrated Theory defines the conceptual adjustments relating the various levels of value to each other (control premiums and minority interest discounts and marketability discounts) in terms of the discounted cash flow analysis summarized by the Gordon Model. Importantly, the Integrated Theory also describes the conditions necessary for the relevant valuation premiums or discounts to exist.

COMMON QUESTIONS

Not every question posed here is answered (or addressed) in this chapter. However, the framework for addressing these and other valuation-oriented questions is established here in Chapter 3.

1. What is the source of value for an *interest* in a business enterprise?
2. If a minority interest is worth less than its pro rata share of an enterprise, what causes this diminution in value?
3. What are the theoretical reasons for the existence of a control premium?
4. In the context of fair market value, should control premiums be applied "automatically" in developing controlling interest value indications?

    a. If a control premium is applied, what types of data from the marketplace should be used to estimate it?

    b. If appropriate, to what valuation base should a control premium be applied?

    c. How can the reasonableness of control premiums be evaluated?

    d. Do control premiums determine value or merely describe valuation results?

5. What factors give rise to "financial control premiums"?

6. What factors give rise to "strategic control premiums"?

7. When applying the DCF method, should appraisers apply control premiums when developing controlling interest values? If so, why? And where?

8. What does the term *marketable minority* level of value mean in the context of public security values?

9. When valuing minority interests of private companies, should appraisers normalize earnings?

    a. What are normalizing adjustments?

    b. What kinds of normalizing adjustments should be made?

    c. What is the objective of making normalizing adjustments?

    d. What is the difference between normalizing and control adjustments?

10. When using guideline public company multiples, should appraisers apply control premiums to the resulting "marketable minority" value indications?

11. Are marketability discounts applicable to 100% controlling interests of companies?

12. What are the economic factors that give rise to the marketability discount?

13. Using the levels of value framework, can the following phenomena be explained or described?

    a. The existence of control premiums when public companies sell.

    b. Most public companies do not sell in any given period.

    c. Illiquid minority interests often sell for less than their pro rata share of enterprise value.

    d. Private companies often sell for less than public company multiples in their industries.

    e. Strategic buyers may pay more than financial buyers for the same company.

    f. Financial buyers may outbid strategic buyers for a given company.

14. What are the similarities and differences between a restricted stock discount observed when public companies issue restricted shares and marketability discounts applicable to minority interests in private companies?

15. What is the relationship between the standard of fair market value and the strategic control level of value?
16. In valuing nonmarketable interests in private businesses, why do appraisers normally begin with appraisals at the marketable minority level of value?
17. Why is the concept of the expected holding period an integral element in the valuation of nonmarketable minority interests in enterprises?
18. What is the relationship between the discount rates applicable to minority interests in a business enterprise and the discount rates applicable to the enterprise as a whole?

THE GORDON MODEL

In Chapter 1, we provided background information on the Gordon Model. This model is a single-period income capitalization model that summarizes the way securities are valued in the public markets. The Gordon Model is shown again as a beginning point for discussing of the Integrated Theory of Business Valuation.

$$V_0 = \frac{CF_1}{r - g} \tag{3.1}$$

The Gordon Model defines the value of a business or interest as the next period's expected cash flow divided by an appropriate capitalization rate (the discount rate less the expected growth rate of the specified cash flow). As we have previously shown, this formula is a summary of the discounted cash flow method of valuation under the following conditions:

- The cash flows are expected to grow at the constant rate of g, and
- All cash flows are either distributed to shareholders or reinvested in the firm at the discount rate, r.

The discounted cash flow model as summarized by the Gordon Model provides an ideal basis for the Integrated Theory of Business Valuation.

EARLY VIEWS OF THE LEVELS OF VALUE

The so-called levels of value chart first appeared in the valuation literature some time around 1990.[1] However, the general concepts embodied in the chart were accepted by appraisers (and courts) prior to that time. Even

---

[1] Z. Christopher Mercer, "Do Public Company (Minority) Transactions Yield Controlling Interest or Minority Interest Pricing Data?," *Business Valuation Review*

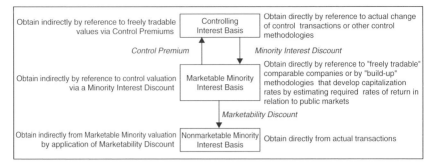

EXHIBIT 3.1 The Traditional Levels of Value

today, many discussions regarding levels of value in the valuation literature are very general, lacking any compelling logic or rationale regarding the factors giving rise to value differences at each level.

The early levels of value chart showed three conceptual levels, as indicated in Exhibit 3.1. The chart is so important to an understanding of valuation concepts that analysts at Mercer Capital have included it in virtually every valuation report since about 1992.

We, like most appraisers, assumed the existence of the conceptual adjustments referred to as the control premium, the minority interest discount, and the marketability discount. We relied on market evidence from control premium studies to help ascertain the magnitude of control premiums (and minority interest discounts). And we relied on certain benchmark studies, the so-called Pre-IPO Studies and the Restricted Stock Studies, as the basis for estimating marketability discounts. In hindsight, this reliance contributed to our failure to understand the basis for the premiums and discounts being estimated.[2]

Vol. 9, No. 4 (1990). This article was written in response to an insightful article by Eric Nath, published earlier that year. See Eric W. Nath, "Control Premiums and Minority Interest Discounts in Private Companies," *Business Valuation Review*, Vol. 9, No. 2 (1990). See also James H. Zukin, *Financial Valuation: Business and Business Interests* (New York: Maxwell MacMillan, 1990), pp. 2–3. While the concepts of the levels of value had been around for some time prior to 1990, to the best of our knowledge, the levels of value chart was not published until the Mercer article in 1990 and in the Zukin text that same year.

[2]By the early 1990s, we became increasingly uncomfortable with the prevailing methodologies for developing marketability discounts. The Quantitative Marketability Discount Model, which is based on our early development of the Integrated Theory, was introduced in speeches beginning in 1994 and in a book in 1997. See

The purpose of this chapter is to integrate the Gordon Model with how the markets value companies and the conceptual framework of the levels of value. In other words, this chapter introduces the Integrated Theory of Business Valuation, which is designed to:

- Provide a conceptual description of each level of value in the context of the Gordon Model.
- Use the components of the Gordon Model to define the conceptual adjustments between the levels of value, the control premium (and its inverse, the minority interest discount) and the marketability discount.
- Reconcile the resulting integrated valuation model to observed pricing behavior in the market for public securities (the marketable minority level), the market for entire companies (the controlling interest level(s) of value), and the market for illiquid, minority interests in private enterprises (the nonmarketable minority level of value).

With these objectives in mind, we proceed with the development of the Integrated Theory of Business Valuation.

THE MARKETABLE MINORITY INTEREST LEVEL OF VALUE

The Gordon Model provides a shorthand representation of the value of public securities at the marketable minority interest level of value. For privately owned enterprises, it indicates the same level of value (the "as-if-freely-traded" level). In developing the Integrated Theory, we use the Gordon Model to analyze how the levels of value relate to each other. To do so, we introduce a symbolic notation to designate which elements of the model relate to each level of value. Equation 3.2 introduces the conceptual math of the benchmark level of value—the marketable minority value.

$$V_{mm} = \frac{CF_{e(mm)}}{R_{mm} - G_{mm}} \qquad (3.2)$$

We just described the marketable minority level of value as the "benchmark" level of value. The marketable minority level of value is the benchmark to which control premiums are added to derive controlling

---

Z. Christopher Mercer, *Quantifying Marketability Discounts* (Memphis: Peabody Publishing, LP, 1997). The various studies mentioned in this paragraph are summarized in Chapters 1–3 of that book, and are briefly discussed in Appendix 7-A of this book.

interest indications of value, and from which marketability discounts are subtracted to reach the nonmarketable minority level of value.

Equation 3.2 is defined as follows:

- V_{mm} is the equity value of a company at the marketable minority level of value, whether public or private. This is the benchmark, observable value for public securities. The as-if-freely-traded value for private enterprises is a *hypothetical* value. By definition, it is not observable for nonmarketable interests of private enterprises because there are no active, public markets for the shares. Appraisers develop indications of value at the marketable minority level as a first step in determining other levels of value. Such indications of value are developed either by direct reference to the public securities markets (using the guideline public company method)[3], or indirectly, using the Adjusted Capital Asset Pricing Model or other build-up methods.[4]
- $CF_{e(mm)}$ is the expected cash flow of the enterprise at the marketable minority level for the next period. The marketable minority level of cash flow reflects enterprise earnings, "normalized" for unusual or nonrecurring events and having an expense structure that is market-based, at least in terms of owner/key shareholder compensation.[5] Public companies attempt to keep investors focused on their "normalized" earnings. Many public companies, for example, disclose pro forma earnings, or earnings after adjusting for unusual or nonrecurring (and sometimes not so nonrecurring) items. A more detailed discussion of the importance of normalizing earnings in developing marketable minority value indications is found in Chapter 4. The need to adjust for unusual or nonrecurring items is intuitively apparent. In Chapter 4, we discuss the other frequent type of normalizing adjustment—adjusting owner and/or officer compensation and perquisites to market levels. At this point, we ask the reader to accept this assumption and then consider the more detailed treatment in Chapter 4.

---

[3] See "SBVS-1 The Guideline Public Company Method," *ASA Business Valuation Standards* (Washington, D.C., American Society of Appraisers, November 2005), p. 32.

[4] See Chapter 6 for further discussion of discount rate development.

[5] Otherwise, there would be potential for excess returns through the acquisition of public companies and the realization of normalized earnings. The 1990 Nath article, discussed in a later section of this chapter, makes this point clearly. Eric W. Nath, "Control Premiums and Minority Interest Discounts in Private Companies," *Business Valuation Review*, Vol. 9, No. 2 (1990): pp. 39–46.

- R_{mm} is the discount rate at the marketable minority level of value. While it is not directly observable, it can be inferred from public pricing or estimated using the Capital Asset Pricing Model or other models. For private companies, R_{mm} is most often estimated using one of several build-up approaches.[6]
- G_{mm} is the expected growth rate of core earnings for the enterprise under the assumption that all earnings are distributed to shareholders (or g_e from Chapter 1). As shown previously, it is the compounding effect of reinvested earnings that enables a company to grow its reported earnings (and value) at rates (g^* from Chapter 1) in excess of its underlying core earnings growth rate. For reasons discussed in Chapter 1, G_{mm} is not equal to the expected growth rate of earnings published by stock analysts for public companies. The analysts' g (g^*) includes the compounding effect of the reinvestment of cash flows on the expected growth of earnings.

At this point, we can begin to connect the mathematics of valuation theory with the conceptual levels of value chart. The marketable minority level of value is the conceptual value from which other levels of value are derived. Exhibit 3.2 presents the conceptual math of the marketable minority level of value.

We refer to the marketable minority level of value as an *enterprise level* of value. We do so because $CF_{e(mm)}$ is defined as the cash flow of the

	Conceptual Math	Relationships	Value Implications
Marketable Minority Value	$\dfrac{CF_{e(mm)}}{R_{mm} - G_{mm}}$	$G_v = R_{mm} - \text{Div Yld}$	V_{mm} is the benchmark for the other levels

EXHIBIT 3.2 Conceptual Math of the Marketability Minority Level of Value

---

[6]Z. Christopher Mercer, "The Adjusted Capital Asset Pricing Model for Developing Capitalization Rates: An Extension of Previous 'Build-Up' Methodologies Based Upon the Capital Asset Pricing Model," *Business Valuation Review*, Vol. 8, No. 4 (1989): pp. 147–156. Some writers make a distinction between the ACAPM and the *build-up* method, which is identical to the ACAPM under the assumption that beta is equal to 1.0. This distinction is artificial because it should be apparent that the build-up method is based on the Capital Asset Pricing Model, just as is the ACAPM. See the more detailed discussion of discount rates in Chapter 6.

enterprise.[7] All the shareholders of a publicly traded enterprise, controlling or minority, share the benefit of all of its cash flows (as they are capitalized in the public stock markets every day). The importance of this definition will become clear as the remaining mathematical relationships of the conceptual levels of value are built.

We build the Integrated Theory from the base found in Exhibit 3.2 (and the in-depth discussion of the discounted cash flow model and the Gordon Model in Chapter 1).

- First, the conceptual math is illustrated. In Exhibit 3.2, that math is the familiar Gordon Model with the added notation of Equation 3.2. We will develop the conceptual math for the other levels of value as the chapter progresses.
- The next column is labeled Relationships. Here we see that the expected growth in value, G_v, is equal to the discount rate, R_{mm}, less the expected dividend yield (recall Equation 1.8). We will follow the progression of relationships between expected cash flows, risk, and growth as we develop the other levels of value.
- The final column is labeled Value Implications. In Exhibit 3.2, the conceptual math yields the benchmark marketable minority value, or V_{mm}. The value implications of the other levels of value will be explored in relationship to V_{mm} in this column.

The marketable minority level of value is that level to which appraisers have almost automatically applied control premiums to develop controlling interest indications of value. It is also the level from which appraisers have subtracted marketability discounts to derive indications of value at the nonmarketable minority level of value. Refer back to Exhibit 3.1. The control premium and the marketability discount are conceptual adjustments enabling appraisers to relate the marketable minority level of value with the controlling interest level (control premium) and the nonmarketable minority level (marketability discount). The minority interest discount also relates the controlling interest and marketable minority levels.

As pointed out clearly by Pratt, Reilly, Schweihs, and others, no valuation premium or discount has meaning unless we understand the base to

---

[7]As the discussion of the Integrated Theory progresses, we will consistently discuss the market value of the equity of business enterprises. The term *enterprise value* is sometimes used to describe the market value of the total capital of a business, inclusive of equity and debt. When we refer to *enterprise* levels of value, we consistently focus on market values of equity at each level of value where equity is a function of the cash flows to equity of the enterprise.

which it is applied.[8] The marketable minority value is the benchmark level of value for the enterprise in the Integrated Theory of Business Valuation.

A review of the valuation literature prior to the latter part of the 1990s yields little insight into the theoretical basis for applying the well-known conceptual premiums and discounts. Practically, appraisers applied control premiums because they were frequently observed when public companies changed control. And marketability discounts were applied because it was observed that restricted stocks of public companies traded at prices lower than their freely traded counterparts. Only in recent years have appraisers begun to understand and to articulate *why* control premiums and restricted stock discounts exist, and consequently, to understand the theoretical basis for their existence. The Integrated Theory explains the *why* behind the generally accepted valuation premiums and discounts.

THE CONTROL LEVELS OF VALUE

There is a growing consensus that there are at least two conceptual levels of value above the marketable minority level:

- *Financial Control.* The first control level describes what a financial buyer is able (and perhaps willing) to pay for control of a business. Financial buyers acquire companies based on their ability to extract reasonable (to them) rates of return, often on a leveraged basis.
- *Strategic Control.* The second control level is referred to as the strategic, or synergistic, level of value. Strategic buyers can (and do) pay more for companies than financial buyers because they expect to realize synergies

---

[8]Shannon P. Pratt, Robert F. Reilly, and Robert P. Schweihs, *Valuing a Business: The Analysis and Appraisal of Closely Held Companies*, 4th ed. (New York, NY: McGraw-Hill, 2000).
Shannon P. Pratt, Robert F. Reilly, and Robert P. Schweihs, *Valuing a Business: The Analysis and Appraisal of Closely Held Companies*, 3rd ed. (Chicago, IL: Irwin Professional Publishing, 1996).
Shannon P. Pratt, *Valuing a Business: The Analysis and Appraisal of Closely Held Companies*, 2nd ed. (Homewood, IL: Dow Jones-Irwin, 1988).
Shannon P. Pratt, *Valuing a Business: The Analysis and Appraisal of Closely Held Companies*, 1st ed. (Homewood, IL: Dow Jones-Irwin, 1981).
Z. Christopher Mercer, "Valuation Overview," *Valuing Financial Institutions* (Homewood, IL: Business One Irwin, 1992), pp. 193–206.

from acquisitions (e.g., perhaps through eliminating duplicate expenses or achieving cross-selling benefits) that increase future cash flows.[9]

This emerging consensus, supported by evidence from change-of-control transaction data, has led to conceptual levels of value charts with four, rather than three, levels. A general comparison of the two charts is shown in Exhibit 3.3. Further refinements of the comparison follow at Exhibit 3.5.

The left side of Exhibit 3.3 presents the traditional, three-level chart, including the conceptual premium and discounts that enable appraisers to relate the three levels to each other. The right side of Exhibit 3.3 presents the expanded, four-level chart. Note that the "financial control premium" on the right and the "control premium" on the left are the equivalent conceptual premiums.[10] As a result, the minority interest discounts shown on the left and right sides of Exhibit 3.3 are the same conceptual discount. We have called the conceptual premium relating the financial control value to the strategic control value the "strategic control premium."[11] Note that no name is

---

[9]Steven D. Garber, "Control vs. Acquisition Premiums: Is There a Difference?" (Presentation at the American Society of Appraisers International Appraisal Conference, Maui, HI, June 23, 1998).

Z. Christopher Mercer, "A Brief Review of Control Premiums and Minority Interest Discounts," *The Journal of Business Valuation*, (Toronto: Carswell Thomas, 1997), pp. 365–387.

M. Mark Lee, "Premiums and Discounts for the Valuation of Closely Held Companies: The Need for Specific Economic Analysis," *Shannon Pratt's Business Valuation Update*, August 2001.

[10]This flows from the general belief that fair market value is a financial concept based on the hypothetical negotiations of hypothetical willing buyers and sellers, and that the "strategic control premium" reflects the consideration of specific buyers who benefit from particular synergies or strategies. The strategic control level of value might become the appropriate level for fair market value if the *typical buyers* are strategic buyers. This situation existed during much of the last two decades in the consolidating banking industry and in numerous other consolidating industries.

[11]Shannon P. Pratt, Robert F. Reilly, and Robert P. Schweihs, *Valuing a Business: The Analysis and Appraisal of Closely Held Companies*, 4th ed. (New York, NY: McGraw-Hill, 2000). Note that the strategic control premium is referred to as the "strategic acquisition premium" in their chart at page 347. The authors state, regarding the chart:

"The diagram presented in Exhibit 15-1 reflects the value influence of the ownership characteristics of control versus the noncontrolling stockholder's situation as discussed in Chapter 16. This schematic usually would represent the *fair market value standard of value* on a *going-concern basis*

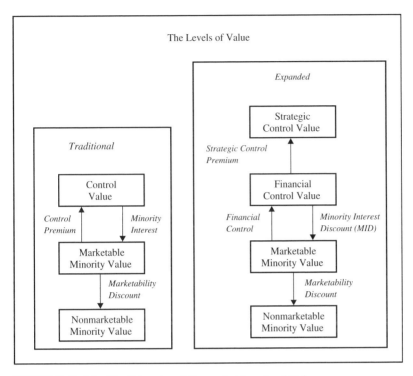

The Levels of Value

Expanded

Traditional

Strategic
Control Value

Strategic Control Premium

Control
Value

Financial
Control Value

Control Premium   *Minority Interest*

Financial Control   *Minority Interest Discount (MID)*

Marketable
Minority Value

Marketable
Minority Value

Marketability Discount

Marketability Discount

Nonmarketable
Minority Value

Nonmarketable
Minority Value

EXHIBIT 3.3 The Traditional and Expanded Levels of Value

provided for the conceptual discount that would reduce the strategic control to the financial control value. Further, note that this conceptual discount *is*

----

premise of value. In some cases, there may be yet another layer of value, which may reflect synergies with certain third-party buyers (as examples of: (1) reducing combined overhead by the consolidation of operations or (2) raising prices by reducing competition). There is not yet a widely used term for this additional layer of price premium over fair market, going-concern value. However, this price premium—when combined with the owner-ship control premium—is sometimes called an *acquisition premium*. The standard of value reflecting these synergies usually would be considered *investment value*. This is because it reflects the *value to a particular buyer*, generally referred to as the *synergistic buyer*, rather than value to the hypo-thetical willing buyer. This "hypothetical" typical willing buyer acquires the subject company strictly because of its financial merits, and is generally referred to as a *financial buyer*." (emphasis in original)

not the minority interest discount relating the financial control value with the marketable minority level of value.

As we move up from the marketable minority level to the levels of financial control and strategic control, we see that it is possible that a controlling shareholder may make adjustments to expected cash flows based on the expected ability to run an enterprise more efficiently (financial control) or differently (strategic control). Such *control adjustments* could have the effect of increasing value if such adjustments would normally be negotiated between hypothetical (or real) buyers and sellers. In other words, from a conceptual viewpoint, *control adjustments* are those that, if appropriate, increase enterprise cash flow *above that of the (normalized) marketable minority level.* As Exhibit 3.3 indicates in a conceptual sense, the value of the expected cash flows of the enterprise from the viewpoint of either a financial control buyer or a strategic control buyer may be greater than the value of the normalized expected cash flow of the enterprise.

Careful review of the control (or acquisition) premium data available to appraisers indicates such premiums generally result from transactions motivated by strategic or synergistic considerations. Consequently, the available control premium data more generally reflects the *combination of the financial control premium and the strategic control premium* (see Exhibit 3.2).[12] This observation suggests the following conclusions:[13]

- Use of available control premium studies as a basis for inferring minority interest discounts in a fair market value context is conceptually incorrect, except where strategic buyers are the norm. The improper use of such data would tend to *overstate* the magnitude of minority interest discounts.
- When applied to financial control values, such discounts would not yield marketable minority interest levels of value, but rather something below that level (with no clear conceptual definition).
- And finally, the application of a "standard" marketability discount to that lower (and conceptually undefined) value would tend to *understate* the value of illiquid interests of private enterprises.

---

[12] *Mergerstat/Shannon Pratt's Control Premium Study.* This study is available in print versions and online at www.BVMarketData.com.
[13] Z. Christopher Mercer, "Understanding and Quantifying Control Premiums: The Value of Control vs. Synergies or Strategic Advantages," *The Journal of Business Valuation,* (Toronto: Carswell Thomas, 1999), pp. 31–54.

THE FINANCIAL CONTROL LEVEL OF VALUE

With this conceptual backdrop, we can examine the controlling interest levels of value. Equation 3.3 illustrates the conceptual math of the first control level of value—*the financial control value*. Equation 3.3 introduces notation that we will use to discuss the levels of value in the context of the Integrated Theory. Each symbol is defined in the following list.

$$V_{e(c,f)} = \frac{CF_{e(c,f)}}{[R_f - (G_{mm} + G_f)]} \tag{3.3}$$

As with the marketable minority level of value, the terms found in Equation 3.3 are defined as follows:

- $V_{e(c,f)}$ is the value of the equity of an enterprise as a whole from the viewpoint of financial control buyers who do not expect to achieve strategic benefits relative to the marketable minority value. Traditionally, appraisers have developed the financial control level of value in two ways: 1) directly, by comparison with change of control transactions of similar businesses (the guideline transaction method); and 2) indirectly, by application of control premiums to indications of marketable minority value.
- $CF_{e(c,f)}$ is the expected cash flow of the enterprise from the viewpoint of the financial buyer. The first step in developing $CF_{e(c,f)}$ is to derive $CF_{e(mm)}$ by normalizing the earnings stream as described in Chapter 4. Note that the normalization of earnings is not a "control" process, but one of equating private company earnings to their as-if-public equivalent.[14] The second step involves judging the ability of a control buyer to *improve* the earnings stream beyond the normalization process. This could involve the ability of a specific buyer to improve the existing operations or to run the target company more efficiently. However, unless there are competing financial buyers, a single buyer would likely be unwilling to share the benefit of all expected cash flow improvement

---

[14]The issue of normalizing earnings is discussed at more length in Chapter 4. However, normalization is an integral part of public securities pricing. It is not uncommon to find companies with well above-peer group price/earnings multiples based on trailing 12-month earnings, yet with near average multiples of forward (next year's) earnings. Commonly, investigation reveals an unusual, nonrecurring item in the most recent period that the market is "normalizing" and pricing based on the expectation of more normal earnings next year.

with the seller. In the real world, there would be a negotiation to determine the extent of such sharing.[15]

- R_f is the discount rate at the financial control level of value. In the real world, R_f may be identical to R_{mm}, as other writers have observed.[16] While market forces will tend to equate R_f and R_{mm}, R_f is distinctly specified to allow for potential differences. Financial control buyers may bid up prices in competition with other financial or strategic buyers, causing R_f to fall below R_{mm}. Certain buyers may consciously lower R_f to secure a deal, leading to potential overvaluation. Alternatively, specification of R_f in excess of R_{mm} recognizes that the value of an enterprise to financial control buyers may be less than the freely traded value. In the public markets, this result could occur, for example, when speculative trading pushes a stock's price above financial control values. In the context of various control premium studies, this specification of R_f helps explain the existence of occasional *negative* control premiums in acquisitions, or acquisition prices below the before-announcement trading prices of targets.

- $(G_{mm} + G_f)$ is the expected growth rate of earnings for the financial control buyer. The first factor is the same G_{mm} found at the marketable minority level. The second factor (G_f) is the increment in the growth rate of earnings that a financial control buyer expects to generate. The second factor may not be relevant in determining the value of an enterprise for either of two reasons: 1) the universe of buyers may not expect such an increment in growth; or 2) a specific buyer who can accelerate growth may not share that expected benefit in a negotiation.[17] Nevertheless, this component of expected growth needs to be specified in order to understand market behavior. Financial control buyers might expect to augment growth by better managing the relationship between the growth of revenue and expenses, more productive use of facilities, better processes, and the like. Note that, unlike strategic synergies, these internal opportunities for cash flow enhancement do not depend on a specific combination with another business.

---

[15]Note that the negotiation between buyers and sellers affects the purchase price and not the expected after-acquisition cash flows. This suggests that observed takeover premiums do not reflect the expected total change in cash flow, but only the portion negotiated and shared with sellers.

[16]Shannon P. Pratt, *Cost of Capital* (New York: John Wiley, 1998), pp. 111–112.

[17]Multiple financial buyers in an auction process may end up competing with each other such that the seller gains all or most of the growth benefit from the second-highest estimate of G_f.

	Conceptual Math	Relationships	Value Implications
Financial Control Value	$\dfrac{CF_{e(c,f)}}{R - [G_{mm} + G_f]}$	$CF_{e(c,f)} \geq CF_{e(mm)}$ $G_f \geq 0$ $R_f = R_{mm(+/-\ a\ little)}$	$V_{e(c,f)} \geq V_{mm}$
Marketable Minority Value	$\dfrac{CF_{e(mm)}}{R_{mm} - G_{mm}}$	$G_v = R_{mm} - Div\ Yld$	V_{mm} is the benchmark for the other levels

EXHIBIT 3.4 Conceptual Math of the Marketable Minority and Financial Control Levels of Value

We now have a conceptual model describing the financial control level of value, consistent with the previously specified conceptual model for the marketable minority level of value. The relationship between the two levels of value is shown in Exhibit 3.4.

The conceptual differences in value at the marketable minority and financial control levels of value can be discerned by examining Exhibit 3.4. This analysis illustrates that control premiums (or other conceptual adjustments) are not automatic, but are based on expected differences in cash flows, risk, and/or growth. Based on Exhibit 3.4, the financial control value would exceed the marketable minority value if, all other things being equal, one or more of the following conditions were true:

- $CF_{e(c,f)}$ *is greater than* $CF_{e(mm)}$. This would be true if the buyer of the enterprise could be expected to improve the operations of the enterprise (and would share that expected benefit with the seller). Note that $CF_{e(c,f)}$ will not exceed $CF_{e(mm)}$ because of above-market salaries paid to owners of a business. Such adjustments were required to derive $CF_{e(mm)}$.[18]
- G_f *is greater than zero.* If the financial control buyer expects to augment the future growth of cash flows (and will share that benefit with the seller), then $V_{e(c,f)}$ can exceed V_{mm}.
- R_f *is less than* R_{mm}. Conceptually, R_f could be less or greater than R_{mm}. Either condition could be true for a specific buyer; however, it is

---

[18]Appraisers often assume that in valuing minority interests of private companies, no adjustments should be made for above-market owner salaries or perquisites "because the minority shareholder lacks the power to change the cash flows." The upcoming discussion of the minority interest discount and the treatment of normalizing adjustments (Chapter 4) will address this common misconception.

likely that market forces would force the relevant universe of buyers to expect a return no greater than R_{mm} as the appropriate discount rate. The specification of R_f does provide an explanation for financial control premiums that might be paid for enterprises based on competition between private equity funds. Such funds have the capacity to bid up prices by accepting lower returns on individual deals.[19]

Once again, the point of this analysis is that the financial control premium is not automatic. Sellers have a history of earnings (appropriately adjusted) that provides the basis for future cash flow expectations. Buyers have the benefit of that history and may perceive greater future cash flows. Any differential in value is the function of negotiations between buyers and sellers of enterprises. The conceptual analysis of the Integrated Theory does not predict financial control value, but does provide a vocabulary to describe the economic behavior of rational market participants. The Integrated Theory also provides the conceptual and analytical framework within which appraisers can estimate financial (or strategic) control value in appropriate situations.

Financial Control Premium

At this point, the control premium relating the price a financial control buyer might pay to the marketable minority value can be specified in terms of differences (from the marketable minority level) in expected cash flow, risk and/or growth.

$$\mathbf{CP}_f = \frac{V_{e(c,f)} - V_{e(mm)}}{V_{e(mm)}} \qquad (3.4)$$

Equation 3.4 defines the financial control premium as the difference in value between the financial control and the marketable minority levels. Several observations regarding the relationship between value at the marketable minority and financial control levels of value follow.

Application of financial control premiums should be limited to situations in which the hypothetical willing buyer reasonably expects to:

---

[19]In fact, financial buyers have been shown to compete with strategic buyers. See "Control Premium Study Shows Decline in Market Multiples," *Shannon Pratt's Business Valuation Update*, October 2001, pp. 6–7. Such capacity of private equity funds to bid up deals is likely correlated to the supply of investable funds at their disposal.

- Increase cash flows relative to normalized cash flows of the enterprise; and/or,
- Increase expected growth of cash flows of the enterprise; and/or,
- Accept a return less than R_{mm}; and,
- Be willing to share all or a portion of the expected benefits of these items with seller.

In the absence of any of the preceding conditions, the financial control value will be the same as the freely traded, marketable minority value. Further, values derived by applying guideline public company multiples to normalized earnings of privately owned enterprises will approximate financial control values. This assumes, of course, that the public multiples are properly adjusted for fundamental differences in expectations (primarily for risk and growth) between the guideline public companies and the subject private enterprises. The concept of the fundamental adjustment and its role in the Integrated Theory is discussed in Chapter 5.

The financial control premium is clearly a range concept. The financial control premium that might be paid for a particular enterprise will vary with potential buyers based on their unique circumstances and the degree of competitive bidding.

We have come a long way catching up to Eric Nath's startling suggestion in 1990 that the public market multiples of guideline companies yielded controlling interest values.[20] Suffice it to say that many appraisers thought this observation was nothing short of heresy. Mercer was in that group![21] The Integrated Theory reconciles Nath's position of control multiples coming from the public markets if the financial control premium is zero.

We have defined $V_{e(c,f)}$ from the viewpoint of financial control buyers. $V_{e(c,f)}$ sets the upper boundary for negotiation of price with sellers (unless a particular buyer is willing to reduce R_f). The greater the positive differences between $V_{e(c,f)}$ and $V_{e(mm)}$, the greater the potential for the consummation of transactions. Nath's observation was that, given the relatively low number of acquisitions in any year relative to total number of public companies, the

---

[20]Eric W. Nath, "Control Premiums and Minority Interest Discounts in Private Companies," *Business Valuation Review*, Vol. 9, No. 2 (1990): pp. 39–46.

[21]Z. Christopher Mercer, "Do Public Company (Minority) Transactions Yield Controlling Interest or Minority Interest Pricing Data?," *Business Valuation Review*, Vol. 9, No. 4 (1990): pp. 123–126. In this article, Mercer charged to the defense of public multiples providing marketable minority value indications. Nath's view is reconciled with the Integrated Theory under the assumption that no value-enhancing factors are available to the financial control buyer, and the financial control premium is therefore zero. Mercer did not recognize this potential for reconciliation in 1990.

difference, in most instances, must be zero (or not large enough to warrant the interest of financial buyers). This suggests that public market pricing could reflect both marketable minority and financial control pricing. There is a growing consensus among appraisers that there is a difference between financial and strategic control values, and a growing recognition that, to the extent they exist, financial control premiums are likely small.

Prerogatives of Control (Introduction to the Minority Interest Discount)

We now turn to corollary implications of the analysis of the financial control premium. The *minority interest discount* necessary to adjust a financial control value to a marketable minority value in an operating company may be zero, or quite small. This conclusion follows from the discussion of the conceptual elements of the financial control premium.

Developing and articulating reasonable financial control premiums and minority interest discounts is difficult outside the conceptual framework of the Integrated Theory. Consider the discussion of the value of control in the most recent edition of Pratt/Reilly/Schweihs. Many appraisers cite the list of prerogatives of control found in each of the Pratt/Reilly/Schweihs books (and other books) as support for the application of a substantial minority interest discount. The prerogatives of control include the ability to unilaterally:[22]

1. Appoint or change operational management
2. Appoint or change members of the board of directors
3. Determine management compensation and perquisites
4. Set operational and strategic policy and change the course of the business
5. Acquire, lease, or liquidate business assets, including plant, property, and equipment
6. Select suppliers, vendors, and subcontractors with whom to do business and award contracts
7. Negotiate and consummate mergers and acquisitions
8. Liquidate, dissolve, sell out, or recapitalize the company
9. Sell or acquire treasury shares
10. Register the company's equity securities for an initial or secondary public offering
11. Register the company's debt securities for an initial or secondary public offering

---

[22]Shannon P. Pratt, Robert F. Reilly, and Robert P. Schweihs, *Valuing a Business*, 4th ed (New York: McGraw-Hill, 2000), pp. 347–348. The list is growing with succeeding editions.

12. Declare and pay cash and/or stock dividends
13. Change the articles of incorporation or bylaws
14. Set one's own compensation (and perquisites) and the compensation (and perquisites) of related-party employees
15. Select joint venturers and enter into joint venture and partnership agreements
16. Decide what products and/or services to offer and how to price those products or services
17. Decide what markets and locations to serve, to enter into, and to discontinue serving
18. Decide which customer categories to market to and which not to market to
19. Enter into inbound and outbound license or sharing agreements regarding intellectual properties
20. Block any or all of the above actions

In short, the controlling shareholder is empowered with the rights to manage a business enterprise for the benefit of the controlling shareholder. Appraisers (and courts) have long thought that control buyers pay control premiums for the prerogatives of control just listed. The Pratt/Reilly/ Schweihs text concludes the presentation of this list, which first appears in Chapter 15, "Control and Acquisition Premiums," with the following comment:

> *From the above list, it is apparent that the owner of a controlling interest in a business enterprise enjoys some very valuable rights that the owner of a noncontrolling ownership interest does not enjoy.*[23]

The authors present two levels of value charts at the same point in the text. The first chart is the three-level one used for several years in editions of *Valuing a Business* and other publications. The second is the modified and expanded four-level chart presented in Exhibit 3.3.[24] In other words, the control premium in view is the same conceptual premium as the financial control premium indicated in Exhibit 3.3.

---

[23] Ibid, p. 349.
[24] Ibid, p. 347. Citing Jay E. Fishman, Shannon P. Pratt, *Guide to Business Valuations*, 10th ed. (Fort Worth, TX: Practitioners Publishing Company, 2000). Also, at p. 348, citing Z. Christopher Mercer, "Understanding and Quantifying Control Premiums: The Value of Control vs. Synergies of Strategic Advantages," *The Journal of Business Valuation* (Toronto: Carswell Thomson, 1999), p. 51.

We will see shortly that the statement just quoted may be true as it relates to a controlling owner of a private company and a minority (noncontrolling) shareholder in the same company. It is likely not true (or is not relevant) as it relates to the managements and boards of directors of well-run public companies and the corresponding minority shareholders holding publicly traded shares.

Examination of the conceptual math shown in Exhibit 3.4 reveals no direct consideration of the aforementioned prerogatives of control. What, then, is a control buyer paying for? We observe the following from Exhibit 3.4, which defines the financial control premium:

- The financial control premium is created by any differential in cash flows or growth that the control buyer is willing to price into a deal. In other words, the conceptual model suggests that a control buyer would pay a financial control price based only on the expectation of greater future cash flows than expected at the marketable minority level.

  Rather than having some inherent value, the value of the various prerogatives of control is manifest in more favorable expectations with respect to expected cash flows, growth, or risk. Control premiums are paid for the right to run the enterprise differently to achieve enhanced cash flow or accelerated growth. The price is paid for the expected cash flow and not for the naked right, or prerogative.

- There is no specific portion of the value of an enterprise that should be allocated solely to the prerogatives of control.

We conclude, therefore, that control buyers augment the marketable minority level of cash flow through the exercise of the prerogatives.

We have observed thus far that unless the control buyer expects to achieve augmented levels and growth of cash flows, the financial control premium could be zero, or at least, quite small. The reason is simple: If a substantial premium were paid with no expectation of augmented cash flows, then the control buyer would have to accept a substantially lower return.

The Minority Interest Discount

The conceptual difference between the financial control value and the marketable minority value is the financial control premium (see Exhibit 3.3). If that premium is zero (or quite small), it is also true that the minority interest (or lack of control) discount is quite small.[25] Several observations

---

[25] "Definitions," *Business Valuation Standards* (Washington, D.C.: American Society of Appraisers, June 2005), pp. 21–31. This lack of control discount is theoretically consistent with eliminating a financial control premium.

about the relationships between the marketable minority and financial control levels of value are summarized here:

- Minority shareholders of public companies lack control, which is vested with managements and boards of directors. Yet we have observed (practically as with Nath, and conceptually with the Integrated Theory) that the marketable minority value and the financial control value may approximate each other for most public companies. Again, otherwise there would be strong financial incentive for the takeover of many public companies. Absent such a level of activity, it is reasonable to assume that the marketable minority and financial control values for most public companies approximate each other.

- The implication of this line of reasoning is that there is no (or very little) discount for lack of control considered in the pricing of public securities. This makes sense because investors in the public markets are not investing to gain control—they invest in companies and expect managements to run them in the best interests of the shareholders. Otherwise, the shareholders would exercise the control they do have—selling their shares and putting downward pressure on market prices, creating opportunities for takeovers by financial buyers.

- Further, observe that at the marketable minority level, all the cash flows of public enterprises are expected to be distributed to the shareholders or reinvested in the enterprises at their discount rates. Share prices are not reduced because minority shareholders do not control or have direct access to enterprise cash flows, since minority shareholders have access to the benefit of the market's capitalization of all expected future cash flows in the current market price. At any time, a minority shareholder in a public enterprise can place a sale order and achieve current market value in three days.

- This reasoning suggests that the public securities markets eliminate most, if not all, of any discount for lack of control.

The logical inference following these observations is that unless there are cash flow–driven differences between the enterprise's financial control value and its marketable minority value, there will be no (or very little) minority interest discount.[26] Market discipline causes most public companies to be run in reasonable fashion, with cash flows being optimized and either

---

[26]The capital structure of an enterprise may include voting and nonvoting stock. If the vote is perceived to decrease risk somewhat relative to the nonvoting shares, voting shares may trade at a small premium to nonvoting shares. Stated alternatively, nonvoting shares may trade at a small discount to voting shares.

reinvested or distributed to achieve appropriate returns to shareholders. The minority interest discount will exist only if the typical control financial buyer can expect to augment cash flows from properly normalized cash flows at the marketable minority level.[27]

The financial control premium was defined in Equation 3.4. The related minority interest discount from the financial control value (MID_F) is defined in Equation 3.5.

$$MID_F = \left(1 - \frac{V_{mm}}{V_{e(c,f)}} \right) \tag{3.5}$$

The conceptual analysis thus far suggests that Exhibit 3.3 should be modified to reflect the conceptual relationship between the financial control and marketable minority levels of value (see Exhibit 3.5).

The expanded, modified chart in Exhibit 3.5 depicts the much smaller (or non-existent) difference between the financial control and marketable minority levels of value suggested by our analysis.

The strategic control value will be developed to round out the enterprise levels before proceeding to the shareholder level (nonmarketable minority value). However, we do pause to observe that what can be large differences between the enterprise and shareholder levels of value is not attributable to the familiar prerogatives of control, but rather the lack of marketability.

STRATEGIC CONTROL LEVEL OF VALUE

Equation 3.6 introduces the conceptual math describing the second control level of value—the strategic control value.

$$V_{e(c,s)} = \frac{CF_{e(c,s)}}{[R_s - (G_{mm} + G_s)]} \tag{3.6}$$

As with the other levels, we define the terms in Equation 3.6:

---

[27]These observations are made in relationship to operating companies. Their relevance for asset holding entities needs to be addressed further. The logic of the Integrated Theory suggests that there is no reason for minority interest discounts related to asset holding entities to be of great magnitude. In practice, we have used minority interest discounts in the range of 0% to 15% for several years when valuing asset holding entities. The issue of minority interest discounts seldom arises when valuing operating companies, because most valuation methods, other than comparison with guideline transactions of whole companies, yield marketable minority level indications of value.

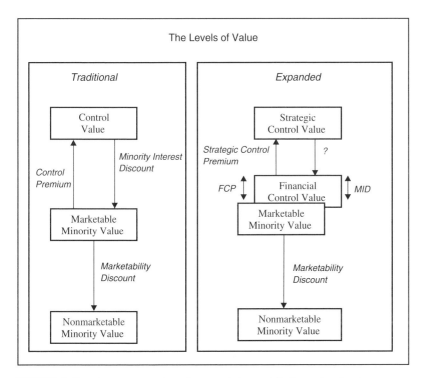

EXHIBIT 3.5 The Traditional and Expanded, Modified Levels of Value

- $V_{e(c,s)}$ is the value of the equity of an enterprise from the viewpoint of strategic control buyers who expect to achieve unique synergistic or strategic benefits relative to the financial control value (and the marketable minority value). As noted in the quote from Pratt/Reilly/Schweihs shown earlier, strategic control value is that perceived by particular buyers, rather than the typical buyers in the fair market value context. As such, $V_{e(c,s)}$ is generally more akin to investment value than fair market value.

- $CF_{e(c,s)}$ is the cash flow of the enterprise from the viewpoint of strategic control buyers. As with $CF_{e(c,f)}$, the first step in developing $CF_{e(c,s)}$ is to normalize earnings to derive $CF_{e(mm)}$. Additional adjustments may then be appropriate to reflect:

  ○ Improvements that typical financial buyers might expect to make by running the company better (to derive $CF_{e(c,f)}$);

  ○ Expected synergies (generally related to cost reductions); and/or,

  ○ Expected strategic benefits (e.g., from selling more of the acquirer's products through the target's existing distribution channels).

In other words, in addition to expectations of running the existing company more efficiently, strategic control buyers may take into consideration expected benefits related to adding the company to the buyer's existing portfolio.

- R_s is the discount rate of potential strategic buyers. R_s can be lower than R_{mm} or R_f for at least two reasons. First many strategic buyers are considerably larger in size than the smaller public and private companies that they may desire to acquire, and therefore have lower costs of capital than their smaller targets.[28] Second, other strategic acquirers may expect business risk to decrease as the result of a strategic combination, and therefore be willing to accept a lower return.

- $(G_{mm} + G_f)$ is the expected growth rate of earnings for the strategic control buyer. The first factor is the same G_{mm} found at the marketable minority level. The second factor is the increment in the growth rate that a strategic control buyer may expect to create. In other words, expected synergies can impact both the level of cash flow ($CF_{e(c,s)}$) and the growth of those cash flows.

The conceptual model now includes the strategic control level of value. It builds on the base created by the other two enterprise levels, marketable minority and financial control. The relationship between the three enterprise levels of value is illustrated in Exhibit 3.6.

The strategic control value will be greater than the financial control value if one or more of the following conditions hold:

- *$CF_{e(c,s)}$ is greater than $CF_{e(c,f)}$*. In other words, a strategic purchaser of an enterprise expects to achieve synergies or strategic benefits unavailable to the financial control buyer. Consider, though, that a lone strategic buyer has no incentive to pay any more than necessary to outbid the most aggressive financial buyer.[29] In other words, there may be a considerable difference in what a particular strategic buyer is *able* to pay and what that buyer is *willing* to pay in an acquisition.

---

[28] Whether strategic buyers should give benefit to their lower costs of capital in strategic acquisitions is a separate question. However, if the market consists of numerous, competing strategic buyers some or all of that benefit may be transferred to the seller.

[29] Mr. Gilbert A Matthews, ASA, currently of Sutter Securities, Inc. and for many years an investment banker with Bear, Stearns & Co., made this observation years ago. The conceptual analysis presented here should confirm the relevance of this observation in the context of fair market value determinations.

	Conceptual Math	Relationships	Value Implications
Strategic Control value	$\dfrac{CF_{e(c,s)}}{R_s - [G_{mm} + G_s]}$	$CF_{e(c,s)} \geq CF_{e(c,f)}$ $G_s \geq 0$ $R_s \leq R_{mm}$	$V_{e(c,s)} \geq V_{e(c,f)}$
Financial Control Value	$\dfrac{CF_{e(c,f)}}{R_f - [G_{mm} + G_f]}$	$CF_{e(c,f)} \geq CF_{e(mm)}$ $G_f \geq 0$ $R_f = R_{mm(+/-\text{ a little})}$	$V_{e(c,f)} \geq V_{mm}$
Marketable Minority Value	$\dfrac{CF_{e(mm)}}{R_{mm} - G_{mm}}$	$G_v = R_{mm} - \text{Div Yld}$	V_{mm} is the benchmark for the other levels

EXHIBIT 3.6 Conceptual Math of the Enterprise Levels of Value?

- G_s *is greater than zero.* If a strategic control buyer expects to augment the future growth of cash flows (and will share that benefit with the hypothetical seller), then value can exceed the financial control or marketable minority levels.
- R_s *is less than* R_f. If a strategic buyer considers its own discount rate (cost of capital), which may be lower than that of a target, in pricing an acquisition, strategic control value can be greater than at the other enterprise levels.

If a strategic control buyer is willing to consider expected cash flow enhancements (either one-time increases in level and/or increases in growth from that new level) *and* its own lower discount rate in pricing an acquisition, $V_{e(s,c)}$ can be substantially higher than V_{mm} or $V_{e(c,f)}$. If multiple strategic buyers are seeking the same (public or private) business, then strategic value is more likely to be achieved by that seller, and pricing can sometimes seem almost irrational.[30]

---

[30] Mercer has often said in speeches that there are *three* kinds of buyers of businesses: financial buyers, strategic buyers, and irrational buyers. What every seller wants to find is an irrational buyer. Unfortunately, when they are really needed, they are hard to find. However, fair market value is a rational concept, not an irrational one. Appraisers need to keep these concepts in mind when determining fair market value at the financial control level.

CRITICAL INSIGHTS FOR CORPORATE FINANCE PROFESSIONALS, MANAGEMENTS, AND BOARDS

Corporate finance professionals, managements, and boards of directors of acquisitive companies responsible for the pricing of acquisitions should take note of these observations. Finance theory suggests that the appropriate discount rate is that of the investment, rather than the investor. Strategic purchasers who substitute their own discount rates (R_s) for the discount rates of acquisition targets $(R_{mm}$ or $R_f)$ may overpay for acquisitions relative to the risks assumed. Overpayment is even more likely if expected strategic or synergistic cash flow benefits are considered in acquisition valuation models through adjustments either to the level or the expected growth of a target's cash flows. In such cases, there remains no incremental reward for accepting all of the operational and execution risks of achieving the anticipated benefits. If execution is not flawless, shareholder returns will suffer.

In other words, strategic buyers should acknowledge the impact of using their own discount rates (R_s) to value potential acquisitions. Acquirers that start negotiations at the strategic level of pricing transfer wealth to sellers and accept the future execution risks without adequate compensation.

Strategic Control Premium

The premium that a strategic control buyer might pay (CP_s) relative to the marketable minority value can now be defined. We specify the premium in this way because there is no observable market for financial control values (other than if public companies are trading at their financial control values).[31] Note that this premium includes any financial control premium. CP_s is specified in Equation 3.7.

$$CP_s = \frac{V_{e(c,s)} - V_{e(mm)}}{V_{e(mm)}} \qquad (3.7)$$

---

[31] We can observe the net pricing of private companies in the acquisition markets; however, the marketable minority base is not observable, and therefore the extent of any control premium cannot be observed directly.

The strategic control premium is the excess of strategic control value over the marketable minority value as a percentage of the marketable minority value.

Strategic control premiums exist only if one or more of the following conditions hold:

- The strategic buyer expects to be able to enhance cash flows from the normalized, marketable minority level.
- The strategic buyer is willing to accept a lower return than that available at the marketable minority level.
- There is a single, motivated strategic buyer who is willing to share the expected synergistic or strategic benefits with a seller.[32]
- There are multiple strategic buyers who will compete in a bidding process.
- Elements of motivation or irrationality enter into the bidding process.

For public companies, the marketable minority value is the base from which strategic control prices are negotiated. Private company transactions tend to be negotiated directly, because there is no observable freely traded value to serve as a base. These same principles are manifest, however, within negotiated private company transactions.

Having developed the strategic control premium, we can briefly discuss the discount that would translate strategic control value to marketable minority value. Note the question mark between the strategic control and financial control levels of Exhibit 3.5. We have already observed that the question mark is not the minority interest discount, which relates the financial control and marketable minority levels, but does subsume the minority interest discount. It would represent the minority interest discount only if strategic transactions are the norm for an industry. Rather than attempting to give this nameless discount a moniker, we leave it for further consideration by appraisers in specific valuation situations.

ENTERPRISE LEVELS VS. THE SHAREHOLDER LEVEL OF VALUE

Thus far, the enterprise levels of value—marketable minority, financial control, and strategic control—have been addressed. These conceptual

---

[32]Note that owners that are not particularly motivated to sell may be able to extract some or all of the potential strategic control premium if there is only a single strategic buyer—if that buyer is motivated.

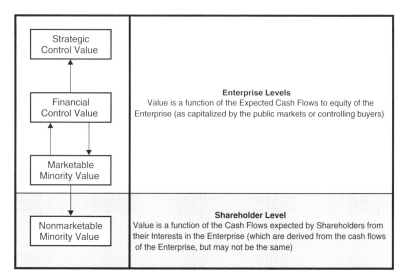

EXHIBIT 3.7   The Enterprise and Shareholder Levels of Value

levels are called enterprise levels because each is determined on the basis of (potentially) differing market perceptions and valuations of the cash flows to equity of the enterprise. As illustrated in Exhibit 3.7, the Gordon Model posits that value is a function of the expected cash flows of the enterprise, all of which are available for distribution or for reinvestment.

The fourth conceptual level of value is the nonmarketable minority level. In contrast to an enterprise level of value, this level is referred to as the *shareholder level of value*. Value to a shareholder is determined based on the expectation of cash flows to the shareholder. This important distinction is, unfortunately, often overlooked.

For years, appraisers have called the difference between the marketable minority and nonmarketable minority levels of value the *marketability discount*, or the *discount for lack of marketability*. The marketability discount is defined in the *ASA Business Valuation* Standards as an "amount or percentage deducted from the value of an ownership interest to reflect the relative absence and marketability."[33]

We wrote an article in 2001 discussing the logical basis for the marketability discount. The following excerpt focuses on the distinction between enterprise and shareholder values:[34]

---

[33]Ibid, p. 23.

[34]Z. Christopher Mercer and Travis W. Harms, "Marketability Discount Analysis at a Fork in the Road," *Business Valuation Review*, Vol. 20, No. 4 (2001): pp. 21–22.

There is almost unanimous agreement in the valuation profession that the value of a business, at the marketable minority level, where most valuations originate, is the present value of the expected future benefits to be generated by the business, discounted to the present at an appropriate, risk-adjusted discount rate. In other words, the value of a business depends on the expected cash flows of the business (including their expected future growth), and the risk of generating those cash flows (manifested in the discount rate).

Likewise, a nonmarketable minority interest in a business is a financial asset whose value must derive from the same factors determining the value of the business: expected cash flows (including their expected future growth), and the risk of generating those cash flows (as manifested in the discount rate).

- The expected cash flows to the holder of a nonmarketable minority business interest have as their source the cash flows generated by the business. The cash flows received by the nonmarketable minority investor may be less than, or equal to, but may be no greater than the cash flows generated by the business.
- Since the expected cash flows generated by the business are the source of the nonmarketable minority investor's cash flows, the risks faced by the nonmarketable minority investor encompass the risk of the business generating those cash flows, as well as incremental risks arising from the illiquidity of the investment. Therefore, the embodiment of risk for valuation purposes, the relevant discount rate, must for nonmarketable investors be greater than or equal to, but cannot be less than, the discount rate applicable to the valuation of the business.
- From the standpoint of the nonmarketable minority investor, this confluence of circumstances (he may not receive all the cash flows of the business, and he faces additional risks not borne by the business) leads to the almost inevitable conclusion that his nonmarketable interest is worth less than (or possibly the same as) his pro rata share of the business. The difference in value is the "amount or percentage" from the definition of the marketability discount quoted earlier.
- The preceding discussion should make clear the logical and theoretical basis for the existence of a disparity between the value of illiquid business interests and the value of the corresponding business. Without any reference to empirical observation, the fact of marketability discounts is undeniable. Given any two investments, if it is known that one has both less cash flow (and corresponding growth) expectations *and* greater risk, its value will be lower than its counterpart.

We now proceed to discuss the nonmarketable minority level of value and the associated marketability discount.

THE NONMARKETABLE MINORITY LEVEL OF VALUE

Equation 3.8 introduces the conceptual math describing the shareholder—or nonmarketable minority—level of value.

$$V_{sh} = \frac{CF_{sh}}{R_{hp} - G_{v}} \tag{3.8}$$

As with the other levels of value, the terms in the conceptual definition of value at the nonmarketable minority level are defined:

- V_{sh} is the value of minority equity interest of an enterprise that lacks an active market for its shares, from the viewpoint of the owner of the interest. Appraisers typically develop indications of value at this level by subtracting a marketability discount from a marketable minority interest value. Appraisers also examine transactions in the stock of companies without public markets as another means of developing indications of value at the nonmarketable minority level.

- CF_{sh} is the portion of the enterprise cash flow expected to be received pro rata by the shareholders, including both interim distributions and any expected terminal value.[35]

- R_{hp} is the discount rate of the minority investor in a nonmarketable equity security for the expected holding period, or the *required holding period return*. The concept of holding period risk is discussed in more detail in the context of the Quantitative Marketability Discount Model

---

[35]CF_{sh} is a symbolic notation to describe all expected interim cash flows and any expected terminal value at the end of the holding period for the investment. In other words, Equation 3.8 cannot be literally used to determine the value of a nonmarketable minority business interest. Actual notation for the two-stage, shareholder level DCF model can be shown as follows:

$$V_{sh} = \left(\frac{CF_{sh,1}}{(1 + R_{hp})} + \frac{CF_{sh,2}}{(1 + R_{hp})^2} + \frac{CF_{sh,3}}{(1 + R_{hp})^3} + \cdots + \frac{CF_{sh,f}}{(1 + R_{hp})^f} \right) + \left(\frac{\left(\frac{CF_{e,f+1}}{R_{mm} - G_e} \right)}{(1 + R_{hp})^f} \right)$$

$$\text{PVICF} \qquad\qquad\qquad\qquad\qquad\qquad\qquad\qquad\qquad\qquad\qquad \text{PVTV}$$

The left portion of the equation represents the present value of interim cash flows (PVICF) for a finite expected holding period ending in year f. The right portion of the equation represents the present value of the terminal value (PVTV), which is the marketable minority value at the end of year f. We discuss these concepts further in Chapter 7.

(QMDM) in Chapter 7. However, as noted earlier, logic suggests that R_{hp} will be equal to or greater than R_{mm}. This required return can be stated symbolically as in Equation 3.9, where HPP is the indicated *holding period premium*. Note that if HPP is equal to zero, meaning there are no holding period risks, as with a liquid, publicly traded security, then R_{hp} is equal to R_{mm}.

$$R_{hp} = R_{mm} + \text{HPP} \tag{3.9}$$

- G_v is the *expected growth rate in value* of the enterprise, which yields the terminal value of the enterprise at the end of the expected holding period for the investment. In the preceding chapter on the basics of the discounted cash flow method, we concluded that for a publicly traded security, the expected growth rate in value is equal to R_{mm} less the dividend yield. If not all enterprise cash flows are distributed to, or invested for the benefit of, the minority shareholders (if, for example, above-market compensation is paid to a controlling shareholder), then G_v will be less than R_{mm} (adjusted for the dividend yield). The same result will occur if a company's expected reinvestment rate is less than its discount rate (e.g., as with the accumulation of low-yielding cash assets, vacation homes, or other assets providing no yield or a yield less than the discount rate).[36]

  Enterprise valuation is a perpetuity concept. Value today is the present value of all expected cash flows attributable to an enterprise discounted to the present at an appropriate discount rate. In contrast, shareholder level values depend on expected holding periods. Investors expect finite holding periods, even if the precise holding period is not known or knowable. The expected growth in value is the means of estimating the future exit value of a nonmarketable investment.

We now have a conceptual model to describe the nonmarketable minority level of value. The model anticipates that the appraiser will initially develop an indication of value at the marketable minority level. In so doing, we will have developed a thorough understanding of the expected enterprise cash flows, their expected growth, and their risks. Grounded in this analysis, the appraiser can then assess the expected benefits to be derived by the minority shareholder of the enterprise. We will further develop this conceptual model in Chapter 7. These relationships are symbolized in Exhibit 3.8.

---

[36] For a more in-depth discussion of this issue, see Z. Christopher Mercer and Travis W. Harms, "Marketability Discount Analysis at a Fork in the Road," *Business Valuation Review*, Vol. 20, No. 4 (2001): pp. 21–22.

	Conceptual Math	Relationships	Value Implications
Marketable Minority Value	$\dfrac{CF_{e(mm)}}{R_{mm} - G_{mm}}$	$G_v = R_{mm} - \text{Div Yld}$	V_{mm} is the benchmark for the other levels
Nonmarketable Minority Value	$\dfrac{CF_{sh}}{R_{hp} - G_v}$	$CF_{sh} \leq CF_{e(mm)}$ $G_v \leq R_{mm} - \text{DivYld}$ $R_{hp} \geq R_{mm}$	$V_{sh} \leq V_{mm}$

EXHIBIT 3.8   Conceptual Math of the Marketable Minority and Nonmarketable Minority Levels of Value

Relying on the framework presented in Exhibit 3.8, we can analyze the conceptual differences between the marketable minority andnonmarketable minority levels of value. The nonmarketable minority value, or value to the shareholder V_{sh}, will be less than V_{mm} if, all else equal, one or more of the following conditions hold:

- *CF_{sh} is less than $CF_{e(mm)}$*. The expected shareholder cash flows will be less than the expected enterprise cash flows if the enterprise cash flows are either reinvested in the business or distributed on a non–pro rata basis to certain shareholders.[37]
- *G_v is less than R_{mm}*. The expected growth rate in value is a function of the expected growth rate of core earnings g_e from Chapter 1), and the effect of reinvestment of enterprise cash flows. If the reinvestment rate is equal to the discount rate, then, as shown in Chapter 1, G_v will be equal to the discount rate, or R_{mm} (adjusted for dividend yield). To the extent that cash flows are not reinvested in the enterprise or are reinvested suboptimally (at rates less than the discount rate), then G_v will be less than R_{mm}, resulting in a lower expected terminal value and lower nonmarketable minority value.[38]

---

[37]Recall that the benchmark marketable minority value is determined under the assumption that all cash flows are paid out to shareholders pro rata or reinvested in the enterprise to achieve a return equal to the discount rate. After this determination is made, the appraiser then estimates CF_{sh}, which may be less than the cash flow of the enterprise ($CF_{e(mm)}$).

[38]Note that the expectation of suboptimal reinvestment, and the accompanying reduction of expected growth in value, impacts both controlling and noncontrolling shareholders. The difference between the two situations is that the controlling

- R_{hp} *is greater than* R_{mm}. Few observers question that the owner of an illiquid asset bears greater risk than the owner of an otherwise identical asset with an active, public market.[39] We have given a name to the compensation necessary for an investor to accept this incremental risk—the holding period premium, or HPP. HPP accounts for numerous risks, including the potential for a long and indeterminate holding period and many other risks that flow from the holding period or from the factual situation in any valuation. Other things being equal, greater risk implies lower value.

We have clarified the circumstances under which the nonmarketable minority value will be less than the marketable minority value. We now examine the marketability discount, which is the name given to the difference in value.

THE MARKETABILITY DISCOUNT

The marketability discount (MD) that investors demand when purchasing nonmarketable minority interests in enterprises is defined in Equation 3.10.

$$MD = 1 - \frac{V_{sh}}{V_{mm}} \qquad (3.10)$$

Conceptually, Equation 3.10 confirms that if the shareholder level value (V_{sh}) is equal to the marketable minority value (V_{mm}) there is no marketability discount. Frequently, owners of nonmarketable securities anticipate each potential source of diminished value:

1. Cash flow to the shareholder (CF_{sh}) less than that of the enterprise ($CF_{e(mm)}$);
2. Expected growth in value less than the discount rate (adjusted for dividend yield); and,

---

shareholder can change the reinvestment and/or distribution policies in order to maximize value while the noncontrolling shareholder cannot make those changes. Said another way, the value, today, of a business to a controlling shareholder can exceed the value of the expected business plan.

[39]This should have been obvious to appraisers years ago (Mercer included) based on the observed discounts or restricted stock studies. If the restricted shares were identical in all respects save restrictions (for a period of time) under Rule 144, the only reason for discounts to market prices of freely traded shares relates to perceived incremental risk over the time horizon until restricted shares become marketable.

3. Incremental risks associated with illiquidity during the expected holding period.

In such cases, the appropriate marketability discounts can be quite large. In other cases, however, as with fully distributing entities, or in cases where the expected growth rate in value is relatively high and holding period risks are not large, the appropriate marketability discounts can be quite small.

Conceptually, no portion of the marketability discount is attributable to not possessing the prerogatives of control. The marketability discount reflects, rather, differences between the expected cash flows of the enterprise and those to shareholders, expected growth in value less than the underlying discount rate, and holding period risk in excess of the risks associated with the enterprise.

Note that the minority investor in a public company has no more direct control over the enterprise than does the minority investor in a private company. However, as previously noted, the public minority shareholder does have an element of *personal control* that the private minority shareholder lacks. He has the ability to sell his investment and receive cash in three days through the public securities markets at the marketable minority level (the present value of all expected cash flows of the enterprise).

APPLICATION OF MARKETABILITY DISCOUNTS TO CONTROLLING INTERESTS

Theoretical Basis

Some appraisers have attempted to define a marketability discount applicable to controlling interests of companies.

The conceptual relationships of the three enterprise levels of value in Exhibit 3.6 suggests that such a discount does not exist. The conceptual math for each enterprise level indicates that value is a function of expected cash flow, risk, and expected growth. If an appraiser adequately measures expected cash flow and the risks and growth of those cash flows, the result is an enterprise value.[40]

---

[40]See *Quantifying Marketability Discounts* (Memphis, TN, Peabody Publishing, LP, 1997), Chapter 11, "Marketability Discounts and the Controlling Interest Level of Value." This chapter primarily consisted of a reprint of a previous article: Z. Christopher Mercer, "Should 'Marketability Discounts' be Applied to Controlling

The argument against the existence of a marketability discount applicable to controlling interests is simple. If enterprise value is determined based on expected cash flows, expected growth of those cash flows, and the riskiness of those cash flows, then what additional factors would support a discount from this value? The Integrated Theory suggests there are none.

Arguments for Controlling Interest Marketability Discounts

The marketability discount for controlling interests is discussed in Pratt/Reilly/Schweihs[41] in the context of U.S. Tax Court decisions, which have recognized marketability discounts for controlling interests in several cases, one of which is cited:[42]

> *Even controlling shares in a nonpublic corporation suffer from lack of marketability because of the absence of a ready private placement market and the fact that flotation costs would have to be incurred if the corporation were to publicly offer its stock.*

We suggest that an opinion of the Tax Court, based on the evidence presented to it relative to a specific case, does not provide economic evidence for appraisers. It is the job of appraisers to instruct the Tax Court (or any court) on valuation issues, and not the reverse.

Pratt/Reilly/Schweihs then suggest that controlling interests are typically liquidated by consummating initial public offerings or in private sales of entire companies or controlling interests. It is the rare private company that successfully completes an IPO, so we focus on the private transactions market.

Pratt/Reilly/Schweihs also suggest that there are five "transactional considerations" faced by owners of closely held businesses desiring to sell

---

Interests of Private Companies?" *Business Valuation Review*, June 1994, pp. 55–65. These articles elaborated on a position taken in *Valuing Financial Institutions* (at p. 205), published in 1992, which concluded: "In any event, appraisers applying 'marketability discounts' to controlling interest values should be clear as to the objective basis for their discounts or run the danger of having their discounts (and their valuation conclusions) considered illogical and/or arbitrary."

[41]Pratt, Reilly, and Schweihs, *Valuing a Business*, 4th ed., previously cited, pp. 411–414.

[42]Ibid, p. 412, quoting *Estate of Woodbury G. Andrews*, 79 T.C. 938 (1982).

their controlling interests.[43] Each consideration is presented here followed by our comments:

1. *Uncertain time horizon to complete the offering or sale.* This suggestion is analogous to considering a holding period for the liquidation of a controlling interest. This ignores the controlling shareholder's ability to direct and to distribute enterprise cash flows during any period of sale.[44] Further, to account for such a risk, appraisers would have to assume that the risks of the holding period exceeded the discount rate of the enterprise. If the enterprise discount rate was properly specified, there is no basis for a discount for lack of marketability for controlling ownership interests.

2. *Cost to prepare for and execute the offering or sale.* These costs include auditing and accounting fees, legal costs, administrative costs, and transaction costs. Such costs impact the proceeds from the sale of an enterprise but not its value. Some appraisers have advanced the further argument that the marketability discount for controlling interests relates to the costs of getting a company "ready for sale." In other words, a company that is not ready for sale (needs audited financial statements, consulting to improve operations, capital expenditures to enhance productivity, and the like) could be discounted for its lack of marketability. This argument falls short, as well, because a company that is not "ready for sale" is, well, not ready for sale, and it is not worth as much as one that is ready. Why? Because it has lower cash flows and lower growth potential for those cash flows, and perhaps, greater risk.

3. *Risks concerning eventual sale price.* These risks relate to market uncertainties regarding pricing, which definitely influence value. But these risks would only give rise to discounts from some hypothetical, higher price that cannot be observed or even explained. Discount rates or earnings multiples for controlling interest appraisals are based on

---

[43] Ibid, p. 413.

[44] We recognize that when deals get down to the letter of intent or definitive agreement stages, the controlling owners may agree, for the short time to expected closing, not to make distributions and to run the business in the "ordinary course of business" or upon specific agreement with the buyer regarding taking specified management actions. Such periods of restriction typically come at the very end of the holding period during which enterprises are marketed, are typical of the way deals are done, and seem unlikely to give rise to a "discount for lack of marketability for controlling ownership interests."

market evidence that reflects similar uncertainty. So further discounting might properly be perceived as "double-dipping."

4. *Noncash and deferred transaction proceeds.* The text notes that some transactions have deferred payments, or other noncash elements. These elements do not give rise to discounts from some higher value, but simply reflect, in terms of their then present values, the actual value of transactions.

5. *Inability to hypothecate.* It is suggested that controlling interests in closely held businesses may not be good bank collateral, and that, during the holding period, an owner may not be able to borrow funds for liquidity needs. The suggestion may or may not be true, depending on the particular enterprises under consideration, but would ultimately be a component of the holding period risk discussed in the first item in this list.

Cynics could argue that the only reason there is no marketability discount for controlling interests in the Integrated Theory is because we have not drawn boxes for them on the levels of value chart. However, as should be clear from the preceding discussion regarding the marketable minority, financial control, and strategic control levels of value, each box is defined in terms of risk, expected cash flows, and their expected growth. There are no boxes for marketability discounts for controlling interests because the risks, expected cash flows, and expected growth have already been accounted for.

There is no theoretical justification or explanation for marketability discounts for controlling interests. The common explanations for the discount fall short, and there is no evidence or guidance as to how to determine the magnitude of such a discount. Finally, the base value from which the discount for lack of marketability for controlling ownership interest could be applied is not specified.

No discount or premium is meaningful without a clearly defined valuation base to which it is applied. The "marketable controlling interest" base value, to which a marketability discount for controlling interests would be applied, has not been defined. Therefore, the discount itself is not meaningful. Appraisers should apply such a discount only with caution—and then they should be prepared to justify the reasons for the discount and why it is applicable to the base value from which it is taken.[45]

_____

[45]We discuss the rare exceptions in which the marketability of a business may be sufficiently tainted as to justify application of a marketability discount to a controlling interest in Chapter 5.

	Conceptual Math	Relationships	Value Implications
Strategic Control Value	$\dfrac{CF_{e(c,s)}}{R_s - [G_{mm} + G_s]}$	$CF_{e(c,s)} \geq CF_{e(c,f)}$ $G_s \geq 0$ $R_s \leq R_{mm}$	$V_{e(c,s)} \geq V_{e(c,f)}$
Financial Control Value	$\dfrac{CF_{e(c,f)}}{R_f - [G_{mm} + G_f]}$	$CF_{e(c,f)} \geq CF_{e(mm)}$ $G_f \geq 0$ $R_f = R_{mm(+/-\text{ a little})}$	$V_{e(c,f)} \geq V_{mm}$
Marketable Minority Value	$\dfrac{CF_{e(mm)}}{R_{mm} - G_{mm}}$	$G_v = R_{mm} - \text{Div Yld}$	V_{mm} is the benchmark for the other levels
Nonmarketable Minority Value	$\dfrac{CF_{sh}}{R_{hp} - G_v}$	$CF_{sh} \leq CF_{e(mm)}$ $G_v \leq R_{mm} - \text{DivYld}$ $R_{hp} \geq R_{mm}$	$V_{sh} \leq V_{mm}$

EXHIBIT 3.9 The Integrated Theory of Business Valuation

THE INTEGRATED THEORY OF BUSINESS VALUATION

We have now examined the four conceptual levels of value in depth. Exhibit 3.9 incorporates all four levels into a single chart to present the conceptual math of the levels of value and summarizes the Integrated Theory of Business Valuation.

The Integrated Theory accomplishes several objectives. It enables business appraisers to:

- Explain each level of value in the context of financial and valuation theory.
- Define the conceptual adjustments relating the various levels of value in terms of that theory. Specifically, the financial control premium and the related minority interest discount, the strategic control premium, and the marketability discount have been defined in financial and economic terms.
- Explain why the integrated model is illustrative of pricing behavior observed in public and nonpublic markets for equity interests.
- Understand the value of control and, conversely, the economic consequences of lack of control. Specifically, it clarifies that a nonmarketable

minority interest in a business is worth less than its actual or hypothetical marketable minority value not because of the inability to control the enterprise, but rather because of the lack of marketability.

■ Confirm Eric Nath's observation in 1990 that the public market pricing of securities offers, at least in many instances, a controlling interest level of pricing. The Integrated Theory does not confirm Nath's conclusion that appraisers should take both a minority interest and marketability discount from the public/control price to arrive at the nonmarketable minority level of value. There is no incentive for financial buyers to exercise control over well-managed public companies to achieve greater earnings and value. In other words, the implied minority interest discount is equal to zero. In this case, the conceptual analysis suggests that only one discount, the marketability discount, is appropriate.

CONCLUSIONS

The Integrated Theory of Business Valuation presented in this chapter is valuable to business appraisers for several important reasons:

1. The Integrated Theory defines each of the levels of value, explains observed pricing behavior in the public markets, and provides a framework within which to discuss the appraisal of privately held companies and interests therein.

2. The Integrated Theory does not relate to any particular standard of value (fair market value, fair value, or investment value). Rather, it enables the appraiser to focus on what determines value in the context of any standard of value.

3. The Integrated Theory allows appraisers to focus more clearly on the relationships between financial control value and marketable minority value.

4. The Integrated Theory raises significant questions about, and objections to, the use of control premium data to estimate minority interest discounts.

5. The Integrated Theory explains the relationship between the marketable minority and nonmarketable minority levels of value in financial and economic terms.

6. The Integrated Theory, when applied to the nonmarketable minority level of value, provides the economic and financial rationale for quantitative, rate of return analysis (of which the QMDM is one example) to determine marketability discounts.

7. The Integrated Theory of Business Valuation exposes the inadequate conceptual support for another discount frequently used by appraisers— a marketability discount applicable to controlling interests of companies. There is no conceptual basis for a marketability discount applicable to controlling interests of companies. Financial control and strategic control values should be determined based on the economic factors outlined previously. If an enterprise faces particular risks that may impinge on the owner's ability to transact with another control buyer, those risks should be estimated in terms of the impact on the enterprise discount rate and ultimately, on the enterprise value.

Case Study — Acquisition Pricing and the Integrated Theory

(WHY MANY ACQUISITIONS DO NOT ENHANCE SHAREHOLDER VALUE)

The Situation

A hypothetical public company ("Company") made an acquisition of a smaller company in its industry ("Target"). This case study re-creates the internal analysis and discussion leading to the final price paid.

1. Target's capital structure was similar to that of Company's. The acquisition was a cash purchase of the stock of Target. Therefore, the objective of the exercise is to develop estimates of Target's equity value for purposes of the acquisition. To the best of the CFO's knowledge, there were no other *strategic purchasers* bidding for Target, so the bidding competitors, if any, were *financial purchasers*.

2. Target had *normalized* net earnings of $1,000 (as discussed in Chapter 4). Staff of Operations at Company (supporting the acquisition) normalized the earnings of Target, adding back excess owner compensation (over and above her expected, ongoing salary post-acquisition). In addition, adjustments for nonrecurring items were made. Company's CFO agreed that these normalizing adjustments were reasonable.

3. Finance Staff developed an equity discount rate of 15% *for Target*, based on its particular risks. Company's equity discount rate component of its cost of capital was 13%, so this estimate made sense to the CFO.

4. Finance Staff also estimated that Target's earnings could reasonably grow at the rate of about 7% for the foreseeable future based on historical performance and discussions with Operations Staff. There

was actually a detailed discounted cash flow model, but this single-point estimate was used to illustrate value using the Gordon Model.

$$V_{mm} = \frac{CF}{R_{mm} - G_{mm}} \qquad \boxed{\begin{aligned} CF &= \$1{,}000 \\ R_{mm} &= 15\% \\ G_{mm} &= 17\% \end{aligned}}$$

$$V_{mm} = \frac{\$1{,}000}{15\% - 17\%} = \boxed{\$12{,}500} \qquad (3\text{-}A.1)$$

Based on these assumptions, the Finance Staff prepared an initial valuation for Target as follows. The valuation is at the marketable minority (V_{mm}) level in terms of the levels of value discussed in Chapter 3.

The conclusion of $12,500, reflecting a multiple of 12.5x net earnings (about 7.5x pre-tax earnings), was the base valuation from which the CFO planned to assess all bids suggested by Operations Staff. Company was currently trading at 22x next year's earnings, so a successful acquisition at this level would clearly be accretive to earnings per share.

BIDDING ANALYSIS

Finance Staff held discussions with Operations Staff about the adjustments that competing financial buyers might consider reasonable for Target. It appears that there were potential efficiencies because Target's operating margin was a bit lower than industry norms. Financial buyers (and Company) might therefore reasonably consider that earnings could be increased by $50, or 5%. In addition, the Operations Staff suggests that earnings growth could likely be enhanced by 1% or so if management were a bit more aggressive.

$$V_f = \frac{CF + \Delta CF_f}{R_{mm}(G_{mm} + \Delta G_f)} \qquad \boxed{\begin{aligned} CF_f &= (CF + \Delta CF_f) \\ G_f &= (G_{mm} + \Delta G_f) \\ CF &= \$1{,}000 \\ R_{mm} &= 15\% \\ G_{mm} &= 7\% \\ \Delta CF_f &= \$50 \\ \Delta G_f &= 1\% \end{aligned}}$$

$$V_f = \frac{\$1{,}000 + \$50}{15\% - (7\% + 1\%)} = \boxed{\$15{,}000} \qquad (3\text{-}A.2)$$

As result of these discussions, Finance Staff valued Target at the financial control Level V_f of value.

After adjusting cash flow for the $50 (5%) increment and expected growth for the 1% increment, the financial control value is $15,000, or 20% higher than the initial valuation. That price reflects a multiple of 15x normalized net earnings for Target, and 14.3x earnings adjusted for the potential better margins.

This did not mean, however, that other financial buyers would automatically offer prices in the range of $15,000 for Target's equity. After all, that value is dependent on their ability to operate Target better than present management, and they would have to accept all execution risk if that price was paid. So Finance Staff had developed a negotiating range of $12,500 to $15,000 for the equity of Target. Given Company's position as a strategic purchaser, CFO was comfortable with pricing within this range, and he knew that paying at even the top-end range would provide for an accretive transaction.

Based on the preceding analysis, which was provided to Operations Staff, the CFO informally approved a bidding range up to $15,000 for Target's equity.

OPERATIONS' STRATEGIC CONSIDERATIONS

The CFO did not hear anything from Operations Staff for some time, but then was informed that the deal for Target had been struck at $24,000. Realizing that he did not have decision-making authority in the matter, he was nevertheless upset and perplexed. He went to the COO to discuss the rationale for the purchase price.

When they met, the COO handed him a valuation analysis performed by Operations Staff. That analysis mirrored the earlier analysis prepared by Finance Staff, but valued Target at the strategic control level. As the CFO reviewed the analysis, he saw that it had been based on the earlier analysis, but made the following additional assumptions:

1. As a strategic buyer, Company could expand sales through new channels, therefore increasing potential earnings and cash flow by another $50, raising expected earnings to the level of $1,100 (from the normalized level of $1,000 and the financial control level of $1,050).
2. In addition, Operations Staff had assumed that earnings growth could be expanded by another 1% (because of growth into new channels), to 9% per year.
3. Finally, Operations Staff, knowing that Company's cost of equity was 13.0%, used that discount rate as the cost of equity for Target.

As a result of these assumptions, the valuation prepared by Operations Staff was considerably higher, and valued Target at $27,500, or more than double the marketable minority value and nearly double the financial control value.

$$V_s = \frac{CF + \Delta CF_f + \Delta CF_s}{R_s - (G_{mm} + \Delta G_f + \Delta G_s)}$$

$$CF_s = (CF + \Delta CF_f + \Delta CF_s)$$
$$G_s = G + \Delta G_f + \Delta G_s$$

$$CF = \$1{,}000$$
$$G_{mm} = 7\%$$

$$\Delta CF_f = \$50$$
$$\Delta G_f = 1\%$$

$$\Delta CF_s = \$50$$
$$R_s = 13\%$$
$$\Delta G_s = 1\%$$

$$V_s = \frac{\$1{,}000 + \$50 + \$50}{13\% - (7\% + 1\% + 1\%)} = \boxed{\$27{,}500} \tag{3-A.3}$$

The COO was proud of his accomplishment. He observed that at $24,000, he had negotiated a price some 13% below what Target was worth to Company. He then mentioned the following additional factors as supporting the pricing decision:

1. The deal should earn the Company's cost of equity capital. And Company's return would be even better if additional enhancements, not included in the valuation, were achieved.
2. A price of $24,000 represented a multiple of 21.8x expected earnings, so the multiple paid was right in line with Company's multiple of 22x.
3. This was truly a strategic fit for Company and it should enhance the public markets' impression of the stock.

CFO REFLECTIONS

Back at his office, the CFO bemoaned the fact that the CEO did not require better coordination between Operations and Finance. He hoped that the acquisition of Target would be successful and he saw that if it were, it could have some benefits for Company. However, he was concerned that in this situation, Company had substantially overpaid for the acquisition. He made the following observations about the deal:

- With normalized net earnings of $1,000 and pro forma earnings of $1,100:
  - Company accepted all of the execution risks involved in achieving the improvement.
  - The price/earnings multiple based on normalized earnings is 24x, which exceeds the multiple of Company's stock in the market.
- With normalized expected earnings growth of 7% and pro forma earnings growth of 9%, Company accepted all of the execution risks involved in achieving the increase.
- By basing the pricing on Company's 13% cost of equity, rather than on the Target's discount rate of 15%, Company had no "risk cushion" to absorb integration problems or failures to achieve objectives.
- No one on Operations Staff was responsible for achieving the projected revenue and growth synergies. In fact, unless he asked Finance Staff to do a follow-up analysis in the future, which was particularly difficult, there would be no operational accountability for the assumptions used to establish the purchase price for Target.
- The Company had just overpaid substantially in terms of market value for Target, with the Company bidding against itself in the process.

But life goes on . . .

CHAPTER 4

Adjustments to Income Statements: Normalizing and Control Adjustments

INTRODUCTION

In Chapter 3, we developed the Integrated Theory to explain the conceptual levels of value on the basis of the Gordon Model. Recall the generalized valuation model that flows from the Gordon Model:

$$\text{Value} = \text{Earnings} \times \text{Multiple}$$

The Integrated Theory and generalized valuation model suggest that value indications should be developed by estimating appropriate indications of earning power and a reasonable valuation multiple. It follows that appraisers may need to consider potential adjustments to both earnings and the multiple in order to develop appropriate indications of value.

- *Normalizing Adjustments.* This chapter first explores normalizing adjustments to develop private company earnings that correspond to the valuation multiples of guideline companies to yield marketable minority indications of value.
- *Control Adjustments.* This chapter also considers earnings adjustments that relate to the other enterprise levels of value, namely, the financial control and strategic control levels of value. An important insight arising from the Integrated Theory is that the discount rate applicable to individual private companies should remain (approximately) the same for the various enterprise levels of value. Control adjustments yield a measure of enterprise earnings appropriate to the control levels of value.
- *Fundamental Adjustments.* Discussed in Chapter 5, fundamental adjustments relate appropriate private company valuation multiples to the median or average multiples of guideline company groups. Fundamental

107

adjustments account for differences in risk and expected growth for private companies relative to selected guideline companies.

This chapter and the next lay the theoretical foundation for these adjustments commonly applied in valuation practice.

COMMON QUESTIONS

1. What are the differences between *normalizing adjustments* to the earnings stream and *control adjustments*?
2. In the context of fair market value, should control premiums always be applied to develop controlling interest value indications?
   a. If a control premium is applied, what data should be used to estimate it?
   b. How can the reasonableness of control premiums be tested?
   c. Are control premiums economic drivers or merely valuation results?
3. When applying the DCF method, should appraisers apply control premiums to develop controlling interest values? If so, why? And where?
4. Why are normalizing adjustments appropriate?
5. What does the term *marketable minority level of value* represent in the context of public security values?
6. When valuing minority interests in private companies, should appraisers normalize earnings?
   a. If yes, what kinds of normalizing adjustments should be made?
   b. What is the objective of making normalizing adjustments?
7. When using guideline public company multiples, should appraisers apply control premiums to the resulting marketable minority value indications?
8. Should appraisers rely on *Mergerstat/Shannon Pratt's Control Premium Study* and other control premium studies to determine the magnitude of control premiums applicable to "marketable minority" value indications?
9. Should those same control premium studies be used to estimate minority interest discounts for operating companies?
10. Should those same control premium studies be used to estimate minority interest discounts for asset holding entities?
11. In valuing illiquid interests in private businesses, why do appraisers normally begin with appraisals at the marketability minority level of value?

THE INTEGRATED THEORY AND INCOME STATEMENT ADJUSTMENTS

In Chapter 3, we developed mathematical expressions for each of the various levels of value. The Gordon Model summarizes each of the four levels of value in Exhibit 4.1.

Cash flow of the enterprise at the marketable minority level is represented by $CF_e(mm)$. This cash flow is assumed to be normalized to approximate that of comparable well-run public companies. Otherwise, if there were, for example, excessive compensation or other discretionary expenditures of an ongoing, egregious nature, there would be pressure from shareholders for the earnings stream to be normalized.

The summary expression for the nonmarketable minority level of value is reproduced at the bottom of Exhibit 4.1. As noted in the "Relationships" column, cash flow to shareholders (CF_{sh}) may be less than or equal to, but not greater than, the cash flow of the enterprise (at the marketable minority level). This should not be surprising. As we saw in Chapter 3, one component of the diminution in value from the marketable minority level to the nonmarketable minority is the potential for agency costs, or non–pro rata distributions to selected shareholders. Agency costs also include excess perquisites and other discretionary expenditures.

	Conceptual Math	Relationships	Value Implications
Strategic Control Value	$\dfrac{CF_{e(c,s)}}{R_s - [G_{mm} + G_s]}$	$CF_{e(c,s)} \geq CF_{e(c,f)}$ $G_s \geq 0$ $R_s \leq R_{mm}$	$V_{e(c,s)} \geq V_{e(c,f)}$
Financial Control Value	$\dfrac{CF_{e(c,f)}}{R_f - [G_{mm} + G_f]}$	$CF_{e(c,f)} \geq CF_{e(mm)}$ $G_f \geq 0$ $R_f = R_{mm}(+/-$ a little$)$	$V_{e(c,f)} \geq V_{mm}$
Marketable Minority Value	$\dfrac{CF_{e(mm)}}{R_{mm} - G_{mm}}$	$G_v = R_{mm} -$ Div Yld	V_{mm} is the benchmark for the other levels
Nonmarketable Minority Value	$\dfrac{CF_{sh}}{R_{hp} - G_v}$	$CF_{sh} \leq CF_{e(mm)}$ $G_v \leq R_{mm} -$ Div Yld $R_{hp} \geq R_{mm}$	$V_{sh} \leq V_{mm}$

EXHIBIT 4.1   The Integrated Theory of Business Valuation

It should be clear that such costs should be normalized, so that the resulting enterprise cash flows approximate the expected enterprise cash flows (assuming any nonrecurring items in historical earnings have been eliminated). We classify adjustments for both agency costs and nonrecurring items as *normalizing adjustments*.

As we move up the levels of value chart from the marketable minority level to the levels of financial control and strategic control, we see that it is possible that a controlling shareholder *may* make adjustments to expected cash flows based on the expected ability to run the existing enterprise more efficiently (financial control), or to modify or manage the enterprise differently (strategic control). Such adjustments are *control adjustments*, and increase value if such adjustments would normally be negotiated between buyers and sellers. In other words, *control adjustments* are those that, if appropriate, increase enterprise cash flow *above that of the (normalized) marketable minority level*. As the conceptual chart indicates, the cash flow of the enterprise from the viewpoint of either a financial control buyer or a strategic control buyer *may* be greater than the normalized cash flow of the enterprise.

TWO TYPES OF INCOME STATEMENT ADJUSTMENTS

Having described the general nature of normalizing adjustments and control adjustments, we now turn to their proper application.

- With normalizing adjustments, we attempt to adjust private company earnings to a reasonably well-run, public company equivalent basis. Normalizing adjustments can be further divided into two types to facilitate discussion and understanding. Normalizing adjustments are *not* control adjustments.
- Control adjustments modify normalized private company earnings to reflect 1) the operational improvements anticipated by the *typical financial buyer*; and 2) synergies or strategies of *particular buyers*. Control adjustments can also be divided into two types.

This nomenclature for income statement adjustments is fairly new.[1] Many appraisers do not distinguish between normalizing and control adjustments or between types of normalizing and control adjustments. The specific

---

[1] Mercer has been using this vocabulary in speeches and articles since the late 1990s. It received first publication in Pratt's *Cost of Capital* (1st), which was published in 1998 (previously cited) in an appendix Mercer wrote dealing with developing discount rates using the Wiley *ValuSource Pro* Software.

vocabulary presented in this chapter is not essential to understanding income statement adjustments. It is, however, helpful in clarifying the nature of and reasons for income statement adjustments.

INCOME STATEMENT ADJUSTMENTS AND THE RELEVANT DISCOUNT RATE

The importance of distinguishing between types of income statement adjustments becomes apparent when we discuss the discount rates applicable to derived earnings. The discount rate or capitalization rate applied to a particular measure of earnings must be appropriate for that measure, whether net income, pre-tax income, debt-free net income, or another level of the income statement. The CAPM (and ACAPM, or build-up) discount rates discussed here apply to either the net income or net cash flows of business enterprises.

There has also been considerable discussion in recent years regarding whether discounted cash flow valuation models yield minority interest or controlling interest indications of value. The two major schools of thought are as follows:

1. The CAPM/ACAPM discount rate is applicable to the net income (or net cash flow) of a business enterprise, and therefore yields a marketable minority indication of value. As a result, control premiums are properly applied to value indications at this level to derive a controlling interest conclusion of value.
2. Appraisers often make control adjustments in developing their projections for DCF methods. If the income stream is "control adjusted," the resulting valuation indication is at the controlling interest level. As a result, no additional control premium is appropriate, and a minority interest discount might be applied to derive a marketable minority value indication.

Appraisers have debated these two viewpoints for years. Depending on the adjustments made, either approach might yield similar results. However, the issue has been a source of confusion, and the debate has found a forum in the Tax Court. A number of recent appraisals submitted to the court have been scrutinized over the very issue of whether a DCF model yields a minority interest or a controlling interest valuation.

Dr. Pratt and others, including Mercer, have suggested that in DCF methods, the value of control is generally developed by adjusting the numerator (the projected cash flows). The following quote from Pratt's *Cost of Capital* illustrates the consensus:

> *The discount rate is meant to represent the underlying risk of a particular industry or line of business. There may be instances in which a majority shareholder can acquire a company and improve its cash flows, but that would not necessarily have an impact on the general risk level of the cash flows generated by that company.*
>
> *In applying the income approach to valuation, adjustments for minority or controlling interest value should be made to the projected cash flows of the subject company instead of to the discount rate. Adjusting the expected cash flows better measures the potential impact a controlling party may have while not overstating or understating the actual risk associated with a particular line of business.*[2]

While the preceding quote is found in a chapter dealing with discount rates, note the suggestion that control adjustments would be made to the marketable minority level of cash flows. If such adjustments are made, the indicated controlling interest value would exceed the marketable minority level.

Properly distinguishing between normalizing and control adjustments in the context of the Integrated Theory of Business Valuation should bring clarity to this issue.

Normalizing Adjustments to the Income Statement

Normalizing adjustments modify the income statement of a private company to reveal a "public equivalent" income stream. If such adjustments are not made, the resulting indication of value is something other than a marketable minority value. For appraisers using benchmark analysis to determine marketability discounts, this would be disastrous, because the restricted stock studies are based on freely traded (marketable minority) stock prices.[3]

---

[2]Ibid, pp. 127–128.

[3]In other words, the value indication derived from the use of non-normalized earnings for a private company and the application of a marketability discount derived from the various restricted stock studies would yield something other than a nonmarketable minority value indication. Because the earnings capitalized were not normalized, and a "normal" marketability discount was applied, the indicated value conclusion would likely be *below* that of the nonmarketable minority level.

Note that, in creating a public equivalent earnings stream for a private company, the subject company need not have all of the characteristics of potential IPO candidates. Another name given to the marketable minority level of value is as-if-freely-traded. This terminology emphasizes that earnings are being normalized to where they would be as if the company were public. The framework does not require that a company be public or even that it have the potential to become public.

A new vocabulary is needed to clarify the nature of normalizing income statement adjustments. As noted earlier, there are two types of normalizing adjustments. Being very original, we call them Type 1 and Type 2.

- *Type 1 Normalizing Adjustments.* These adjustments eliminate one-time gains or losses, other unusual items, discontinued business operations, expenses of non-operating assets, and the like. Every appraiser employs such income statement adjustments in the process of adjusting (normalizing) historical income statements. Regardless of the name given to them, there is virtually universal acceptance that Type 1 Normalizing Adjustments are appropriate.
- *Type 2 Normalizing Adjustments.* These adjustments normalize officer/owner compensation and other discretionary expenses that would not exist in a reasonably well-run, publicly traded company. Type 2 Normalizing Adjustments should not be confused with control adjustments or Type 1 Normalizing Adjustments.

These adjustments reveal the income stream that is the source of potential value for the minority investor. Normalizing adjustments also reveal the base income stream available to the controlling interest buyer who may be able to further enhance that income stream.

Appraisers should not be confused by the fact that minority shareholders of private companies lack the control to make normalizing adjustments. Some have argued that because minority shareholders lack the ability to change, for example, things like excess owner compensation, normalizing adjustments should not be made in minority interest appraisals. We disagree.[4] Minority shareholders of public companies also lack control. However, they expect normalized operations. If management of a public company receives egregious salaries, or fails to reasonably manage expenses, minority shareholders of the public company will invest their money elsewhere. And the market value of such companies normally reflects this lack of investor interest, thereby exposing incumbent management to the threat of hostile takeover (followed shortly thereafter by unemployment).

---

[4]See the more detailed discussion regarding the Integrated Theory in Chapter 3.

NORMALIZE OR NOT?

Let us illustrate with an example Mercer has used in many speeches. First, he poses the following example:

Consider an investment in a partnership. The relevant interest is a 1% limited partnership interest, so there are no elements of control. The partnership pays $100 per unit per year in annual distributions and is certain to be liquidated in exactly five years.

He then asks how much those in the audience would pay for the interest. The responses are invariably the same. Appraisers want to know, for example, what is in the partnership and how much it is worth today. They want to know if it is appreciating, and at what rate. They ask these questions because without answers to them, one does not have sufficient information to make an informed investment decision.

Yet many appraisers suggest that Type 2 Normalizing Adjustments are "control" adjustments and believe they should not be made in minority interest appraisals. In so doing, they put readers of their reports in exactly the same position as the investors for his partnership unit—i.e., lacking sufficient information to make an informed investment decision. In other words, if Type 2 Normalizing Adjustments are not made, readers of reports (and hypothetical investors) do not know the value of the underlying enterprise or its ability to grow into the future. Absent that information, rational investment decisions cannot be made.

Owners of nonmarketable minority interests generally lack this ability to "take my money and run." These considerations have no impact on the value of the enterprise. Rather, they reduce the value of the interest in the enterprise in relationship to its pro rata share of enterprise value. This diminution of value must be considered separately from, but in conjunction with, the valuation of the enterprise.

NORMALIZING ADJUSTMENTS ILLUSTRATED

While some appraisers disagree regarding the applicability of Type 2 Normalizing Adjustments, we find the arguments supporting their use compelling. Consider the following example:

ABC, Inc. Normalizing Adjustments ($000s)		Normalizing Adjustments		
		Type 1	Type 2	
		Nonrecurring	Normalize to	
	Reported	Items	Public Equivalent	Normalized
Sales	$10,000	$0	$0	$10,000
COGS	$5,800	$0	$0	$5,800
Gross Profit	$4,200	$0	$0	$4,200
Litigation Settlement	$200	($200)	$0	$0
Selling (Cousin Joe)	$800	$0	($100)	$700
G&A (Cousin Al)	$1,800	$0	($100)	$1,700
Owner Comp (Big Daddy)	$900	$0	($600)	$300
Chalet (Big Daddy's Vacation Home)	$200	$0	($200)	$0
	$3,900	($200)	($1,000)	$2,700
Operating Profit	$300			$1,500
Operating Margin (No debt)	3.0%			15.0%

EXHIBIT 4.2 ABC, Inc. Normalizing Adjustments

In Exhibit 4.2, ABC, Inc. is a company reporting sales of $10 million and operating profit of $300,000.

Assume that we are appraising ABC and are now considering normalizing adjustments. There is one Type 1 Normalizing Adjustment to be made in this particular appraisal. There are also several Type 2 Normalizing Adjustments that relate to the owner and the controlling shareholder of the business.

- Type 1 Normalizing Adjustment (Nonrecurring Items):
  ○ The company settled a lawsuit regarding damages when one of its vehicles was in an accident. The settlement, inclusive of attorneys' fees, was $200,000 in the most recent year. Expenses associated with the lawsuit are eliminated from operating expenses.
- Type 2 Normalizing Adjustments (Agency Costs and Other Discretionary Expenses):
  ○ Our examination of selling expenses reveals that Cousin Joe is on the payroll at $100,000 per year and he is not doing anything for the good of the business. An adjustment is clearly called for regarding Cousin Joe. His compensation must be eliminated in order to see the "as-if-freely-traded" income stream.
  ○ In the Administrative Department, Cousin Al comes to work every day, but it is clear that the department is being run by someone else

and that Cousin Al is not productive. We adjust by removing his $100,000 salary.
- ○ Big Daddy takes a substantial salary out of the business. Based on a salary survey, earnings should be adjusted by $600,000 for his excess compensation to lower the expense to a normal, market level of compensation.
- ○ Finally the business owns a chalet for Big Daddy's vacation needs, which costs the company about $200,000 a year. Expenses associated with Big Daddy's vacation home are adjusted accordingly.

Summing the Type 1 and Type 2 adjustments, adjustments to operating expenses of $1.0 million have been identified. These adjustments raise the adjusted operating profit to the level expected were this company publicly traded (even though it likely never will be!). The normalized operating margin is 15%.[5]

Before proceeding to examine control adjustments, we should carry the discussion of normalizing adjustments a step further in order to address any lingering concerns. Some appraisers remain convinced that Type 2 Normalizing Adjustments are really control adjustments and that they should not be made when valuing minority interests.

Why, they ask, should we not value the minority interest directly and forego making Type 2 Normalizing Adjustments? Consider that if we do not make these adjustments:

- The resulting earnings stream is not comparable to those of public companies (or "as-if-freely-traded").
- A discount rate based on guideline company analysis would not be appropriate and the resulting value indication would not be at the marketable minority level.
- Marketability discounts referencing restricted stock and pre-IPO transactions involving public companies would be inappropriate if relevant Type 2 Normalizing Adjustments are not made. The various restricted stock and pre-IPO studies are based on marketable minority values

---

[5]Note that this appraisal process would not ignore the valuation impact of the agency costs associated with Big Daddy and his family if the objective were a nonmarketable minority value indication. The economic impact of the excess compensation (effectively a non–pro rata distribution) would substantially impact the expected growth in value of the business and the dividend policy (key assumptions of the Quantitative Marketability Discount Model). The risks of nonmarketability over an appropriate expected holding period would also be considered.

and the resulting, non-normalized base would not be at the marketable minority level.

- There is an implicit assumption that the shareholder will never realize his or her pro rata share of the value of the enterprise. In the alternative, there is no basis to estimate what that future terminal value might be. There would be no basis, for example, to estimate the expected growth in value of the enterprise over any relevant expected holding period, because the base marketable minority value is not specified.

The bottom line is that, absent making appropriate Type 2 Normalizing Adjustments, an appraiser cannot assure users that his or her conclusion is at the nonmarketable minority level of value, which is typically the objective of minority interest appraisals. The bottom, bottom line is that failure to make Type 2 Normalizing Adjustments when valuing nonmarketable minority interests provides neither the appropriate theoretical nor practical bases for their conclusions.

CONTROL ADJUSTMENTS TO THE INCOME STATEMENT

We suggested at the beginning of this chapter that there are two types of control adjustments to the income statement. Control buyers assess how they can exercise the various prerogatives of control to enhance the normalized earnings of the enterprise. Exhibit 4.3 summarizes the control adjustments applied to ABC, Inc.

ABC, Inc. Control Adjustments ($000s)	As if Publicly Traded Normalized	*Financial Control*		*Strategic Control*	
		Financial Control Adjustment	As Adjusted Type 1	*Strategic Control Adjustment*	As Adjusted Type 2
Sales	$10,000	$0	$10,000	$0	$10,000
COGS	$5,800	$0	$5,800	($200)	$5,600
Gross Profit	$4,200	$0	$4,200	$200	$4,400
Litigation Settlement	$0	$0	$0	$0	$0
Selling	$700	($150)	$550	$0	$550
G&A	$1,700	$0	$1,700	($250)	$1,450
Owner Comp	$300	$0	$300	$0	$300
Chalet	$0	$0	$0	$0	$0
	$2,700	($150)	$2,550	($250)	$2,300
Operating Profit	$1,500		$1,650		$2,100
Operating Margin (No debt)	15.0%		16.5%		21.0%

EXHIBIT 4.3   ABC, Inc. Control Adjustments

The two types of control adjustments:

■ *Financial Control Adjustments.* Financial Control Adjustments modify private company earnings for the economies or efficiencies available to the typical financial buyer, but not present on the as-if-freely-traded basis.

Prospective financial control buyers may consider adjustments that can improve the normalized earnings stream. As noted earlier, these adjustments generally occur from implementation of more efficient management practices, which may also impact the expected growth rate of adjusted earnings.

Financial Control Adjustments are appropriate if the typical buyer could expect to manage the existing company more efficiently. We live in an expectational world. If a prospective financial buyer reasonably believes that a particular change will improve earnings and/or growth, that buyer may be willing to share a portion of that benefit with the seller. If there are other purchasers with similar expectations, market value may be bid up shifting a significant portion of that benefit to the seller. The Financial Control Adjustment may reflect expected financial economies from better management or more rapid growth from more aggressive management.[6]

For example, ABC, Inc. reports selling costs of $700,000, or 7% of sales. Selling costs for the most efficient companies in the industry run on the order of 5.5% of sales, so there is a potential benefit of $150,000 from a reorganization or restructuring of the selling process. Recognizing this potential, financial and/or strategic buyers may consider adjusting the income statement for such expected benefits. Such a reorganization would be a Financial Control Adjustment. That reorganization could increase earning power by as much as $150,000, as illustrated in Exhibit 4.3.

ABC's earnings, after appropriate normalizing adjustments, increased from $300,000 to $1,500,000, and the operating margin increased from 3.0% to 15.0%. With the consideration of Financial Control Adjustments, expected operating income increases by an additional $150,000 to $1,650,000, or to 16.5%. As it turns out, ABC, Inc. is actually a very profitable company and can likely be even more profitable under control of new buyers.

---

[6]Financial Control Adjustments might be reflected in a negotiation or in an appraisal at the controlling interest level if the indicated economies or growth prospects are generally available to multiple buyers and bidding competition transfers those benefits to the seller.

"READY FOR SALE" AND ADJUSTMENTS

Should appraisers consider possible financial restructurings as part of the earnings normalization process? This question is raised by the distinction between the Type 2 Normalizing Adjustment related to Cousin Al and the potential reorganization of the Administrative Department treated here as a Financial Control Adjustment.

This question is tantamount to asking whether a company that is "ready for sale," and operating efficiently with reasonable margins, is worth more than one that is not ready for sale? Logically, the Company that is ready should be worth more. Clearly, if ABC, Inc.'s earnings already reflected the potential reorganization, normalized earnings would be $150,000 higher than adjusted in Exhibit 4.3. And those earnings would be capitalized and reflected in as-if-freely-traded value.

The potential reorganization is treated in Exhibit 4.4 as a Type 1 Control Adjustment because it represents only potential value to the shareholders of ABC, Inc. *If* competing financial buyers recognize this potential *and if* they bid the price up to share all or part of the capitalized benefit, *then* that benefit may be reflected in a higher financial control value. Otherwise the appropriate valuation of ABC, Inc. should reflect only the normalizing adjustments. ABC, Inc. is not "ready for sale," and its value should reflect that fact.

■ *Strategic Control Adjustments.* Strategic control adjustments reflect changes stemming from an expected interaction between the subject company and other assets in the strategic buyer's portfolio. Such benefits may arise from several sources, including consolidation of general and administrative expenses, lower costs of goods sold because of higher volume purchasing, benefits from horizontal or vertical integration, the ability to achieve lower financing costs, and others. Essentially strategic buyers do not contemplate operating the acquired business on a stand-alone basis, but rather in conjunction with other businesses currently owned (or expected to be acquired). Strategic buyers may also seek beachheads in an industry, thinking it cheaper to "pay up" by anticipating future synergies rather than to build from scratch. Other considerations include the preemption of other competitors from obtaining a certain "space."

With ABC, Inc., one or more strategic buyers might reasonably believe that their larger purchasing volumes could lower cost of goods sold by $200,000, and that a consolidation of general and administrative expenses could eliminate an additional $250,000 of expenses. So the strategic buyer is looking not at $300,000 of reported earnings for ABC, Inc., at $1,500,000 as normalized, or at $1,650,000 with Financial Control Adjustments, but potentially at $2,100,000, with Strategic Control Adjustments, as shown in Exhibit 4.3.

We have now developed four distinct measures of operating income for ABC, Inc. ranging from $300,000 to $2,100,000. We now discuss the potential value impact of these earnings adjustments.

POTENTIAL VALUE IMPACT OF EARNINGS ADJUSTMENTS

Income statement adjustments are important in providing estimates of earnings for capitalization using methods under either the income or market approaches to valuation, as well as for providing a base level of earnings from which to forecast when using discounted future benefits methods.

Appraiser judgment is obviously required in the assessment of potential income statement adjustments. Hopefully, the vocabulary and analysis of this chapter, together with the previous conceptual discussion of the Integrated Theory, have highlighted the importance of income statement adjustments and the judgments made in developing them.

Exhibit 4.4 summarizes an analysis of each of the measures of ABC, Inc.'s operating income. Each level of adjusted earnings is capitalized using a pre-tax multiple of 5.0x. As discussed earlier, we assume that the enterprise discount rate does not change across categories of investors (we also assume a common outlook for expected growth in earnings).

Enterprise-level values are developed at the respective levels of value and premiums or discounts to the marketable minority value are presented. Marketability discounts are applied to the "as reported" and normalized marketable minority values. Explanatory comments are also provided.

We make the following observations from Exhibit 4.4:

■ If the objective of an appraisal is to develop an indication at the nonmarketable minority level of value, appraisers who fail to normalize in situations like that summarized in Exhibit 4.4 have little chance to develop a reasonable indication of value. In the present case, the capitalization of reported operating income yields a result that is

	Types of Income Statement Adjustments and Levels of Value			
	As Reported	**"Public Equivalent" Normalized**	**Financial Control**	**Strategic Control**
Operating Income	$300,000	$300,000	$1,500,000	$1,650,000
Net Adjustments	*none*	*$1,200,000*	*$150,000*	*$450,000*
Adjusted Operating Income	$300,000	$1,500,000	$1,650,000	$2,100,000
Implied Operating Margins	*3.00%*	*15.00%*	*16.50%*	*21.00%*
Types of Adjustments Considered	*None*	*Type 1 Normalizing Type 2 Normalizing*	*Financed Control*	*Strategic Control*
Assumed Multiple of Operating Income (*No Debt; Discount Rate and Growth Prospects Remain Unchanged*)	5.0	5.0	5.0	5.0
Implied Value Indications	$1,500,000	$7,500,000	$8,250,000	$10,500,000
Implied Level of Value	*Unknown*	*Marketable Minority*	*Financial Control*	*Strategic Control*
Implied Differences Over/Under "Public Equivalent" Normalized	*−80.0%*	*"Public Equivalent"*	*10.0% "Financial Control" Premium*	*40.0% "Strategic Control" Premium*
Implied Multiples of "Public Equivalent" Normalized	*1.00x*	*5.00x*	*5.50x*	*7.0x*
Value Indications	$1,500,000	$7,500,000	$8,250,000	$10,500,000
Level of Value	*unknown*	*Marketable Minority*	*Financial Control*	*Strategic Control*
Differences Over/Under Normalized	*−80.0%*	*"Public Equivalent"*	*10.0% "Financial Control" Premium*	*40.0% "Strategic Control" Premium*
Multiples of Normalized	*1.00x*	*5.00x*	*5.50x*	*7.0x*
Assumed Marketability Discount	**35.00%** *"Typical Benchmark"*	**60.00%** *Based on QMDM*		
Nonmarketable Minority Indications	$975,000	$3,000,000		
Implied Multiples of "Public Equivalent" Normalized Comments	0.65x Clearly unreliable. Masks underlying value of enterprise. Crux of the problem is the failure to consider appropriate normalizing adjustments.	2.0x Large marketability discount reflects the agency costs (i.e., foregone cash flows to minority shareholders) of Big Al and expected holding period.	Analysis provides logical explanation for a fairly wide range of observed control premiums as well as for the attractiveness of finding competing strategic buyers when a company is being sold. Absent a market with competing strategic buyers, there would appear to be little rationale for large control premiums over normalized (marketable minority) levels of value.	

EXHIBIT 4.4 Summary of Income Statement Adjustments and the Levels of Value

20% of the appropriate nonmarketable minority value ($1,500,000 vs. $7,500,000). In other words, failure to normalize earnings suggests that nonmarketable minority investors will be burdened by the identified agency costs indefinitely.

- The application of typical marketability discounts based on benchmark analysis only exacerbates the problem just noted.
- The example illustrates that it is quite possible for different types of buyers to see different income potential—to them—when examining the same company.
- It is important to distinguish between the types of adjustments in order to understand the level of the income stream being developed. For example, if it is unlikely that there are any strategic buyers for a particular company, including Strategic Control Adjustments would overstate value.
- A corollary to the preceding point is that the blind application of a so-called typical control premium of 40% or so to an indication of

value derived using a normalized income stream would tend to result in overvaluation if no competition among strategic buyers is expected for the property.

- Wide variations in value indications can result between appraisers at the nonmarketable minority level based on assumptions made regarding appropriate normalizing and control adjustments to enterprise earnings.
- It is inappropriate to apply a control premium to a value indication that considers Financial or Strategic Control Adjustments—such a premium is already embedded in the capitalized value.
  - The application of a control premium in cases where no control adjustments are made implies that such benefits do exist and that, in the case of fair market value, typical buyers are willing to pay for them.
  - For example, the strategic control value of $10,500,000 could be developed as indicated or by applying a 40% control premium to the marketable minority value of $7,500,000. In either case, there is an assumption that a total of $600,000 in combined Financial and Strategic Control Adjustments is available.
- Further when using discounted future benefits methods:
  - No control premium is applicable to value indications developed based on forecasts that included Financial or Strategic Control Adjustments.
  - If the forecast does not include control adjustments to income, it may be proper to consider the application of an *appropriate* control premium. However, that premium should relate to the expectation of benefits that buyers would pay for—else it could lead to overvaluation.

THE NATURE OF CONTROL PREMIUMS

Control Premiums and Fair Market Value

Combining the practical analysis of this chapter with the conceptual analysis of the Integrated Theory in Chapter 3, we now consider several questions business appraisers should ponder when developing controlling interest value indications under the standard of fair market value.

- Are the typical buyers financial buyers?
  - The appraiser may need to evaluate the market for similar enterprises to ascertain the nature of the so-called *typical buyers* in a fair market value determination.

- ○ Financial buyers *may* believe they can improve the earnings stream, and this belief may be reflected in the pricing.
- ○ If there are no cash flow improvements available, there may be little or no premium to the marketable minority value (i.e., to the value developed using normalized cash flows).
- Are the typical buyers strategic buyers?
  - ○ Again, the appraiser may need to evaluate the market for similar enterprises to ascertain the nature of typical buyers.
  - ○ Strategic buyers may believe they can alter and improve the earnings stream, and may reflect this belief in pricing, particularly if there are other strategic buyers who may be in competition for the same business.
  - ○ Strategic buyers may pay a premium in excess of that available to typical financial buyers, however, as previously noted, a rational strategic buyer will willingly pay no more than necessary to win the deal from the next most capable strategic buyer.
  - ○ Consideration of strategic buyers may be irrelevant in the context of fair market value determinations. For example, if there are no strategic buyers in a particular market, it would likely not be appropriate to consider a control premium based on strategic cash flows incorporating the effect of strategic control adjustments. Alternatively, if the likely buyers are strategic, for example, in consolidating industries, it may be appropriate to consider potential strategic control adjustments in the context of a fair market value determination. Once again, appraisers must make appropriate judgments in the context of their overall analysis of a subject enterprise and the likely market for the subject enterprise.
- What accounts for control premiums?
  - ○ The appraiser may consider appropriate premiums over marketable minority value, but such control premiums are not automatic. Appraisers must make appropriate judgments in the context of fair market value appraisals.
  - ○ A buyer's desire to "get a deal done" can cause the price offered to increase, resulting in a larger observed premium. If this occurs, there may be elements of compulsion involved in establishing the price limiting the relevance of such transactions in the determination of fair market value.
  - ○ Irrational buyers can pay any price that they can afford to pay, but this provides poor support for assessing fair market value.
  - ○ Elements of compulsion and irrationality should not be considered in fair market value determinations according to the very definition of fair market value.

Control Premiums: Valuation Results, Not Value Drivers

At this point, it is appropriate to recall the conceptual discussion of control premiums in the context of this practical discussion of adjustments to the earnings stream. A control premium (CP) is observed when a public company is acquired at a price in excess of its pre-announcement, freely traded price. The announced acquisition price of a public enterprise, or control value (CV) can be shown as a function of its marketable minority, or pre-announcement value (MMV) as:

$$CV = MMV * (1 + CP)$$

Prior to the announcement, marketable minority value reflected a given multiple of normalized earnings (or $Earnings_n$):

$$CV = (Earnings_n * M) * (1 + CP)$$

Alternatively, the control value can also be expressed in terms of the control buyer's earnings expectation. As we have demonstrated, control values are based on expected *earning power from the viewpoint of prospective acquirers*, where the earning power is the level of earnings expected post-acquisition based on economies or synergies available to that purchaser ($Earnings_c$). Therefore, the announced control value can also be expressed, from the viewpoint of the acquirer, as:

$$CV = Earnings_c * M$$

Combining these two expressions yields the following:

$$(Earnings_n * M) * (1 + CP) = Earnings_c * M$$

This expression clarifies that the control premium relates two expressions of value, the public market price on the left side of the equation and the announced acquisition price on the right. Observed control premiums are not value drivers—rather they reflect the valuation result of underlying economic and financial factors. Appraisers should be very careful in applying control premiums, particularly larges ones, in valuations.

Finally, if we assume that the acquirer's discount rate and growth expectations (embedded in M) are the same as the market discount rate for the public company, the relationship can be simplified to the following:

$$Earnings_n * (1 + CP) = Earnings_c$$

Because the control premium is the observed link between normalized enterprise cash flows for a public entity and the expected cash flows available to acquirers, it should further be clear that we should not apply control premiums without also examining the underlying multiples of earnings that were paid in acquisitions (or the implied multiples of the earnings of subject enterprises represented by resulting value implications). Observed control premiums represent the benefit of the increment in expected earnings of a public enterprise that is to be received by selling shareholders. (See Appendix 4-A.)

CONCLUSION

This chapter revisits concepts discussed in the Integrated Theory of Business Valuation from a practical viewpoint. We are not suggesting that appraisers who do not use the chapter's vocabulary for income statement adjustments are wrong. We are suggesting, however, that this vocabulary regarding Type 1 and Type 2 Normalizing Adjustments and Financial and Strategic Control Adjustments can help appraisers consider the impact of valuation adjustments on their conclusions. This vocabulary also clarifies the level of value that a particular valuation method yields.

In the next chapter, we address another type of valuation adjustment, the fundamental adjustment that may be appropriate when using guideline public company data or guideline transactions as the basis for developing capitalization factors.

A Cautionary Tale

We were asked recently to review a valuation prepared by another firm. While multiple methods were employed in the appraisal, two are relevant for this story—the guideline transaction and the guideline company method. Because the appraisal was on a controlling interest basis, the appraiser developed a marketable minority value indication using the guideline company method and applied a control premium.

The subject company's industry was in a consolidation phase and there was considerable acquisition activity of both private and public companies. In this industry, the focus was on the multiples of EBITDA paid in acquisitions. The appraiser's research indicated many acquisitions of similar companies in recent years—nearly one hundred. Over the entire time period leading to the valuation date, the average and median multiples paid for companies was on the order of 11x EBITDA, which was the approximate multiple used by the appraiser in the guideline transaction method.

A marketable minority value was developed for the guideline company method. Interestingly, the multiple of normalized EBITDA implied by this indication was about 10.0x. The appraiser next reviewed control premium data found in the *Mergerstat Control Premium Study*. Two transactions were identified involving similar companies, and the observed control premiums were on the order of 100% each. Based on a discussion of a short paragraph or so, the appraiser concluded that a range of control premiums of 60% to 90% was appropriate. Splitting the difference, the appraiser applied a control premium of 75%.

The result of the guideline public company method was substantially higher than other indications of value in the valuation. In fact, it reflected a multiple of 17x to 19x EBITDA (i.e., $10.0 \times (1 + 75\%)$). Recall that the median and average multiples of EBITDA in the many transactions examined in the guideline transactions method was about 11x. The appraiser should have attempted to reconcile the difference between 19x and 11x but, unfortunately, did not.

As it turns out, the two acquisitions examined from *Mergerstat Control Premium Study* were reflected among the transactions examined for the guideline transactions method. The EBITDA multiples recorded for these two transactions were 10.0x and 11.0x, respectively. There was no justification for a value indication at 19x EBITDA, and the report lost credibility because of the failure to reflect an understanding of the economics of pricing in the subject company's industry.

CHAPTER 5

Fundamental Adjustments to Market Capitalization Rates

INTRODUCTION

Thus far, we have discussed two types of valuation adjustments used by appraisers:

1. Conceptual Adjustments (Chapter 3)
   - Control premiums
   - Minority interest discounts
   - Marketability discounts
2. Adjustments to the Earnings Stream (Chapter 4)
   - Normalizing adjustments (Type 1 and Type 2)
   - Control adjustments (Financial and Strategic)

The Integrated Theory contributes to a thorough understanding of the conceptual adjustments. We have defined the conceptual adjustments in the context of the fundamental valuation elements of cash flow, risk, and growth. Value at the enterprise level is a function of enterprise cash flows, risks, and growth potential. Value at the shareholder level is a function of the cash flows expected to be received by shareholders, the risks faced by shareholders, and the growth (capital appreciation) potential of the subject interest.

It is critical to understand the adjustments that are made to the income stream in conducting an appraisal—why and when certain adjustments are appropriate or not. We demonstrated, for example, that *not making* normalizing adjustments in *minority interest* appraisals leads to unreliable valuation results.

We now consider a third category of valuation adjustments, *fundamental adjustments*. These adjustments are used by appraisers applying the guideline company method. We have been exploring the concept of fundamental adjustments for some time. In *Valuing Financial Institutions*, published in 1992, we framed the issue as follows:

129

Business and bank appraisers face a difficult task in developing capitalization rates in situations where they are unable to identify a comparable group of public companies to use as a foundation. The ACAPM (Adjusted Capital Asset Pricing Model, discussed in Chapter 6) provides some assistance in this regard.

But the analyst sometimes faces an equally imponderable task in assessing where, relative to a public comparable group, to "price" the earnings of a valuation subject. The analytical question is straightforward: How can the analyst justify a significant discount to the P/E multiples derived from public comparables even when it seems obvious that the subject should command a considerably lower multiple?

While a public company comparable group provides an objective basis for comparing a subject company's results, either with measures of the group average (such as the mean or median) or with regard to the performance of specific companies in the group, appraisers often end up applying what amounts to a large judgmental discount to the comparable group average (e.g., "... on the order of 50 percent based on our detailed analysis") to obtain a correct (i.e., more reasonable and realistic) valuation multiple to be applied to the subject company.[1]

We originally referred to fundamental adjustments as *fundamental discounts*. Along the way, however, we learned that private companies can compare both favorably and unfavorably with groups of guideline companies, so we began using the term *fundamental adjustments*.

COMMON QUESTIONS

1. What are fundamental adjustments, and how should appraisers determine and apply them?
2. What are the differences in fundamental adjustments applied to equity versus total capital valuation metrics?
3. In valuing illiquid interests of private businesses, why do appraisers normally begin with appraisals at the marketability minority level of value?

---

[1] Z. Christopher Mercer, "Minority Interest Valuation Methodologies," *Valuing Financial Institutions* (Homewood, IL: Business One Irwin, 1992), p. 235.

THE GRAPES OF VALUE REVIEWED

A brief review of the GRAPES of Value is appropriate as we begin to address the concept of fundamental adjustments. We begin with A (*alternative investment world*) because of its direct relationship to the guideline company method. While the examples in the following discussion are drawn from the guideline public company method, the concepts are applicable to guideline transactions involving entire companies, to guideline transactions involving restricted shares of public companies, or any other relevant comparisons of private enterprises with market transactions.

A—The world of value is an *alternative investment* world. We value private enterprises and interests in private enterprises *in relationship to alternative investments*. In using the guideline company method, we look, for example, at groups of similar (or comparable) publicly traded companies to develop valuation metrics for application to private enterprises.

G—The world of value is a *growth* world. Investors purchase equity securities with the expectation that the underlying enterprises will grow and that their investments will grow in value. This suggests that it is important, when comparing private enterprises with groups of guideline public companies, to examine the underlying growth prospects for each.

R—The world of value is a world in which *risk* is both charged for and rewarded. This suggests that in making comparisons with guideline companies, appraisers should account for differences in the relative riskiness of subject enterprises and the guideline groups.

P—The world of value is a *present value* world. To the extent that one investment is riskier than another, the impact of that greater risk dampens the present value of expected future cash flows, and therefore, value.

E—The world of value is an *expectational* world. If it is important for appraisers to understand the growth prospects of both guideline public companies and the subject enterprise, it is also important to examine the impact of *differences in expectations* on the value of the subject enterprise.

S—The world of value is a *sane and rational* world. While pockets of presumed irrationality may always exist in the public markets, on balance, free markets are unsparingly rational. It is incumbent on the analyst to decipher the underlying rationale reflected in market transactions.

The seventh principle in the GRAPES of Value is *knowledge*. This review frames the following discussion of fundamental adjustments used when developing valuation multiples for private enterprises based on comparisons with public companies (or other guideline transactions).

A CONCEPTUAL OVERVIEW OF FUNDAMENTAL ADJUSTMENTS

In Chapter 3, we illustrated the levels of value conceptually using the Gordon Model. The basic valuation of any business enterprise was summarized as:

$$V = \frac{CF}{r - g} \tag{5.1}$$

When we examine price/earnings *multiples* from guideline public companies, the observed multiples are a composite of the market's view of each company's r and expected g. Using the market approach, analysts generally examine market multiples directly and do not attempt to derive either r or g specifically. There is an implicit assumption that reported public company earnings are normalized.[2] In some cases, the analyst may actually make normalizing adjustments to individual public companies before calculating earnings multiples.

When valuing a private company, appraisers capitalize the enterprise's normalized cash flows based on the appropriate discount rate for that private enterprise and its expected growth in core earnings.

In other words, appraisers can develop reasonable valuation indications if the discount rate and expected growth of cash flows are appropriately estimated.

Risk Differentials Cause Fundamental Adjustments

When comparing a subject private company with public guideline companies, the objective is to ascertain the appropriate discount rate or capitalization rate for the subject private company. In doing so, appraisers must contemplate that the appropriate discount rate for the subject private

---

[2]Even if there are unusual or nonrecurring items in the most current (twelve months) earnings of a public company, the public markets effectively normalize these results by focusing on *next year's* earnings.

company may be less than, equal to, or greater than those of the guideline public companies.

Quite often, the subject private company is riskier than the public guideline companies. For example, it may be smaller, have key person risks, customer concentrations, or other risks not present in most or all of the selected guideline companies. Skeptical readers might suggest that in such circumstances the selected guideline companies are not sufficiently comparable to the private enterprise. However, by common practice (and judicial and client expectation), if there are publicly traded companies somewhat similar to the subject, even if considerably larger, they will need to be considered.

As discussed at length in Chapter 6, it is common practice when using income methods to "build up" a discount rate. Analysts routinely add a small stock premium to the base, CAPM-determined market premium to account for the greater riskiness of small companies relative to large capitalization stocks. In addition, analysts routinely estimate a specific company risk premium for private enterprises, which is added to the other components of the build-up discount rate. In other words, analysts adjust public market return data (from Ibbotson Associates or other sources) used to develop public company return expectations to account for risks related to size and other factors. Stated alternatively, they are making *fundamental adjustments* in the development of discount rates. Analysts do so to develop credible valuation indications for the subject enterprises.

Now, consider the guideline public company method. Assume that the subject enterprise is riskier than the public guideline companies. Other things being equal (like expected growth in earnings), the direct application of guideline public multiples to the subject private enterprise would result in an *overvaluation* of the private enterprise.

Why? Because the cash flows are normalized to a public equivalent basis and growth expectations are comparable. However, the lower r from the public group was applied to the normalized cash flows of the private enterprise—and the higher (relative) risk of the private enterprise was not captured in the public guideline multiple.

Expected Growth Differentials Cause Fundamental Adjustments

Like risk, the growth expectations for the subject private enterprise may be the same, greater than, or less than the growth expectations underlying the public company multiples. Quite often (indeed, more often), it is the case that the realistic growth expectations for the subject private enterprise are less than the growth expectations embedded in public market pricing.[3] Familiarity with public markets is crucial when examining relative growth expectations between private and public companies.

- For private companies, examination of historical growth may provide the best evidence relating to future growth expectations, although "hockey stick" projections are seen quite often in private company appraisals. The question in such cases is: "How realistic are the forecasted results in light of history and the current condition of the private enterprise?"
- For a public company, examination of historical growth may provide little indication of the expectations for future growth underlying its stock price. These expectations can, however, be inferred from the price/earnings multiples. Further, analysts covering many public companies publish estimates for one-year, two-year, and perhaps, five-year earnings growth.[4]

In direct capitalization methods, analysts estimate expected future growth to convert their estimated discount rates into capitalization rates. Growth expectations are normally based on analysis of historical financial results, assessment of current economic and industry conditions, and evaluation of the company's productive capacity, management resources, and operating capabilities. Based on personal experience, discussions with hundreds of appraisers and reviews of hundreds of appraisal reports, it is fair to say that expected growth for private companies is typically less than 10%. When a DCF model is used, this observation is also true when direct capitalizations are used to develop terminal value indications.

However, the effective, long-term G_e embedded in the pricing of public companies is often close to, or even a bit more, than 10%. Appraisers who use lower expected growth in income methods are implicitly applying fundamental adjustments.

Other things (like risk) being equal, overvaluation is caused by application of valuation multiples from guideline public companies directly

---

[3]Analysts may compare the *historical* growth patterns of a subject private company with public guideline companies and find similarity in levels and/or patterns. Under such circumstances, it could be tempting to apply median or typical public multiples to the private company. This will result in error, however, if the growth expectations embedded in current public market pricing are significantly different than the past and higher than the expectations for the subject private company. Remember the E of the GRAPES—the world of value is an *expectational* world.

[4]Recall from Chapter 1 that analysts' EPS growth estimates are not equal to the growth in core earnings of the Gordon Model.

to performance measures of private enterprises having lower growth expectations. (The opposite holds when the private company's growth expectations exceed those of the public companies.) Therefore, analysts must consider whether a *fundamental adjustment* is appropriate to account for differing growth expectations.

Fundamental Adjustments by Another Name

Most appraisers, even those who have never employed the term "fundamental adjustment" have used the same concept in appraisals. In fact, any appraiser who has selected guideline company multiples other than the median (or perhaps, the average), whether above or below, has implicitly applied the concept of the fundamental adjustment. Based on comparisons with the subject company, appraisers often select multiples above or below the measures of central tendency for the public group. In so doing, they are applying the concept of the fundamental adjustment no less than others who quantify specific adjustments.

The next section provides practical examples of developing fundamental adjustments whether using a quantitative methodology or selecting valuation multiples other than the median (or average) of a guideline company group for application to private company performance measures.

PRACTICAL TECHNIQUES FOR DEVELOPING FUNDAMENTAL ADJUSTMENTS

Quantifying Fundamental Adjustments Using the ACAPM

Consider two companies in the same industry, Publico and Privateco: Privateco is somewhat smaller than Publico, having issues with customer concentration and with key person dependency on the majority shareholder. Using these two companies, and the broader guideline group, we can illustrate one potential means of developing an appropriate fundamental adjustment when using the guideline company method.

Compare Publico and Privateco The market for Publico stock is relatively liquid for a small capitalization company. At the valuation date, its current share price represents a price/earnings multiple of 17.0x, as seen at Line 6 in Exhibit 5.1. This observed multiple corresponds to a range of potential expectations with respect to the discount rate and expected growth in core earnings. After directly estimating either rate, we can infer the other. For example, as shown in Exhibit 5.1, the observed P/E multiple of 17.0x is

Compare Publico with Privateco
Derive Publico Discount Rate and Adjust for Privateco

Line	Capitalization Rate Components	Publico	Privateco	
1	Base Discount Rate (R)	15.5%	15.5%	Derived for Publico
2	Specific Company Risk (SCR)	0.0%	2.0%	Greater risks
3	Equity Discount Rate (R)	15.5%	17.5%	
4	Expected Growth (G_e)	–9.6%	–7.0%	Slower growth expectations
5	Capitalization Rate ($R - G_e$)	5.9%	10.5%	
6	P/E Multiple $1/(R - G_e)$	17.0	9.5	Lower implied P/E for Privateco
		Observed Multiple		
7	**Effective Fundamental Adjustment**	–44.0%		

EXHIBIT 5.1   Comparison of Publico and Privateco Capitalization Rates

equal to a capitalization rate of 5.9%. If the discount rate is assumed to be 15.5%, the implied growth rate in core earnings is 9.6%.

Relative to Publico, it is clear that Privateco is riskier, principally because of unique key person and customer concentration risks. Assuming that an appropriate risk premium of 2.0% (Line 2) is added to the base Publico discount rate, the resulting discount rate for Privateco is 17.5% (Line 3). If we now assume that the appropriate core earnings growth expectation (G_e) for Privateco is 7.0% (Line 4), the resulting capitalization rate of 10.5% and the corresponding price/earnings multiple of 9.5× are calculated on Lines 5 and 6.

The fundamental adjustment is the difference between the observed multiple for Publico and the estimated multiple of Privateco based on the specific consideration of Privateco's discount rate and growth expectations. The indicated fundamental adjustment based on this analysis (borrowed from the income approach) is −44%.

Fundamental analysis indicates that Privateco is both riskier and expected to grow at a slower rate than Publico. Given these fundamental differences, appraisers must adjust the 17.0× multiple observed for Publico in some fashion to develop an appropriate indication of value for Privateco.

In practice, appraisers develop fundamental adjustments in several ways:

- Develop quantitative analysis of risk and growth differentials as described previously.
- Omit obvious outlier multiples (very high or very low) and select a multiple based on an adjusted median or average.

- From a range of multiples for a particular earnings measure, select a multiple from one company that is most appropriate in the appraiser's judgment.
- From a range of multiples for a particular earnings measure, select a multiple that the appraiser thinks is most appropriate.

Regardless of the technique used, the concept of the fundamental adjustment is used any time a valuation multiple other than the median or mean of the guideline group is applied to the subject company. The salient question is not whether fundamental adjustments are warranted, but rather how they are best estimated and supported.

In the following section, we elaborate on one suggested technique (based on estimated risk and growth differentials) for specifying appropriate fundamental adjustments.

Determine a Fundamental Adjustment Using ACAPM   The method outlined in the comparison of Publico and Privateco can be a useful means of quantifying the appropriate fundamental adjustments in many applications of the guideline company method. After estimating appropriate public company discount rates, the Gordon Model can then be used to estimate the long-term G_e embedded in guideline public company share prices.[5] Exhibit 5.2 develops the 15.5% discount rate for Publico that was assumed in Exhibit 5.1.

Estimate Long-Term Growth Rate of Public Guideline Group
Publico Represents the Median of a Guideline Company Group

Line	Guideline (Public) Company Growth Analysis				Sources/Comments
1	Long-Term Government Bond Yield-to-Maturity		4.9%		As of March 2003
2	Ibbotson Common Stock Premium	6.2%			Per Mercer Capital analysis
3	x Industry Beta	1.2			
4	Beta-Adjusted Common Stock Premium	7.4%			
5	+ Ibbotson Small Stock Premium	3.2%			Per Mercer Capital analysis
6	= Total Equity Premium		10.6%		
7	Industry Discount Rate (required rate of return)		15.5%		
8	− Industry P/E and Resulting Cap Rate (1/P/E)	17.0	5.9%		Based on median guideline p/e
9	= Implied Long-Term Growth Rate for Public Companies		9.6%		

EXHIBIT 5.2   Derivation of Discount Rate for Publico

---

[5]The model may be used to estimate either variable for a given public company, but not both simultaneously.

Determine a Fundamental Adjustment
  Use the ACAPM to Narrow the Range of Judgment
  Privateco in Relationship to Guideline Company Group

Line	Subject Company Analysis	Medians for Public Group	Privateco ACAPM Build-up	Step 1 Set Risk = Privateco GROWTH = Public	Step 2 Set G = Privateco RISK = Public	Step 3 GROWTH = Privateco RISK = Privateco
1	Long-Term Government Bond Yield-to-Maturity	4.9%	4.9%	4.9%	4.9%	4.9%
2	+ Total Equity Premium (Line 6 from Exhibit 5-2)	10.6%	10.6%	10.6%	10.6%	10.6%
3	+ Specific Company Risk Premium	0.0%	2.0%	2.0%	0.0%	2.0%
4	= Discount Rate (required rate of return)	15.5%	17.5%	17.5%	15.5%	17.5%
5	– Growth Rate Estimates	−9.6%	−7.0%	−9.6%	−7.0%	−7.0%
6	= Implied Capitalization Rates	5.9%	10.5%	7.9%	8.5%	10.5%
7	Implied P/E Multiples	17.0	9.5	12.7	11.8	9.5
8	*Implied Adjustment from Guideline Median P/E*	na		−25.4%	−30.8%	−44.0%

9   Step 4: Selected Fundamental Adjustment   −35.0%

EXHIBIT 5.3   Derivation of Fundamental Adjustment

Assume now that there are several other public companies in Publico's industry that are suitable for inclusion in the guideline public group for Privateco. Assume further, for purposes of this illustration, that Publico's market multiples represent the median of the broader group.

Exhibit 5.3 presents the ACAPM summary build-up for Publico (the median guideline company) and Privateco. Then, in four steps, a methodology is presented to develop a fundamental adjustment for Privateco.

Step 1. Using the discount rate for Privateco, which includes 2.0% of company-specific risk factors, substitute the implied G_e for the public group into the build-up of a capitalization factor for Privateco. This captures the valuation impact of the differing risk assessments between Privateco and the public guideline companies. Given the discount rate for Privateco of 17.5% (Line 4, Step1), the expected growth for the guideline public group of 9.6% is substituted for the 7.0% expected growth for Privateco (on Line 5). The result is a capitalization rate of 7.9% (Line 6) and a price/earnings multiple of 12.7× (Line 7), which represents a discount of 25.4% relative to the median public multiple of 17.0×. Stated another way, relative to the median of the guideline group, the consideration of 2.0% of incremental risk for Privateco would justify a −25.4% fundamental adjustment to the median public multiple.

Step 2. Using the discount rate for the guideline group, i.e., excluding Privateco's specific risk premium, and setting the expected growth at the 7.0% level for Privateco (Lines 4 and 5), we develop a capitalization rate of 8.5% (Line 6) and a resulting price/earnings multiple of 11.8× (Line 7). Considering only slower growth expectations relative to the guideline group median justifies a −30.8% fundamental adjustment.

Step 3. Now, we consider the combined effects of Privateco's slower expected growth and its higher riskiness. Step 3 replicates the 44.0% discount illustrated in Exhibit 5.1.

Step 4. The first three steps have created a range of potential fundamental adjustments, from −25.4% (based on extra risk), to −30.8% (based on slower expected growth), to −44.0% (based on the combination of extra risk and slower expected growth). In Step 4, the analyst must reach a conclusion for the appropriate fundamental adjustment. Obviously, there is a difference between a −25% and a −44% adjustment—it is rare in valuation when a set of calculations provides such a precise result that the need for judgment is eliminated. The calculations in Steps 1–3 have, however, established a reasonable range for the appropriate fundamental adjustment. The analyst must reach a conclusion within this range based on other quantitative comparisons, qualitative comparisons, and, ultimately, judgment. In this case, a 35% fundamental discount was selected.[6]

By analyzing the potential impact of risk and growth differentials on valuation multiples, the analyst can develop confidence making the judgments necessary when the guideline company method is used. This method provides a framework within which to adjust public company multiples for private company valuations. While the example illustrated a fundamental discount, similar analysis may in some cases suggest a fundamental premium.

It is important to note that, because this framework uses equity discount rates and core earnings growth rates, the resulting fundamental adjustments relate to equity, rather than total capital valuation multiples.

Application of the Fundamental Adjustment　　The fundamental adjustment is a function of relative differences in risk and expected growth between a subject company and a selected group of public guideline companies.

---

[6]One may argue that if the appraiser believes in both the estimates of higher risk and slower growth, the concluded fundamental discount should be −44%. However, the objective of the analysis is to price a private company "as-if-freely-traded," or close to how the analyst believes the public markets would price that firm if public. The judgments required for this analysis should allow some discretion within a calculated range of potential adjustments.

We have presented a simple framework for estimating the fundamental adjustment for (market value of) equity multiples.

Appraisers often derive total capital valuation multiples when using the guideline method. The fundamental adjustment for total capital multiples is different than that for equity multiples. Leverage influences the appropriate adjustment to total capital multiples. While fundamental adjustments applicable to equity valuation multiples can be adjusted to apply to total capital valuation multiples, we prefer to simply apply the fundamental adjustment to equity values after debt has been deducted from indicated values of total capital. Exhibit 5.4 illustrates application of a fundamental adjustment of 35% to indicated values of equity derived using both total capital and equity valuation multiples.

Application of Fundamental Adjustments to Total Capital
and Equity Value Indications

		Market Value of Total Capital to			Price to Net Income (Market Value of Equity/NI)	
	Derivation of Value	Sales	EBITDA	EBIT	Ongoing/Tr 12	Current FY
1	Appropriate Earnings or Performance Measure	$100,000,000	$15,000,000	$10,500,000	$6,500,000	$8,200,000
2	× Guideline Company Capitalization Factor	1.25	8.10	11.15	16.00	13.50
3	= Capitalized Value: Total Capital	$125,000,000	$121,500,000	$117,075,000	$104,000,000	$110,700,000
4	− Interest Bearing Debt (Operational)	(18,000,000)	(18,000,000)	(18,000,000)		
5	= Capitalized Value: Total Common Equity	$107,000,000	$103,500,000	$99,075,000	$104,000,000	$110,700,000
6	− Fundamental Adjustment −35.0%	(37,450,000)	(36,225,000)	(34,676,250)	(36,400,000)	(38,745,000)
7	= Adjusted Guideline Company Capitalized Value	$69,550,000	$67,275,000	$64,398,750	$67,600,000	$71,955,000
	INDICATED VALUES: Rounded to:					
8	GUIDELINE COMPANY METHOD $10,000	$69,550,000	$67,280,000	$64,400,000	$67,600,000	$71,960,000
9	Concluded Multiples Based on Derived Equity Value	0.876	5.685	7.848	10.400	8.776
10	Effective Fundamental Adjustment to the Guideline Median	−30.0%	−29.8%	−29.6%	−35.0%	−35.0%
11	Adjustment Factor (Equity to Total Capital)	−14.4%	−14.8%	−15.4%		
	− (Market Value of Equity Before Fundamental Adjustment / Market Value of Total Capital) (Line 5 / Line 3)					

EXHIBIT 5.4   Application of Fundamental Adjustments

Note that for the indications of value developed using total capital multiples, the fundamental adjustment (Line 6) is applied to the implied market values of total capital less applicable debt (Line 5), or the derived equity values for each measure. Note also that the fundamental adjustment is applied directly to the indications of value developed using equity multiples to the right of the vertical line separating total capital and net income measures.

Adjusting Equity-Based Fundamental Adjustments for Total Capital Methods

This presentation in Exhibit 5.4 avoids the valuation misstatement that occurs when the equity-based fundamental adjustment is applied to total capital measures. For example, in Exhibit 5.4, in the market value of total capital to sales column, we calculate at Line 9 the implied multiple of total capital to sales based on the concluded equity value (Line 8). A multiple of 0.88x sales would yield an equity value of $69.55 million. This multiple represents a 30% discount to the guideline median multiple of

1.25x sales (Line 10), not a 35% fundamental adjustment, a difference of about 14% (30%/35% − 1).

The conversion factor is easily determined. On Line 11 we calculate the adjustment factor (AF) necessary to convert an equity-based fundamental adjustment (FAE) to a total capital basis. In this case, the adjustment factor is −14.4%. Symbolically, the fundamental adjustment for total capital (FATC) can be represented as follows (where market value of equity is MVE and market value of total capital is MVTC):

$$FATC = FAE \times AF$$
$$AF = (MVE/MVTC)$$

In most cases, we find it simpler to apply the equity-based fundamental adjustment to indicated values of equity (Lines 1 through 8 of Exhibit 5.4).

Using a Factor Other Than the Median or Mean to Determine the Fundamental Adjustment

Without using the vocabulary of fundamental adjustments presented in this chapter, an appraiser may nonetheless judge that the mean or median valuation multiple of the guideline public company group is not applicable to the subject company because of size differences, less favorable growth outlooks, or unfavorable financial comparisons. The framework outlined in the preceding section is one mechanism for identifying a range of reasonable fundamental adjustments. Appraisers using the guideline company method make subjective and objective comparisons between subject companies and the selected guideline companies. In so doing, they may prefer another procedure for adjusting from the median, or typical multiples for a guideline group.

In lieu of such an approach, appraisers may select a measure other than the median or mean as the base multiple. For example, an appraiser might, based on comparisons of revenues, growth, leverage, or other factors, conclude that a private company should most appropriately be compared with a specific portion of the entire guideline group, for example, the lower half of the group's multiples, rather than the entire group. This essentially represents subjecting the guideline public company group to an additional screen by eliminating multiples above the median or mean.[7]

Assume for purposes of illustration that an appraiser has determined that his subject company should be compared, based on his overall analysis, with the lower half of multiples for his guideline group rather than with the

---

[7]This same technique could obviously be used to focus on the multiples above the median (or average) of a guideline public company group.

Guideline Companies	Sample Company Guideline Multiples	
	Revenues	EBITDA
	0.53	14.69
Multiples from Six Selected Guideline	0.53	10.21
Companies Arranged in Descending	0.52	9.67
Order for Ease of Visual Inspection	0.34	7.72
	0.26	7.44
	0.13	5.40
Median Multiples	**0.43**	**8.69**
Average Multiples	**0.39**	**9.19**

1. First Quartile Analysis		
Calculate First Quartiles	**0.28**	**7.51**
Implied Adjustment from Overall Medians	−35%	−14%
Implied Adjustment from Overall Averages	−27%	−18%

2. Lower Half Average Analysis		
	0.53	14.69
Upper Half for Perspective	0.53	10.21
	0.52	9.67
Averages (for Top of Lower Half Range)	**0.39**	**9.19**
	0.34	7.72
Lower Half of Multiples (Including Average)	0.26	7.44
	0.13	5.40
Averages of Lower Half	**0.28**	**7.44**
Implied Adjustment from Overall Medians	−35%	−14%
Implied Adjustment from Overall Averages	−28%	−19%

EXHIBIT 5.5 Alternative Techniques for Adjusting Market Capitalization Rates

entire group. Exhibit 5.5 illustrates two techniques the appraiser may use to determine appropriate valuation multiples.

Using either technique (first quartile or average of lower half), the appraiser has effectively applied a fundamental adjustment to the median observation of the public guideline company group.

Either technique may be used in the context of judgments made in appraisal assignments—if the adjustments are based on the facts and circumstances and are reasonable.[8]

---

[8]Note that there is a difference between the implied fundamental adjustments applicable to the two valuation multiples. This result can occur because the analysis

Conceptual Illustrations of Fundamental Adjustments

In this section, we reconcile the fundamental adjustment with the conceptual levels of value of the Integrated Theory.

Fundamental adjustments relative to the marketable minority level of value can be depicted as shown in Exhibit 5.6.[9]

The following discussion, which compares a series of private companies to a guideline public group, will help illustrate the significance of the fundamental adjustment in an appraisal.

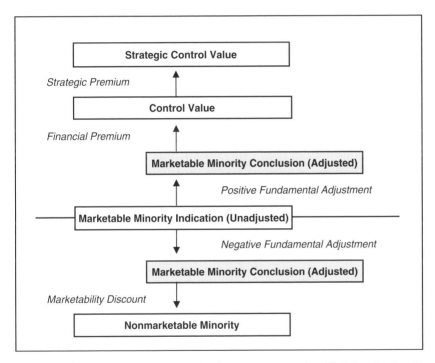

EXHIBIT 5.6 Impact of Fundamental Adjustment on Marketable Minority Level of Value

---

is based on medians and first quartiles of individual multiples, rather individual companies. In practice, this kind of result is not unusual. For example, an individual public company may be the median observation by one measure and above—or below—median for other valuation multiples.

[9]Conceptually, if guideline control transactions form the basis for valuation comparisons, fundamental adjustments can be considered relative to those transactions, which yield value indications at the strategic or financial control levels.

Because application of public market multiples (after application of fundamental adjustment) provides a marketable minority, or "as-if-freely-traded" indication of value, the other levels of value for the private company would tend to shift accordingly. The following illustrations relate the levels of value for private companies to the public guideline groups assuming different fundamental adjustments.

Median Pricing. The analyst "prices" a private company by selecting appropriate multiples based on fundamental comparisons with the guideline information. In this case, the application of median multiples would achieve realistic valuation indications for the subject private company. This scenario is illustrated in Exhibit 5.7.

Above Median Pricing. The analyst may value a particularly attractive private company at the high end of the guideline company range. In Exhibit 5.8, the subject private company is an excellent performer, and its fundamentals suggest that it should be priced above median levels for the guideline group.

Below Median Pricing. Sometimes fundamental comparisons between a guideline public company group and a private company will indicate that the private company is less attractive than the public group due to higher risk, an outlook for slower growth, or both. The subject private company in Exhibit 5.9 is valued below the median levels for the guideline group.

Below the Range of Guideline Multiples. In some cases, comparisons of a private company with selected guideline companies suggest pricing below the range of the public group. While some would argue that this indicates the group is not sufficiently comparable to the private company

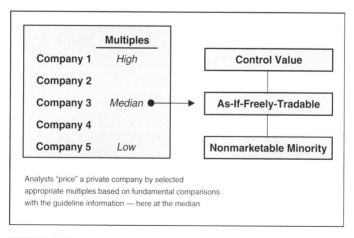

EXHIBIT 5.7 Median Pricing

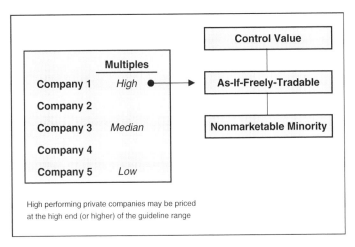

EXHIBIT 5.8 Above Median Pricing

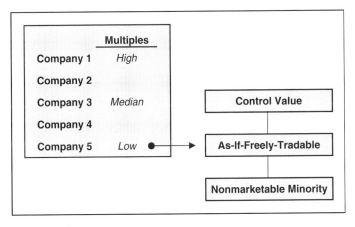

EXHIBIT 5.9 Below Median Pricing

for comparison, such situations do arise. As shown on Exhibit 5.10, the appropriate private company valuation multiples in such cases will be below the range of the public multiples.

Exhibit 5.11 summarizes the comparisons we have just seen, depicting all four situations on a single chart.

Exhibit 5.11 underscores the importance of fundamental adjustments in the guideline public company method. The application of a fundamental adjustment, whether positive or negative, shifts the "as-if-freely-traded"

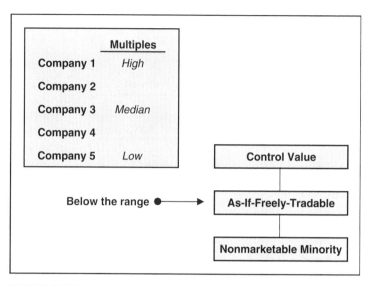

EXHIBIT 5.10 Below the Range of Guideline Multiples

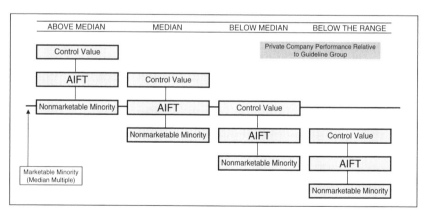

EXHIBIT 5.11 Influence of Fundamental Adjustment on the Various Levels of Value

value for a private company to its appropriate position relative to the public group. From this value, the application of an appropriate marketability discount will yield an appropriate conclusion at the nonmarketable minority level. Similarly, application of an appropriate control premium will yield an appropriate controlling interest conclusion.

The Double-Dipping Argument

Fundamental adjustments are rooted in differences in risk and expected growth. Differences in margin performance, revenue per employee, and so on are already reflected in earnings or cash flow. Such differences are already accounted for by applying unadjusted multiples, particularly if risk and expected growth are considered identical.

For example, assume that the median margin of EBITDA to sales is 15% for a public guideline group, and that the median EBITDA multiple is 10×. The implied multiple of total capital to sales is therefore 150% (15% × 10). If a company with similar risk and growth prospects has an EBITDA margin of 10%, the implied total capital to sales multiple is 100% if the median EBITDA multiple is applied (10% × 10). The valuation penalty of a lower margin is already present without considering a fundamental adjustment. Applying a fundamental adjustment for lower profit margins would add another penalty and, therefore, could be described as double-dipping.

The potential for double-dipping can be alleviated by appropriate screening of public guideline companies for similar performance characteristics as the subject. Analysts should always test the reasonableness of valuation conclusions by making appropriate comparisons with the selected guideline group. While individual adjustments may be questioned, it is important to demonstrate their overall reasonableness in relationship to the selected guideline group.

MARKETABILITY DISCOUNTS FOR CONTROLLING INTERESTS?

Some appraisers apply marketability discounts to controlling interests of companies. In Chapter 3, we examined the lack of any conceptual basis for such a discount. To review, enterprise value is the present value of expected future cash flows. Because control over the cash flows is being transferred, there is no basis for discounting for lack of marketability. Such discounting is an incorrect application of the concept of the marketability discount applicable to minority interests.

When appraisers apply a marketability discount to a controlling interest, it may actually represent the fundamental adjustment necessary to appropriately ascertain the marketable minority value. When faced with value indications that are obviously too high, most appraisers will attempt to resolve the discrepancy in some fashion to reach a reasonable result. We suspect that many applications of marketability discounts to controlling interest value indications reflect such attempts.

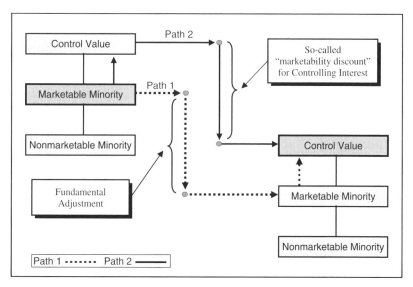

EXHIBIT 5.12   Marketability Discount for Controlling Interests as a Proxy for the Fundamental Adjustment

SHANNON PRATT RESPONDS: MARKETABILITY DISCOUNTS APPLICABLE TO CONTROLLING INTERESTS

"The marketability discount applicable to controlling interests has something to do with the company not being ready for sale. In other words, Grandma is still on the payroll, the equipment has not been cleaned and shined, the accounting statements are not in shape for a buyer to see them credibly, there may be some unresolved lawsuits or questions with some of the contracts with suppliers or customers, there may be some legal work—and all of this takes management time, elapsed time, and the cost of lawyers and accountants and probably other advisors to accomplish. These are the bases on which I quantify the DLOM for controlling interests, at least partially. There may be other reasons. For example, the company may be so unique that it would be hard to find a buyer. Call them what you like, I'm sure that you agree that these are real problems of many companies and you would probably choose to call them by some other name rather than lumping them under the marketability discount, but that is just a semantic argument."

Exhibit 5.12 illustrates how two different appraisers arrived at the same controlling interest value.

Exhibit 5.12 illustrates two possible paths to the "right" controlling interest value for a private company. The first path begins with a public guideline company analysis in the left portion of the Exhibit. A fundamental adjustment is applied to the median public multiples. The effect of the fundamental adjustment is to lower the marketable minority (and other levels of value) of the private company, on the right. A small control premium is added (based on appropriate analysis, of course), and the "right" value is achieved.

The second path begins with the same guideline company analysis and a marketable minority value is developed on the left side of the Exhibit without application of an appropriate fundamental adjustment. After adding a "reasonable" control premium to this marketable minority value, the appraiser derives the (undiscounted) controlling interest value on the left. Realizing from common sense and experience that the resulting value is simply too high, the appraiser applies a sizable "marketability discount" to the left side, which results in the "right" answer.

Path 1 is consistent with the Integrated Theory. Value is based on the present value of expected cash flows at an appropriate discount rate. Path 2 is inconsistent with the Integrated Theory. There is no conceptual justification for the selected "marketability discount," nor is there any market evidence to support it. Appraisers should consider this discussion, together with the theoretical considerations raised in Chapter 3, before blindly applying "marketability discounts" in controlling interest appraisals.

We are a bit less dogmatic than in years past that there cannot be taints on the marketability of private companies. Mercer Capital represented a bank holding company beginning in 1997. We solicited competitive bids and a satisfactory letter of intent was signed. Before the definitive agreement could be signed, a lawsuit was filed against the bank holding company. While it was essentially frivolous, the suit carried a $10 million claim against the company. As result of the suit, the planned merger was not completed. The suit progressed until early 2002, when it appeared that the magnitude of any resolution would be quite small. Discussions were held with a logical strategic buyer who stated that they would be able to isolate the impact of the litigation in pricing. When it became apparent that this would not be possible, we recommended to the company's board that negotiations cease until the suit was resolved.

Some months later, the lawsuit was settled at a nominal cost. Negotiations with the strategic buyer recommenced and a deal was signed at favorable pricing. The sale closed in early 2003, some six years after we initially marketed the bank. During the intervening period, the company was essentially unmarketable. The good news is that management ran the bank exceedingly well during the period of "nonmarketability." Substantial growth occurred and a growing dividend was paid. If an appraisal on a controlling interest basis had been necessary during this period, the taint on marketability resulting from the litigation would properly have been considered in some fashion. However, references to restricted stock studies would not have been a satisfactory means of assessing the value impact of the lawsuit.

Dr. Shannon Pratt was kind enough to review the first edition prior to its publication. He wrote a comment regarding the marketability discount applicable to controlling interests and approved of my including it in the text. The comment appears in the sidebar on page 148.

Most of the factors raised by Dr. Pratt in the sidebar were addressed in the theoretical discussion of marketability discounts applicable to controlling interests in Chapter 3, including the issues of costs to sell (which impact proceeds, not value) and readiness to sell (which definitely influences value in terms of cash flows and their expected growth and risk).

There may be unusual circumstances such as with the bank in litigation just mentioned, but such circumstances should be treated by appraisers for what they are. In any event, we continue to caution appraisers against using the concept of a "marketability discount" applicable to controlling interests.

THE LITERATURE REGARDING FUNDAMENTAL ADJUSTMENTS

We have not been alone in suggesting that fundamental adjustments must be applied when using guideline public company multiples to value private companies. For example, the third edition of *Valuing a Business* contained a brief, conceptual discussion of the concept, although the term fundamental adjustment was not used. The Pratt/Reilly/Schweihs text provides an example illustrating how to adjust for differences in expected growth and risk.

> *We will continue with the example where the guideline company indicated price/cash flow multiple is 8, resulting in a capitalization rate for cash flow of 12.5 percent. Let us assume the comparative risk analysis leads us to conclude the discount rate for the subject company would be five percentage points higher than for the guideline companies, which would bring the capitalization rate to 17.5 percent (12.5+5.0=17.5). On the other hand, let us assume our smaller, riskier company had two percentage points higher*

infinitely sustainable long-term growth prospects than the guideline companies. This offsetting factor would bring the capitalization rate back down to 15.5 percent (17.5−2.0=15.5). This, then, equates to a valuation multiple of 6.5 (1/15.5=6.5).[10]

Given that the adjusted valuation multiple is 6.5x and the beginning guideline multiple is 8.0x, the Pratt/Reilly/Schweihs analysis implies that a fundamental discount of 19% is appropriate in their example. Unfortunately, this analysis does not appear in the fourth edition of *Valuing a Business*.

Fundamental adjustments are receiving increasing attention among business valuation practitioners. The following survey article compares the treatment of fundamental adjustments in recent leading business valuation texts:

- Niculita, Alina, CFA, "Adjusting Public Multiples: A Summary of Theories and Methodologies," *Business Valuation Update*, January 2007.

In this article, Niculita reviews contributions to the topic by Richard Goeldner, Jerry Peters, Shannon Pratt, Jay Fishman, Jim Hitchner, and Chris Mercer.

CONCLUSION

We summarize the discussion of fundamental adjustments with the following observations:

- Fundamental adjustments account for observed differences in size, risk profile, or growth expectations between subject private companies and the guideline company group.
- Fundamental adjustments, positive or negative, are applicable to marketable minority multiples, and may also be applicable to controlling interest guideline multiples.
- Fundamental adjustments can be sizeable. Appraisers use a variety of methods and techniques to identify the need for, and then quantify, the application of fundamental adjustments.

---

[10]Shannon P. Pratt, Robert F. Reilly, and Robert P. Schweihs, *Valuing a Business: The Analysis and Appraisal of Closely Held Companies*, 3rd ed. (Chicago, IL: Irwin Professional Publishing, 1996), pp. 225−226.

- A failure to consider fundamental differences between valuation subjects and selected guideline groups of companies can result in material undervaluation or overvaluation.
- Appraisers selecting valuation multiples within the range (or outside the range) of guideline company multiples are using the concept, if not the vocabulary, of the fundamental adjustment.

In this chapter, we have presented techniques to assist appraisers to quantify and justify fundamental adjustments relative to guideline company multiples.

CHAPTER 6

Developing Appropriate Discount Rates

INTRODUCTION

The three elements of the Gordon Model—cash flow, growth, and risk—define the value of any business enterprise or interest therein. In previous chapters, we have explored the cash flow and growth elements from the perspectives of both the enterprise and minority shareholders. In this chapter we turn our attention to the final element, risk.

The appraiser's assessment of the riskiness of a particular asset is manifest in the estimated discount rate. Appraisers use a variety of related techniques to derive appropriate discount rates. In this chapter, we consider the appropriate discount rate in the context of the Integrated Theory using one such technique, the Adjusted Capital Asset Pricing Model (or ACAPM). We use the term ACAPM because that name was used by Mercer in a 1989 article on developing capitalization rates.[1]

Exhibit 6.1 recaps the conceptual math of the Integrated Theory to provide context for our discussion of the discount rate.

In this chapter, we assume a basic knowledge of the Capital Asset Pricing Model and related methods for estimating discount rates, focusing on practical concerns in discount rate development. Some of the more widely debated theoretical issues and controversies are rendered moot given the range of judgment exercised in discount rate development.

---

[1] Z. Christopher Mercer, "The Adjusted Capital Asset Pricing Model for Developing Capitalization Rates: An Extension of Previous 'Build-Up' Methodologies Based Upon the Capital Asset Pricing Model," *Business Valuation Review*, Vol. 8, No. 4 (1989): pp. 147–156.

	Conceptual Math	Relationships	Value Implications
Strategic Control Value	$\dfrac{CF_{e(c,s)}}{R_s - [G_{mm} + G_s]}$	$CF_{e(c,s)} \geq CF_{e(c,f)}$ $G_s \geq 0$ $R_s \leq R_{mm}$	$V_{e(c,s)} \geq V_{e(c,f)}$
Financial Control Value	$\dfrac{CF_{e(c,f)}}{R_f - [G_{mm} + G_f]}$	$CF_{e(c,f)} \geq CF_{e(mm)}$ $G_f \geq 0$ $R_f = R_{mm}(+/-\text{ a little})$	$V_{e(c,f)} \geq V_{mm}$
Marketable Minority Value	$\dfrac{CF_{e(mm)}}{R_{mm} - G_{mm}}$	$G_v = R_{mm} - \text{Div Yld}$	V_{mm} is the benchmark for the other levels
Nonmarketable Minority Value	$\dfrac{CF_{sh}}{R_{hp} - G_v}$	$CF_{sh} \leq CF_{e(mm)}$ $G_v \leq R_{mm} - \text{Div Yld}$ $R_{hp} \geq R_{mm}$	$V_{sh} \leq V_{mm}$

EXHIBIT 6.1   The Integrated Theory of Business Valuation

COMMON QUESTIONS

1. What are the practical differences, if any, between the discount rates for strategic control investors (R_s) and financial control investors (R_f) and marketable minority investors (R_{mm})?
2. How can business appraisers test the reasonableness of their valuation assumptions and conclusions?
3. What is the conceptual relationship between the discount rates at the marketable minority (R_{mm}) and nonmarketable minority (R_{hp}) levels of value?

THE ADJUSTED CAPITAL ASSET PRICING MODEL

The Adjusted Capital Asset Pricing Model combines elements of the build up or summation methodologies, which have commonly been used to derive earnings capitalization rates for closely held securities, with those of the Capital Asset Pricing Model developed by W. F. Sharpe.[2] See Appendix 6-A for a brief overview of the Capital Asset Pricing Model.

---

[2]W. F. Sharpe, "Capital Asset Prices: A Theory of Market Equilibrium Under Conditions of Risk," *Journal of Finance*, Vol. 19 (1964): pp. 425–442.

The CAPM assumes that specific, or unsystematic, risk associated with any given stock does not contribute to a higher expected return for the stock because of the opportunity for portfolio diversification. The restrictive assumption of adequate diversification is unrealistic when considering investments in closely held companies. For owners of controlling interests of closely held businesses, their interests typically account for major, undiversified portions of their wealth. This lack of diversification cannot normally be remedied by selling interests and diversifying, as there is no ready market for the subdivided minority interests. In addition, many purchasers of controlling interests invariably consider such specific risks, regardless of their degree of diversification elsewhere.

Similarly, both buyers and sellers of illiquid minority interests acknowledge the impact of nondiversifiable risks even if they are otherwise diversified in their portfolios.

The ACAPM includes an incremental return premium for company-specific risk factors because the CAPM assumption of complete diversification often fails with private business enterprises.[3] The ACAPM discount rate, R_{ACAPM}, is developed from the theoretical base of the CAPM and practical experience. R_{ACAPM} is presented symbolically in Equation 6.1, with the symbolic notation discussed following that:

$$R_{ACAPM} = \underbrace{\mathbf{RFR} + \mathit{beta} \times (\mathbf{LSP} - \mathbf{RFR})}_{\substack{\textit{Systematic Risks} \\ \text{The CAPM Expected Return}}} + \underbrace{\mathbf{SSP} + \mathbf{SCR}}_{\substack{\textit{Unsystematic Risks. The} \\ \text{nondiversifiable risks of private} \\ \text{company ownership in excess of} \\ \text{CAPM measure of unsystematic risk}}} \qquad (6.1)$$

1. R_{ACAPM} is the discount rate derived from application of the ACAPM.
2. **RFR** is a risk-free rate, typically that available in the marketplace at or about the valuation date. An intermediate or long-term Treasury yield is most often used as a measure of the base opportunity cost of a long-term

---

[3] Prior to late 1989, there was not a clearly developed, published analysis of how the CAPM could be adjusted to develop discount rates and capitalization rates in the valuation of closely held businesses. See, however, the 1984 publication by Roger J. Grabowski, ASA (*Closely Held Corporations Valuation*, 1984, Steven C. Dilley's Tax Workshops, Inc.) who wrote a precursor description of the ACAPM which, unfortunately, we did not see until 2004. We developed the ACAPM at Mercer Capital in the late 1980s because we had struggled with the concepts and because there was not a clear exposition of how to develop a capitalization rate using the CAPM as a base.

investment in a closely held business. However, some analysts have suggested using a shorter-term Treasury rate. Many analysts assume that the appropriate risk-free rate is the long-term (20-year) Treasury yield to maturity. Others argue for a composite long-term Treasury yield. For purposes of this discussion, RFR is a long-term risk-free rate considered appropriate by the analyst.

3. **beta** is an appropriate industry *beta*, if available. Otherwise it is assumed to be 1.0, or "the risk of the market." *beta* is applied to the excess return of the market (and not to the small stock return).[4] We use the market neutral assumption (beta = 1.0) most commonly in the valuation of small businesses or if no group of sufficiently comparable public companies is available. In such cases, there may be no objective basis to estimate a particular beta. However, use of an industry beta (or a related industry beta), when available, can be helpful in adjusting capitalization factors for certain industries with known risk profiles.

4. **LSP** is the expected return on large capitalization stocks over the risk-free return. Appraisers have traditionally estimated the LSP by reference to the long-run historical performance of large capitalization stocks and U.S. treasury bonds, most typically from 1926 through present. In recent years, financial researchers have begun to suggest that the realized historical return premiums overstate the expected return premium. The principal reason cited by these researchers is the contribution of expanding valuation multiples to the realized historical returns on large capitalization common stocks during the period. These researchers offer a variety of techniques for estimating the prospective return premium, with most concluding that the prospective return premium is between 3.0% and 6.0%, compared to the realized historical premiums on the order of 5.0% to 6.5%.[5]

The emphasis on prospective return premiums has blunted the perennial controversies regarding the choice of historical period analyzed and whether the geometric or arithmetic average returns should

---

[4]The 1989 ACAPM article was less than clear on this point. Thankfully, it is possible to grapple with issues, to learn in the process, and to grow professionally.

[5]Ibbotson Associates, *Stocks, Bonds, Bills, and Inflation: 2006 Yearbook*, Ibbotson Associates, Inc., Chicago, IL, pp. 172–176. Grabowski, Roger J., "Equity Risk Premium: 2006 Update," *Business Valuation Review*, Vol. 25, No. 2 (Summer 2006): pp. 64–68. Arnott, Robert D., and Bernstein, Peter L., "What Risk Premium is 'Normal'?" *Financial Analysts Journal*, (March/April 2002), pp. 64–85. Ibbotson, Roger G., and Chen, Peng, "Long-Run Stock Returns: Participating in the Real Economy," *Financial Analysts Journal*, (January/February 2003), pp. 88–98.

be used. Ibbotson Associates has begun to publish estimates of the prospective return premium in their annual yearbook of historical return data.

5. SSP is the expected return on small capitalization stocks over the return on large capitalization stocks. As with the LSP, appraisers have traditionally estimated the SSP by reference to the long-run historical performance of the two asset classes. With respect to prospective return premiums, the SSP has been the subject of less academic research than LSP. The strongest academic support for the existence of the SSP has come from the various papers by Fama and French exploring factors that predict stock returns as a function of factors in addition to beta.[6]

The realized historical premiums calculated by Ibbotson Associates are on the order of 2.0% to 5.0%, when small capitalization stocks are those with market capitalizations falling into the 9th and 10th size deciles of the New York Stock Exchange. Beginning with the *SBBI 1993 Yearbook*, Ibbotson Associates has published data on the return characteristics of portfolios corresponding to each size decile. In more recent editions, the tenth (smallest) decile has been further segregated into two subgroups (referred to as 10a and 10b).

The most significant practitioner research regarding the magnitude of the SSP has been that published by Roger J. Grabowski, ASA and David W. King, CFA. Grabowski and King began publishing the annual results of their analysis of the relationship between company size and realized returns in 1995, and the research is now updated annually through Duff & Phelps, Inc. Using data from 1963 to the present, Grabowski and King sort public companies into 25 size-ranked portfolios. Importantly, rather than relying on market capitalization of equity alone, Grabowski and King also measure the SSP relative to seven other indications of company size: book value of equity, five-year average net income and EBITDA, the market value of invested capital, total assets, revenue, and number of employees. In addition to aggregate return premiums over the risk-free rate, the authors have also begun to present return premiums over the CAPM-predicted return, permitting appraisers to apply an appropriate beta to the subject business

---

[6]See in particular:

- "The Cross-Section of Expected Stock Returns," *Journal of Finance*, 47 (June 1992), pp. 427–465.
- "Size and Book-to-Market Factors in Earnings and Returns," *Journal of Finance*, 50 (March 1995), pp. 131–156.

enterprise. The Grabowski/King analysis suggests premiums over the CAPM-predicted return for companies in the five smallest portfolios (equity market capitalization less than approximately $500 million) on the order of 4.5% to 5.5%.

Pratt's *Cost of Capital* (2nd ed.) provides a discussion of the "size effect" and provides citations to available studies.[7] This Pratt text also provides a summary of the Grabowski and King study as part of its Chapter 11.

6. **SCR** is the incremental return over the LSP and the SSP that is appropriate for the valuation subject. This (specific company) risk premium is estimated conceptually by comparing the subject company with the universe of relatively small public companies. Direct comparative data for this universe of stocks is not available, so the analyst must be able to conceptualize the risk profile of the alternative investments.[8] One of the factors often cited by appraisers in selecting a specific risk premium is the small size of a subject entity in relationship to the basket of public companies with which it is implicitly being compared. The size-related research helps appraisers quantify this aspect of specific company risk. Appraisers using information from the smallest deciles in Ibbotson's data, or the smallest of the categories from Grabowski and King must carefully relate their estimate of SCR to the measure of SSP used.

In the original ACAPM article, we enumerated several potential specific risk factors, including key personnel issues (or lack of management capability or depth), absolute size, financial structure (leverage), concentrations (related to products, geography, or customers), earnings (margins, stability, and predictability), and other risks associated with a particular company. For the private companies typically valued by appraisers, the total SCR typically runs from 0% to as high as 8%–10% or more. SCR may even be negative for closely held businesses that are larger than the smaller capitalization stocks considered in the development of SSP. Further research on the relationship between company size and return may help appraisers more precisely specify this factor. The selection of the total SCR for a specific valuation assignment requires experience, common sense, and judgment in the context of a detailed analysis of the subject company, as well as a general working knowledge of the public securities markets.

---

[7]Shannon P. Pratt, *Cost of Capital Estimation and Applications*, 2nd ed. (New York: John Wiley & Sons, Inc., 2002). See especially Chapter 11, "Size Effect," p. 90.
[8]SCR premiums in enterprise valuations are analogous to investor-specific risk premiums that must be estimated when valuing shareholder level cash flows.

The discount rate derived using the ACAPM is the sum of these components. This discount rate is consistent with R_{mm} in the conceptual framework of the Integrated Theory.[9]

Appraisers must specify both SSP and SCR when using the ACAPM to develop discount rates. Suppose we know the following:

$$SSP + SCR = 5.0\%$$

Appraiser #1 estimates this portion of the discount rate as:

$$SSP(3.0\%) + SCR(2.0\%) = 5.0\%$$

Appraiser #2 uses a refined size estimate based on the approximate market capitalization of the subject company as:

$$SSP(4.0\%) + SCR(1.0\%) = 5.0\%$$

Both achieved an appropriate result; however Appraisers #1 and #2 estimated SCR from a different base. Further refinements regarding the size premium as it relates to enterprises of differing sizes will force appraisers to focus carefully on SCR and ultimately, on proving the reasonableness of their conclusions. It should be apparent that the indicated refinement in the size effect in the preceding discussion of the ACAPM components should have no impact on the ultimate discount rate, but rather reflects an allocation of a total premium between the two categories (SSP and SCR). In the remainder of this chapter, we focus on assessing the reasonableness of the judgment exercised in estimating the discount rate.

DISCOUNT RATE SENSITIVITY AND JUDGMENT

The ACAPM differs from CAPM in that it attempts to develop a specific discount rate for a private company rather than an expected total return for a publicly traded security in the context of a diversified portfolio of investments. The expected return estimated using the Capital Asset Pricing Model relates the price of the security to expected future dividends

---

[9]The ACAPM was developed as a tool for the use of single period capitalization methods. Accordingly, the focus of the original ACAPM article was the development of appropriate capitalization rates (derived by deducting expected growth in cash flow/earnings from the discount rate).

Discount Rate Sensitivity		Low Estimate	Mid-Point Estimate	High Estimate
Discount Rate Components				
Risk-Free Rate	RFR	5.0%	5.0%	5.0%
Large Stock Premium	LSP	4.0%	5.0%	6.0%
Beta	β	0.9	1.0	1.1
Beta-Adjusted Large Stock Premium		3.6%	5.0%	6.6%
Small Stock Premium	SSP	2.0%	3.5%	5.0%
Specific Company Risk	SCR	2.0%	3.0%	4.0%
Estimated Discount Rate	**R**	**12.6%**	**16.5%**	**20.6%**
less: Estimated Core Earnings Growth	G_e	4.0%	4.0%	4.0%
Estimated Capitalization Rate		8.6%	12.5%	16.6%
Implied Earnings Multiple	**P/E**	**11.6**	**8.0**	**6.0**

EXHIBIT 6.2   Discount Rate Sensitivity

and capital appreciation. The discount rate derived using the ACAPM is applicable to the estimated future cash flows of the enterprise.

Use of the ACAPM or other build-up methods will result in a range of discount rates under differing, but reasonable, assumptions regarding the individual components. Consider Exhibit 6.2, which illustrates the impact of differing estimates, each individually reasonable, on the estimated discount rate. In the context of a single-period capitalization of earnings, the impact on value can be substantial.

JUDGMENT AND REASONABLENESS AND THE ACAPM

The discount rate sensitivity evident in Exhibit 6.2 highlights the informed judgment, common sense, and reasonableness that must be exercised by appraisers. The estimate components were each individually reasonable and defensible, yet 6.0× and 11.6× cannot be equally reasonable and defensible earnings multiples for the same subject enterprise. The resolution to this impasse is the application of informed judgment refined by the appraiser's experience exercised in the context of knowledge of relevant market evidence.[10] Common sense and the intuitive sense of valuation reasonableness also accrue with experience.

Given the discount rate sensitivity illustrated in Exhibit 6.2, how can an appraiser know that he or she is "right" when coming to a conclusion

---

[10]Experience is valuable if it is good experience. There is a world of difference in the experience of two appraisers, where one had ten years of grappling and growing professionally and the other has the same year of experience repeated ten times.

with respect to a specific discount rate? As noted, experience and knowledge assist in the application of judgment. There is no substitute for informed experience and study of available market evidence regarding discount rates from observed pricing of real transactions.

There are now a number of sources providing valuation information regarding actual transactions in public and private companies. These sources include, among others, the following:

- Control Premium Study[11]
- Mergerstat/Shannon Pratt's Control Premium Study[12]
- "Pratt's Stats" [13]
- Done Deals Online[14]
- BizComps[15]

Industry-specific databases provide transactional detail for industry group such as banks, media companies, printing companies, engineering companies, and the like. In addition to use in the market approach, appraisers should search for relevant transaction information as a basis to test the reasonableness of valuation indications from other methods.

Appraisers can also compare valuation conclusions with valuation evidence from guideline company groups selected for their appraisals, yields on similar investments, or, general pricing in the current mergers and acquisitions market.

In the final analysis, appraisers exercise informed judgment when assessing the reasonableness of estimated discount rates (and corresponding value indications) rather than focusing exclusively on the defensibility of individual discount rate components. In our practice, such tests of reasonableness are an integral part of any valuation analysis or report.

Many valuation reports conclude with statements similar to the following:

---

[11] *Control Premium Study* (Santa Monica, CA: *Mergerstat®*). This reference provides certain valuation multiples from public company change of control transactions. For purposes of this discussion, we are referring to this information rather than the observed control premiums that give the study its name.

[12] *Mergerstat/Shannon Pratt's Control Premium Study*. Available at www.bvmarketdata.com.

[13] "Pratt's Stats," (Business Valuation Resources, LLC), www.bvmarketdata.com (accessed May 19, 2004).

[14] "Done Deals Online," (Thompson/Practitioners Publishing Company), www.donedeals.com/pDONHome.asp (accessed May 19, 2004).

[15] Jack R. Sanders, *BizComps* (San Diego, CA, Pacific Services, Inc.). Also available at www.bvmarketdata.com.

Based on our analysis of all the relevant factors related to American Soap Company, Inc., it is our opinion that the fair market value of American's common stock is $100 per share. This conclusion is rendered in connection with (stated purpose), and is rendered on a controlling (or minority) interest basis as of December 31, 2003.

Such a conclusion, while technically proper, fails to help the reader understand the reasonableness of the conclusion. In our opinion, appraisal reports should explain why the concluded value is reasonable, using what we call "tests of reasonableness." The proof can consist of simple comparisons with comparative reference points, including:

- Median or average guideline company multiples across appropriate valuation parameters (sales, EBITDA, EBIT, pre-tax income, net income, book value, and so on).
- Transactions involving the subject company's own stock.
- Comparisons with transaction multiples from the sale of reasonably similar businesses.
- The financial feasibility of a change of control transaction at the appraised value. What financing terms, growth rates, and so on are necessary to provide appropriate debt coverage ratios and (leveraged) equity returns? This test is increasingly significant with the growing influence of private equity investors.
- Tests of the sensitivity of the conclusion to changes in key inputs.
- Other comparisons that can help readers understand the reasonableness of the conclusion, including the use of common sense.

Comparisons such as these help readers and appraisers place the valuation conclusion into perspective. If the valuation conclusion appears relatively high or low, the appraiser and readers should be comfortable that this relative comparison is reasonable in light of the total analysis of the report.

When appraisers provide recurring appraisals of the same company (e.g., for Employee Stock Ownership Plans, gift tax purposes, buy-sell agreements, or other corporate purposes), it is equally important to relate the current appraisal to prior conclusions.

The following quote from a brief article Mercer wrote for *Business Valuation Review* in 1988 describes such an analysis:

We believe a further procedure is necessary with recurring valuation assignments to: 1) insure the intellectual honesty of the analyst (and the firm); 2) allow the reader to understand the basis for significant methodological shifts; and 3) provide the perspective a reader needs to anchor the reasonableness of the current conclusion, not only today, but in light of historical results.

The current methodology is summarized in a table in the report. The table includes all methodologies considered, valuation indicators derived, and weights assigned to each. All discounts or premiums to market multiples applied in the various methodologies are disclosed in the table, as are all marketability or minority interest discounts. The prior year conclusions (one or two years) are then displayed next to the current year data, and changes are noted. Finally, comparative data such as the effective price/earnings, price/sales or price/book value ratios implied by the conclusions, and relevant public market comparisons are included.[16]

Such comparisons are not intended to enforce slavish devotion to prior appraisal methods or assumptions, but rather to illustrate that the consequences of any such changes have been properly considered.

THE ACAPM AND SHAREHOLDER LEVEL VALUATIONS

The focus of this chapter has been the estimation of enterprise discount rates. Recalling the Integrated Theory presented in Chapter 3, the discount rate appropriate to the shareholder (nonmarketable minority) level of value is equal to or greater than the enterprise discount rate.

The enterprise discount rate is the appropriate base from which to develop the required holding period return at the shareholder level. The basis of comparison in the valuation of nonmarketable minority interests is the relevant universe of publicly traded securities. By beginning with the base enterprise discount rate and adding increments of return for shareholder level risks, the subject nonmarketable minority interest is related, from an investment viewpoint, to the relevant universe of alternative investments.

CONCLUSION

Appraisers estimate discount rates to reflect the risks of a particular asset. In Chapter 3, we demonstrated that a single enterprise discount rate is generally applicable at the marketable minority, financial control, and

---

[16]Z. Christopher Mercer, "Issues in Recurring Valuations: Methodological Comparisons from Year-to-Year," *Business Valuation Review*, Vol. 7, No. 4 (1988): pp. 171–173.

strategic control levels of value. In this chapter, we discussed the various assumptions required to estimate a discount rate using a build-up method such as the ACAPM.

Appraisers must exercise common sense, informed judgment, and reasonableness when developing the enterprise discount rate. And there is considerable room for the exercise of judgment. However, appraisers do not exercise judgment in a vacuum. Ken Patton, ASA, has observed many times: "It is quite possible to make the 'right' decisions every time and to achieve an absolutely wrong conclusion or result." Given this possibility, appraisers must consistently demonstrate the overall reasonableness of their conclusions, rather than simply defend the specification of individual discount rate components.

Overview of the Capital Asset Pricing Model (CAPM)

T he Capital Asset Pricing Model describes the relationship between risk and expected returns in the public markets. The essence of the CAPM is expressed in the expected return for an individual security, as seen in Equation 6.2:

$$ER_i = RFR + beta_i(MR - RFR) \qquad (6.2)$$

In this equation:

1. ER_i is the expected return on an equity security$_i$.
2. **RFR** is the risk-free rate.
3. beta$_i$ is a measure of the systematic (or nondiversifiable) risk of a particular publicly traded security, considering both the correlation and volatility of the subject security relative to the broader market (the S&P 500, for example). In other words, *beta* attempts to measure the riskiness of a particular public security in relationship to the broader market.
4. **MR** is the expected return on an investment in the market portfolio (the S&P 500 is often used as a proxy), or the expected return of the market.
5. (**MR −RFR**) is the expected premium in return from an investment in the market portfolio over and above the risk-free rate.

According to the security market line equation (discussed in every basic finance text), the expected return on any security is proportional to its systematic risk. In other words, as systematic risk (*beta*) increases, the expected return (the risk-free rate plus the product of *beta* and the market premium) also increases.

That portion of the security's volatility that is not related to market movements is called *unsystematic risk*. In theory, unsystematic risk can be diversified away by holding a sufficiently large number of assets whose returns are not perfectly correlated with each other. In other words, the *alphas* in a diversified portfolio will sum to zero, with unexpected favorable events in some securities offsetting unexpected unfavorable events in others.[17] CAPM, therefore, considers only that portion of a security's volatility that can be correlated with the volatility of the market.

Sensitivity to the market is called *systematic risk* and is measured in the CAPM by *beta*. A *beta* of 1.0 for a security means that inclusion of that security in a market portfolio neither increases nor decreases the overall risk of the portfolio. For a security with a *beta* of less than 1.0, inclusion of the security on a market portfolio reduces the overall riskiness of the portfolio.[18]

As with any theoretical model, there are several underlying assumptions of the CAPM. These are summarized in most finance texts and include:[19]

1. Investors are interested in maximizing terminal wealth over identical time horizons.
2. Investors are risk averse. They seek to hold diversified portfolios of securities (so that unsystematic risk can be diversified away).
3. Borrowing and lending costs are identical, and investors can borrow or lend at the risk-free rate of interest.
4. There are no investor-related taxes and no transactions costs.
5. Investor expectations are homogeneous with respect to the markets.
6. All assets are perfectly divisible and can be sold in perfectly liquid markets.
7. Investors are price-takers, and their market activities are assumed not to be able to influence the market prices of securities.

---

[17]Note that the CAPM equation expresses the *expected return* for the subject security. The *actual return* in any given period will, of course, differ from the expected return due to unforeseeable factors. This difference, known as *alpha*, may be positive, negative, or zero.

[18]This discussion should not be interpreted to suggest that company-specific risks do not exist for individual public securities. They do. Nor should it be interpreted to suggest that investors in public securities do not care about these risks. They do. The theory of diversification, for which there are logical and mathematical proofs, suggests that in a properly diversified portfolio of publicly traded stocks (in a reasonably efficient market), the adverse consequences of bad things happening to certain stocks in the portfolio will, on balance, be offset by good things happening to others, leaving the investor with the beta-adjusted expected return of the portfolio.

[19]Investment, corporate finance, and valuation texts too numerous to cite contain discussions of the underlying assumptions of the CAPM.

Clearly, not all of the CAPM assumptions hold when investors consider purchasing or selling interests of closely held companies. Time horizons differ, portfolios may not be diversified, borrowing costs can be substantial, and investor taxes and transaction costs are real elements of consideration. Investor expectations are not homogeneous, and no markets exist for the shares of most closely held businesses. Finally, investors may or may not be able to dictate price in real transactions. Nevertheless, the CAPM has been used as a basis for developing discount rates and capitalization rates for closely held businesses and business interests for many years.

This review of the CAPM suggests that there are at least two basic issues that must be addressed in using the model to develop discount rates for use in the valuation of private–public business enterprises.

1. *Specific Risk.* The CAPM assumes a diversified portfolio of investments such that unsystematic (or company-specific) risks are not relevant. When valuing the equity of closely held companies, it may not be appropriate to assume that the specific risks of the subject company are so easily diversified.

2. *beta.* Appraisers must consider the use of *beta* in practical application. One way that appraisers have dealt with the concept of *beta* is to assume that it is $1.0\times$ when building up discount rates. Because this assumption is not always appropriate, the use of *beta* must be carefully considered.

Introduction to the QMDM: The Shareholder Level of Value

INTRODUCTION

In previous chapters, we have explored the implications of the Integrated Theory for valuation at the various enterprise levels (marketable minority, financial control, strategic control). In this chapter we turn our attention to the valuation of specific nonmarketable minority interests in enterprises, or to the shareholder level of value.

The economic determinants of value at the shareholder level are identical to those at the enterprise levels: expected cash flow, growth, and risk. To develop a reasonable shareholder level indication of value, each element must be tailored to the subject interest. In other words, we analyze the cash flows that are expected to accrue to the subject interest, the expected growth, or capital appreciation of the subject interest, and the risk that the expected cash flows and growth will actually be realized over the anticipated holding period.

COMMON QUESTIONS

1. What are the sources of value at the shareholder (i.e., nonmarketable minority interest) level of value?
2. What approaches to valuation should the appraiser consider at the shareholder level?
3. What are the inputs to a shareholder level discounted cash flow analysis?
4. What economic factors contribute to the difference in value between the enterprise and shareholder levels of value?
5. Are agency costs a component of the minority interest discount or marketability discount?

POTENTIAL APPROACHES TO SHAREHOLDER LEVEL VALUATION

As with any other asset, appraisers must consider the relevance of the three basic approaches to valuation for a subject nonmarketable minority interest:

- *Asset-Based Approach.* Within the asset-based approach, appraisers derive indications of value by examining the value of the underlying assets of the enterprise net of its liabilities. For nonmarketable minority interests of operating companies, application of methods within the asset-based approach is generally not appropriate, because the minority shareholder has no access to, or discretion over, the underlying assets and liabilities of the enterprise.[1]
- *Market Approach.* Valuation methods under the market approach compare the subject interest to similar business ownership interests or securities that have been sold. Appraisers often consider a range of valuation methods within the market approach to determine the value of nonmarketable minority interests.

    First, appraisers may attempt to value the subject interest by analyzing prior transactions involving similarly situated nonmarketable minority interests in the subject enterprise. While conceptually appealing, this method is rarely fruitful, as limitations associated with the typically small number of observed transactions, unique motivations of the parties, and timing of such transactions are difficult to overcome.

    Alternatively, appraisers may attempt to ascertain the appropriate discount to the pro rata share of enterprise value for the subject interest by analyzing observations of paired market transactions involving otherwise similar assets having different marketability characteristics. This method is ultimately analogous to the guideline company transaction method, except that the appraiser seeks to "value" the marketability discount rather than the subject enterprise. The market data used in this method consists of the various published pre-IPO and restricted stock studies. Ultimately, we find the comparability of the subject interest to the available market data to be so limited as to render this method unreliable in most cases.

    Finally, appraisers may attempt to define the appropriate marketability discount by reference to empirical studies of published market

---

[1] For asset holding entities, while an asset-based approach beginning with net asset value may be appropriate, the income approach will likely be appropriate to value *interests* in these entities, as will be discussed later.

data. This method generally relies on regression analysis which purports to discern a statistical relationship between the appropriate marketability discount (the dependent variable) and a group of independent variables that describe the subject interest, enterprise, or prevailing economic, industry, or market conditions. While such analyses may provide interesting research insights regarding the body of observed market data, they are rarely sufficiently understood or robust for reliable use in practice.

Application of the market approach requires assessment of whether the available market evidence provides a reasonable basis for comparison to the subject asset. Prevailing business valuation standards and practice provide three principal bases for this assessment: (1) whether there is a sufficient similarity of qualitative and quantitative investment characteristics with the subject asset, (2) the amount and verifiability of data known about the asset being compared to the subject asset, and (3) whether or not the price of the similar investment was obtained in an arm's-length transaction, or a forced or distress sale. Additional factors for consideration include the selection of the time periods used for the underlying market data, and the timing of the price data used in the valuation ratios. When assessed on these bases, the available market data from pre-IPO and restricted stock studies is not sufficiently comparable to most subject interests to justify the use of valuation methods under the market approach.[2]

- *Income Approach.* Within the income approach, appraisers use methods that convert anticipated economic benefits into value. This approach is intuitively appealing for a broad range of assets, including nonmarketable minority interests. The very definition of an asset promulgated by the FASB confirms the general applicability of the income approach: "Assets are probable future economic benefits obtained or controlled by a particular entity as a result of past transactions or events."[3]

The discounted cash flow model is the fundamental expression of the income approach. Appraisers can use the discounted cash flow model to estimate the value of the subject nonmarketable minority interest in the context of the existing enterprise valuation. When the discounted cash flow model is used to value the subject interest, the marketability discount is appropriately viewed as *describing* the relationship between the shareholder and enterprise levels of value rather

---

[2]See the appendix to this chapter for further discussion of the applicability of the pre-IPO and restricted stock studies.
[3]See SFAC 6, *Elements of Financial Statements.*

than *determining* that relationship. In other words, the marketability discount is a valuation result, not a valuation input.

The principal challenge to practical application of the discounted cash flow model is the specification of appropriate, defensible assumptions. While the theoretical support for the income approach is unassailable, inappropriate or unsupported assumptions will generate unreasonable conclusions of value. The proper conclusion from this observation is simply that assumptions must be carefully specified, not that the market approach with insufficient comparable data is preferable. After all, when using methods within the market approach, the appraiser finds no relief from making assumptions, even if those assumptions are not explicitly stated.[4]

The income approach is the most appropriate basis for determining value at the shareholder level.

THE QMDM: A SHAREHOLDER LEVEL DCF MODEL

The Quantitative Marketability Discount Model (QMDM), a shareholder level discounted cash flow model, is a valuation method within the income approach. The QMDM provides a standardized format for analyzing, projecting, and discounting relevant shareholder cash flows that is applicable to almost any subject nonmarketable minority interest.[5]

The QMDM inputs are analogous to those used in traditional enterprise level discounted cash flow models. The two sets of assumptions are compared in Exhibit 7.1.

Each of the discounted cash flow inputs (from the enterprise model on the left side of the Exhibit) are tailored to the considerations of minority shareholders in private enterprises (on the right side). Although the QMDM directly values the subject nonmarketable minority interest, it is not used in isolation, but rather in conjunction with a contemporaneous valuation of the subject enterprise because the shareholder level expectations regarding cash flows, risk, and growth are inextricably linked to the corresponding expectations with respect to the enterprise.

---

[4]For elaboration on this point, see the discussion of fundamental adjustments to guideline company multiples in Chapter 5.

[5]Z. Christopher Mercer, *Quantifying Marketability Discounts* (Memphis, TN: Peabody Publishing, LP, 1997).

Enterprise Level DCF Assumptions	Shareholder Level DCF (QMDM) Assumptions
1. Forecast Period	1. Range of Expected Holding Periods
2. Projected Interim Cash Flows (during forecast period)	2a. Expected Distribution / Dividend Yield 2b. Expected Growth in Distributions / Dividends 2c. Timing (Mid-Year or End of Year)
3. Projected Terminal Value (at end of forecast period)	3a. Growth in Value over Holding Period 3b. Premium or Discount to Projected Enterprise Value
4. Discount Rate	4. Range of Required Holding Period Returns

EXHIBIT 7.1   Enterprise and Shareholder Level DCF Assumptions

THE STRUCTURE OF THE SHAREHOLDER LEVEL DCF MODEL

In Chapter 1, we reviewed the basic structure of the two-stage enterprise level discounted cash flow model, which we expressed mathematically in terms of cash flow (CF), growth (g), and risk (r) as shown in Exhibit 7.2.

EXHIBIT 7.2   The Two-Stage Enterprise DCF Model

$$V_e = \underbrace{\sum_{i=1}^{f} \left[\frac{CF(1 + g_e)^i}{(1 + r)^i} \right]}_{\text{PVICF}} + \underbrace{\left[\frac{CF(1 + g_e)^{(f+1)}/(r - g)}{(1 + r)^f} \right]}_{\text{PVTV}}$$

Recalling the previous discussion in Chapter 1, PVICF, the first term in Exhibit 7.2, is the present value of the interim cash flows during a finite forecast period ending in year f. The second term, PVTV, represents the present value of the terminal value. The terminal value is the value of all future cash flows after year f (into perpetuity), or the projected value of the enterprise at the end of year f. The term r in the model is the enterprise discount rate appropriate for the risk of the expected cash flows, which are growing at the interim rate of g_e and the long-term rate of g (for the terminal period calculation).

The same two-stage discounted cash flow model structure can be used at the shareholder level, as shown in Exhibit 7.3.

Exhibit 7.3 includes each of the shareholder level discounted cash flow inputs enumerated in Exhibit 7.1.

1. *Range of Expected Holding Periods*. The expected holding period is year f in the equation, which is the final year for which discrete cash

EXHIBIT 7.3 The Two-Stage Shareholder DCF Model

$$V_{\text{sh}} = \sum_{i=1}^{f} \left[\frac{\text{CF}_{\text{sh}}(1 + g_d)^i}{(1 + R_{\text{hp}})^i} \right] + \left[\frac{V_e(1 + g_v)^f(1 + P/D\%)}{(1 + R_{\text{hp}})^f} \right]$$

$$\underbrace{\phantom{\sum_{i=1}^{f} \left[\frac{\text{CF}_{\text{sh}}(1 + g_d)^i}{(1 + R_{\text{hp}})^i} \right]}}_{\text{PVICF}} \quad \underbrace{\phantom{\left[\frac{V_e(1 + g_v)^f(1 + P/D\%)}{(1 + R_{\text{hp}})^f} \right]}}_{\text{PVTV}}$$

flow projections are made and the year in which the terminal value is expected to be received.

2a. *Expected Distribution/Dividend Yield.* The expected distribution/ dividend yield defines the initial expected shareholder cash flow (CF_{sh}) in terms of the current enterprise value (V_e).

2b. *Expected Growth in Distributions/Dividends.* The expected growth in distributions/dividends defines the subsequent interim shareholder cash flows in terms of an annual growth rate (g_d) relative to the initial expected shareholder cash flow (CF_{sh}). (Assumptions 1 and 2a–2b specify the numerator in the first term in Exhibit 7.3, or expected distributions during the expected holding period of a nonmarketable asset.)

2c. *Timing (Mid-Year or End-of-Year).* The present value of the projected interim cash flows depends on when shareholders expect to receive them. The timing assumption is manifest in the discounting periods denoted as i in the denominator.

3a. *Growth in Value over Holding Period.* The assumed growth in value over the holding period (g_v) defines the terminal enterprise value in terms of an anticipated annual capital appreciation rate from the current enterprise value (V_e).

3b. *Premium or Discount to Projected Enterprise Value.* The most likely expectation in a shareholder level discounted cash flow model is that the projected terminal value to be received by the minority shareholder is the marketable minority value. In certain circumstances, however, the appraiser may wish to specify that the minority shareholder will receive a terminal value in excess of, or below, the projected enterprise value. This potential premium or discount (P/D%) is applicable to the projected terminal enterprise value. (Assumptions 3a and 3b specify the numerator of the second term in Exhibit 7.3.)

4. *Range of Required Holding Period Returns.* The required holding period return (R_{hp}) is the discount rate of the shareholder level discounted cash flow model. The shareholder level discount rate is the sum of the enterprise discount rate and appropriate holding period premiums necessary to compensate the minority investor for accepting the extra risks associated with investing in a nonmarketable security.

EXHIBIT 7.4 The Marketability
Discount

$$\mathrm{MD} = 1 - \frac{V_{sh}}{V_e}$$

(Assumption 4, when applied in the equation in Exhibit 7.3, yields the PVICF and the PVTV, which together comprise V_{sh}.)

Exhibits 7.2 and 7.3 together illustrate that illiquid minority interests (V_{sh}) can be valued under the income approach using the very same discounted cash flow model as that used to value enterprises (V_e).

As shown in Exhibit 7.4, the marketability discount is defined by the relationship between the values determined in Exhibits 7.2 and 7.3.

Given this discussion, our earlier statement that the marketability discount is not a valuation input, but rather a valuation result, should be clear. In Exhibit 7.4, the marketability discount (MD) describes the relationship between V_{sh}, or shareholder level value, and V_e, or enterprise value. Exhibit 7.4 also illustrates the futility, using inadequate transactional data from restricted stock studies, of estimating MD directly (and therefore, V_{sh} indirectly). It is preferable to estimate V_{sh} directly in the context of V_e to determine MD, rather than to attempt to determine V_{sh} indirectly by estimating MD.

Exhibits 7.2, 7.3, and 7.4 also illustrate what can cause value determined for a particular interest of an enterprise (shareholder level value) to be less than the value of the enterprise. The reasons can be summarized as follows:

- Cash flow to shareholders is less than cash flow of the enterprise ($CF_{sh} < CF$). We noted in the discussion of the Integrated Theory in Chapter 3 that there are two potential agency costs that may create a differential between cash flow to shareholders and enterprise cash flows.
  - *Non–pro rata distributions*. Agency costs are incurred by minority shareholders when there are non–pro rata distributions to certain shareholders, e.g., controlling shareholders, who take bonuses in excess of normalized compensation. These funds are not available for pro rata distributions nor are they available for reinvestment, which drives the expected growth in value.
  - *Suboptimal reinvestment*. Suboptimal reinvestment occurs when the management of an enterprise reinvests funds at less than its cost of capital. We have seen that an important assumption of the Gordon Model is that all enterprise cash flows are either distributed or reinvested in the enterprise at the enterprise discount rate. It is

the reinvestment of earnings that drives the growth of earnings (and value), particularly over defined time horizons, at rates greater than the long-term expected growth in core earnings. Suboptimal reinvestment dampens the expected growth in value and therefore V_{sh}, implying greater marketability discounts, other things remaining the same.

■ *Incremental risks faced by minority investors exceed the risks of the enterprise ($R_{hp} > R$).* In developing marketable minority valuation indications (enterprise level), appraisers develop equity discount rates. These discount rates reflect the appraisers' assessments of the risks related to achieving expected cash flows and growth. Those risks are embodied in the enterprise discount rate, R, and in the enterprise valuation. Minority investors in nonmarketable interests face additional risks, including the uncertainties of the expected holding period (which may be long and uncertain), restrictions on transfer, and, in the case of tax pass-through entities, potential exposure to adverse cash flow (if the entity fails to make tax pass-through distributions).

Any combination of agency costs, or incremental shareholder risks, contribute to reducing V_{sh} relative to V_e, and therefore, to increasing the marketability discount, other things being equal.

A VISUAL REPRESENTATION OF THE SHAREHOLDER LEVEL DCF MODEL

The function of the various QMDM inputs is perhaps more easily demonstrated with a visual representation of the underlying discounted cash flow model using a simple example in Exhibit 7.5. At this point, readers are asked to accept the reasonableness of the assumptions in the example. Chapters 8 and 9 examine how to determine and support QMDM assumptions.

In practice, we compute shareholder level values (and corresponding marketability discounts) over a range of potential holding periods and required holding period returns. Exhibit 7.5 depicts the nonmarketable minority value and marketability discount for only a single set of assumptions for ease of presentation.

1. *Expected Holding Period.* The expected holding period of ten years establishes the length of the discrete forecast period and the point at which the projected terminal value is expected to be received (i.e., when the investment is expected to become marketable).

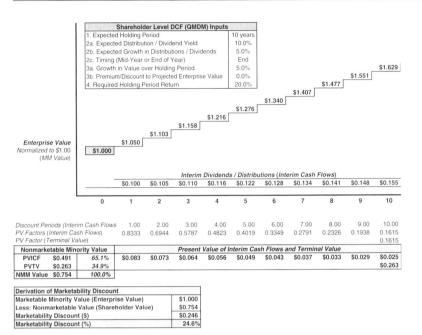

EXHIBIT 7.5   Visual Representation of the QMDM

2a. *Expected Distribution/Dividend Yield.* For ease of exposition and illustration, we develop the shareholder level value relative to a base enterprise value of $1.00 ($V_e$ = $1.00). In this example, the expected distribution/dividend yield of 10.0% establishes the initial shareholder cash flow of $0.100 ($1.00 enterprise value × 10.0% expected yield).

2b. *Expected Growth in Distributions/Dividends.* The expected growth in distributions/dividends of 5.0% defines the subsequent interim shareholder cash flows expectations relative to the initial expected cash flow of $0.10.

2c. *Timing (Mid-Year or End-of-Year).* In this example, the end-of-year cash flow assumption defines the discount periods for the interim cash flows as 1.00 years, 2.00 years, and so on.

3a. *Growth in Value over Holding Period.* The assumed growth in value over the holding period of 5.0% establishes the terminal enterprise value of $1.629 ($1.05^{10}$).

3b. *Premium or Discount to Projected Enterprise Value.* In this example, there is no assumed premium or discount to the projected enterprise value. Had there been, the specified discount or premium would have been applied to the terminal enterprise value of $1.629.

4. *Required Holding Period Returns.* The required holding period return of 20.0% defines the present value factors applicable to each of the projected interim cash flows and terminal value.

The QMDM inputs define the projected cash flows and corresponding present value factors of the shareholder level discounted cash flow model. The mechanics of applying the present value factors to the various cash flows is no different than that of the enterprise level discounted cash flow model, as the bottom portion of Exhibit 7.5 makes clear. The indicated value of the subject nonmarketable minority interest (V_i = $0.754) is the sum of the present value of the projected interim cash flows ($0.491) and the present value of the projected terminal value ($0.263). The corresponding marketability discount of 24.6% calculated at the bottom of Exhibit 7.5 describes, rather than defines, the relationship between the shareholder and enterprise levels of value.[6]

Factors Contributing to Marketability Discounts

While discussing the shareholder level of value in the context of the Integrated Theory, we noted that marketability discounts arise because of the existence of two particular economic factors: agency costs (in the form of non–pro rata distributions to shareholders and/or suboptimal reinvestment of corporate cash flows) and the incremental risks faced by minority investors in private enterprises. Using the previous visual representation, we can illustrate the impact of these two factors upon the marketability discount in Exhibits 7.6, 7.7, and 7.8.

Base Case (Shareholder Value Equal to Enterprise Value) First, we consider the hypothetical case in which neither of the economic factors giving rise to marketability discounts is present, such that the shareholder value is equal to the corresponding enterprise value.

---

[6]In the context of Exhibit 7.4

$$MD = (1 - \frac{V_{sh}}{V_e})$$

$$= (1 - \frac{\$0.754}{\$1.00})$$

$$= (1 - 75.4\%)$$

$$= 24.6\%$$

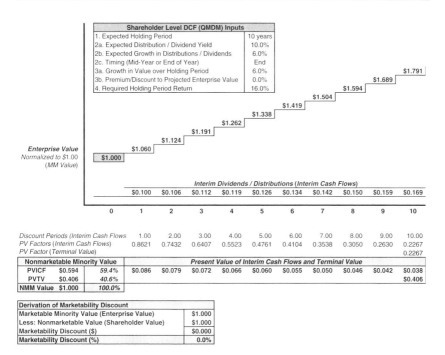

EXHIBIT 7.6   The QMDM with No Agency Costs or Incremental Risks

Assume that the base enterprise value implies growth in core earnings of 6.0% and a total required return, or discount rate, of 16.0%. If there are no agency costs or incremental risks associated with owning a nonmarketable minority interest in the enterprise, the inputs to the shareholder level discounted cash flow model (and the resulting discount) would be those presented in Exhibit 7.6.

The absence of agency costs can be seen by comparing the total projected sources of return to the nonmarketable minority investor (cash flow yield and capital appreciation) to the base enterprise discount rate. Non–pro rata distributions impair the cash flow yield available to the nonmarketable minority investor, while suboptimal reinvestment reduces the anticipated rate of capital appreciation, or growth in value. In this example, the sum of the expected distribution/dividend yield (10.0%) and the growth in value over the holding period (6.0%) is equal to the enterprise discount rate (16.0%).

If there are no incremental risks associated with ownership of a non-marketable minority interest in the subject enterprise, the required holding period return will equal the enterprise discount rate. In other words, investors in the subject nonmarketable minority interest do not earn a premium return relative to the enterprise, or as-if-freely-traded, return. In this example, the required holding period return of 16.0% equals the enterprise discount rate.

In the absence of both agency costs and incremental risks for enduring ownership of a nonmarketable minority interest, the shareholder level discounted cash flow model yields a conclusion of $1.00, implying no discount to the base enterprise value (as calculated at the bottom of Exhibit 7.6).[7]

Impact of Agency Costs   We can now isolate the impact of expected agency costs over the anticipated holding period on the marketability discount. In the example case, the appraiser expects a modest level of suboptimal reinvestment of corporate cash flows, resulting in a downward adjustment in the growth in value (and distributions/dividends) to 5.0% from 6.0%.[8]

As a result, Assumption #2b and #3a are changed from 6.0% in Exhibit 7.6 to 5.0% in Exhibit 7.7.

The impact of suboptimal reinvestment is seen in the projected terminal value, which is $1.629, compared to $1.791 in the absence of agency costs (Exhibit 7.6). In value terms, the agency costs account for a marketability discount of 5.7%, excluding the effect of any incremental holding period premium (as calculated at the bottom of Exhibit 7.7).

This example confirms that the effect of suboptimal reinvestment is not limited to the returns realized by nonmarketable minority investors. Unlike other agency costs against which controlling shareholders may receive an indirect benefit (i.e., excess owner's compensation), suboptimal reinvestment also reduces the returns achieved by the controlling shareholder. In other words, despite controlling the enterprise, the returns of the majority owners also suffer from suboptimal reinvestment over time.

This does not imply, however, that the effect of suboptimal reinvestment should not be a component of the marketability discount. The

---

[7]Enterprise value is determined using the Gordon Model:

$$V_e = \frac{CF_1}{r - g}$$
$$= \frac{\$0.10}{16\% - 6\%}$$
$$= \$1.00$$

[8]An appraiser might make a similar assumption if the enterprise has historically been accumulating excess assets and there is an expectation for a continuation of this policy over the expected holding period.

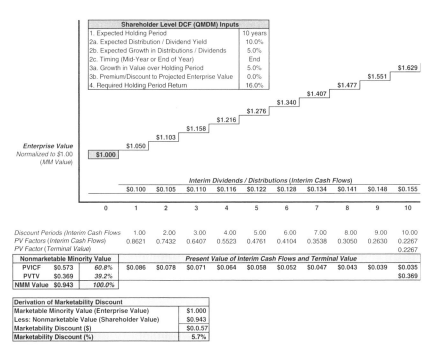

EXHIBIT 7.7 The QMDM with Agency Costs

public company equivalent, or marketable minority, value relative to which marketability discounts are measured is predicated on both normalized current operations and normalized reinvestment practices. The marketability enjoyed by public company minority investors assures that suboptimal reinvestment is not anticipated. Note that this does not mean that certain investments made by public companies will not turn out badly, but rather than such poor performance is not anticipated. If it were, the public share price would be bid down to a level at which incumbent management would be subject to removal, and new managers more responsive to the interests of the shareholders installed.[9]

Impact of Incremental Holding Period Risks We can also isolate the impact of incremental holding period risks over the expected holding period on the

---

[9]We do not suggest that examples of "empire building" or other agency costs are never observed in public companies over even lengthy periods of time, but rather that such examples are exceptions to the typical market discipline faced by public company managers.

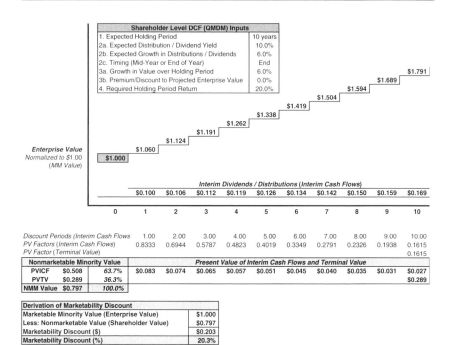

EXHIBIT 7.8 The QMDM with Incremental Risks

marketability discount. In the example case, the appraiser concludes that the incremental holding period risks justify a 4.0% increment to the base enterprise discount, resulting in a required holding period return of 20.0% in Assumption #4. To isolate the impact of incremental holding period risks, we reset the expected growth in value (and distributions/dividends) to 6.0% in Assumption #2b and #3a. These changes are reflected in Exhibit 7.8.

The impact of the incremental holding period risks is manifest in the lower present value factors. Excluding the impact of agency costs, the return premium reflecting the incremental holding period risks generates a marketability discount of 20.3% (as calculated at the bottom of Exhibit 7.8).

Conceptually, the observed discounts in restricted stock transactions of public companies reflect only this component of the overall marketability discount applicable to minority interests in private enterprises. In practice, we are not dogmatic on this point, because the sample of public companies that issue restricted shares consists primarily of small, financially distressed firms trading in relatively inefficient markets for which the discipline described earlier may not be strong enough to eliminate the potential for substantial agency costs.

Combined Impact on Overall Marketability Discount Combining the lower anticipated growth in value and distributions/dividends with the higher required holding period return yields the initial shareholder level discounted cash flow model presented in Exhibit 7.5. Note that the overall marketability discount (24.6%) is modestly less than the sum of the agency costs and incremental holding period risk components (5.7% + 20.3% = 26.0%) because of the interaction of the lower present value factors and lower projected cash flows.

This analysis suggests that the qualitative discussion of the marketability discount applicable to a subject nonmarketable minority interest ought to emphasize the nature and persistence of specific agency costs borne by the shareholders and the specific holding period risks for which the hypothetical willing buyer would demand compensation in the form of a higher required return.

Review of Analysis We can summarize this analysis of the shareholder level DCF model with the following table, reordered to present the enterprise value (0% marketability discount) first. Then, suboptimal reinvestment alone is presented, where the resulting impairment to growth in value generates a marketability discount of 5.7%. Next, incremental risk alone is presented where the required holding period return generates a marketability discount of 20.3%. Finally, we see the combined impact of both suboptimal reinvestment and incremental risk, where the calculated marketability discount is 24.6%.

Exhibit 7.9 illustrates that each assumption of the QMDM is important. It also illustrates that the various assumptions interact and influence calculated marketability discounts.

The marketability discount in column four of 24.6% includes the combined effect of agency costs and incremental shareholder level risks. This discount is lower than the so-called "normal" range of 30% to 40% or more. Why? Note the expected dividend/distribution yield of 10.0% in Assumption #2a. The high current dividend yield serves to mitigate what could otherwise be a substantially higher marketability discount.

CONCLUSION

In this chapter, we have explored the relationship between the enterprise and shareholder levels of value within the context of the Integrated Theory. The Quantitative Marketability Discount Model is a shareholder level discounted cash flow model standardized to accommodate the valuation of nearly all nonmarketable minority interests.

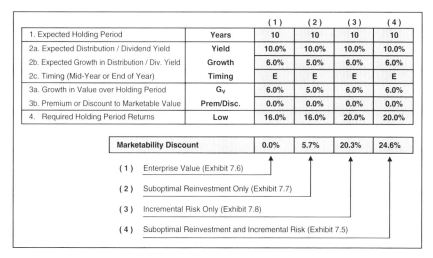

EXHIBIT 7.9   Impact of Agency Costs and Incremental Risk on Marketability Discount

Shareholder level valuation is driven by the same factors as enterprise level valuation: expected cash flow, growth, and risk. Nonmarketable minority interests are generally worth less than the corresponding pro rata portion of enterprise value because of a combination of agency costs (which can affect both the level of, and growth rate in, cash flows) and incremental holding period risks (which cause the required holding period return to exceed the enterprise discount rate).

A Further Look at Pre-IPO and Restricted Stock Studies

As discussed in the introduction to the Quantitative Marketability Discount Model, we find the market evidence available from the pre-IPO and restricted stock studies to be insufficient to support use the market approach to valuation nonmarketable minority interests in private companies. In this appendix, we provide a brief summary of why we find the available market data unpersuasive.

PRE-IPO STUDIES

The various pre-IPO studies compare the prices at which shares of a private company are issued during some period prior to the company's eventual initial public offering with the actual public offering price. The difference in the prices, expressed as a percentage of the actual public offering price, is presumed to reflect the decrement to value associated with the nonmarketable nature of the shares prior to the IPO. As a result, the observed pre-IPO discounts are considered by some analysts to be a proxy for the marketability discount.

The observed pre-IPO discounts, however, likely reflect more than simply the penalty for the absence of marketability. The enterprise valuation multiples are likely to expand as a result of the IPO. There are several potential explanations for such an increase in the enterprise level valuation:

- The new capital raised through the IPO may lead to an expectation of more rapid future earnings growth.
- The new capital raised through the IPO may be used to repay expensive debt, thereby reducing financial risk and increasing pro forma earnings after the IPO.
- Depending on the prevailing conditions in the market, there can be unusually strong demand for and interest in new issues. Depending on the supply of such issues, public offering prices may rise.

The observed differences between pre-IPO stock transactions and the subsequent public offering prices incorporates both changes in the underlying enterprise valuation triggered by the IPO itself as well as incremental premium return demanded by investors in the absence of ready marketability. To the extent the enterprise value increases as a result of the IPO, use of the pre-IPO discount as a proxy for the appropriate marketability discount is likely to lead to undervaluation of the subject nonmarketable minority interest.

RESTRICTED STOCK STUDIES

In addition to the pre-IPO studies, a series of restricted stock studies purport to provide direct evidence regarding the magnitude of marketability discounts applicable to subject nonmarketable minority interests. We have summarized the results of these studies in Exhibit 7.10.

We make the following observations with respect to the available market evidence from restricted stock studies:

- *The number of observed transactions is limited.* The largest study, the FMV Opinions database, reports details for 475 transactions over a 25-year period. Given the difficulty frequently encountered by appraisers attempting to find sufficiently comparable public guideline companies (of which there are more than 10,000) for use in applying the market approach to the enterprise valuation, it is unlikely that appraisers can find sufficiently comparable transactions (either in terms of business models or time) in the various restricted stock studies to apply the market approach at the shareholder level.
- *Much of the data is too old to have any relevance to current appraisals.* The structural differences in the U.S. economy, financial markets, regulatory environment, and business practices between the 1970s and today are dramatic.
- *The range of observed discounts is large.* Appraisers frequently assess the marketability discount applicable to the subject interest relative to a benchmark of 35% or so. While measures of central tendency for the various studies certainly cluster around 35%, the dispersion of actual observations in the studies around this benchmark is wide. There is no objective basis for assessing whether the marketability discount for a particular subject interest should be below, within, or above the benchmark range.
- *Virtually none of the transactions involve companies paying dividends.* While this point is not clear from the summary information

EXHIBIT 7.10 Summary Results of Restricted Stock Studies

Study	Number of Observations	Reporting Dates	Medians	Means	Standard Deviations	Range Low	Range High
SEC Institutional Investor Study	398	1966–1969	24%	26%	na	(15%)	80%
Gelman Study	89	1968–1970	33%	33%	na	<15%	>40%
Moroney Study	146	1968–1972	34%	35%	18%	(30%)	90%
Maher Study	34	1969–1973	33%	35%	18%	3%	76%
Trout Study	60	1968–1972	na	34%	na	na	na
Stryker/Pittock Study	28	1978–1982	45%	na	na	7%	91%
Willamette Management Assoc.	33	1981–1984	31%	na	na	na	na
Silber Study	69	1981–1988	na	34%	24%	(13%)	84%
Hall/Polacek Study (FMV Opinions)	100+	1979–1992	na	23%	na	na	na
Management Planning Study	49	1980–1990	29%	28%	14%	0%	58%
Johnson (BVR) Study	72	1991–1995	na	20%	na	(10%)	60%
Columbia Financial Advisors (pre-1997)	23	1996–1997	14%	21%	na	1%	68%
Columbia Financial Advisors (post-1997)	15	1997–1998	9%	13%	na	0%	30%
FMV Opinions Database	475	1980–2005	19%	22%	19%	na	na
LiquiStat Database	41	2005–2006	32%	31%	16.5%	8%	62%
Averages			33.0%	31.4%			

in Exhibit 7.10, our examination of the underlying transactional data for all the studies for which it is available confirms it. The restricted stock studies (and the pre-IPO studies) do not provide any basis for differentiating marketability discounts for illiquid interests of private enterprises.

The restricted stock studies do provide valuable data regarding the overall return expectations of investors in restricted securities. We discuss this aspect of restricted stock transactions in the next chapter. They do not, however, provide a reasonable basis for applying valuation methods within the market approach to the valuation of subject nonmarketable minority interests.

CHAPTER 8

The QMDM Assumptions in Detail

INTRODUCTION

In the previous chapter we demonstrated the merit of using the income approach to valuation and the discounted cash flow model (method) to value nonmarketable minority interests. We introduced the QMDM as a concise shareholder level discounted cash flow model, and provided a brief overview of the required assumptions. In this chapter, we discuss the assumptions of the QMDM in greater detail. The objectives of this chapter include:

- Discussing the background and rationale for each of the assumptions.
- Illustrating the relative importance of each assumption in developing marketability discounts for nonmarketable minority interests of business enterprises.
- Examining the sensitivity of conclusions drawn from the QMDM to changes in the assumptions made by business appraisers.
- Providing practical guidance for appraisers to assist in developing assumptions in specific valuation situations.

COMMON QUESTIONS

1. Does the expected holding period depend on the characteristics of the subject interest or the current owner of the subject interest?
2. What factors should be considered in assessing the expected holding period?
3. How are distributions from S corporations compared to dividends from C corporations?
4. How does the expected growth in value for public and private companies differ?
5. What specific factors contribute to holding period premiums?
6. How can the reasonableness of the estimated required holding period return be evaluated?
7. Is the QMDM overly sensitive to changes in assumptions?

Assumption #1: Expected Holding Period (for the Investment) (*HP*)

When constructing an enterprise level discounted cash flow model, the appraiser must first determine the forecast horizon, or length of the discrete projection period. Shareholder level discounted cash flow models are no different. In the QMDM, the forecast horizon is referred to as the expected holding period. The expected holding period is the time over which a reasonably informed buyer or seller would anticipate that the subject interest will remain nonmarketable. Note that this is an attribute of the subject interest, and is not necessarily the same as the desired holding period of any specific buyer or seller, including the current owner.

Marketability and the Expected Holding Period

The public securities markets provide the benchmark for assessing the marketability of subject interests. Holders of actively traded stocks can place sale orders with their brokers today at the market price. In three days, cash will be available in their brokerage accounts.[1]

If there is no active market for a private company's shares, investors face considerable uncertainty regarding when and how the shares will become marketable. In the presence of such uncertainty, the value of private company shares becomes a function of the present value of the future cash flows attributable to those securities—if and when they are expected to be achieved. Therefore, appraisers must specifically consider the expected holding period during which the subject interest is expected to remain nonmarketable.

There are several avenues by which a subject interest may become marketable, including:

- *Initial public offering (IPO).* A minority shareholder may have an opportunity to participate in the offering, or his shares may become

---

[1] There are, of course, exceptions to this general statement. It may not be possible to match buyers and sellers immediately if the market for a company's shares is thin or illiquid. Even for highly liquid companies, it can be difficult to sell large blocks of stock immediately, without some "blockage" discount. Large orders hanging over the market can have a depressing impact on share prices of even large market capitalization companies. Nevertheless, the general rule is that the public securities markets provide liquidity in three days, and that is the general standard against which less marketable minority investments are compared.

marketable following the IPO. But relatively few private companies are legitimate candidates to go public.

■ *Sale of the company.* Under normal circumstances, acquirers acquire all the outstanding shares at the same price and on the same terms when companies are sold.

■ *Regular or irregular repurchase activities.* Share repurchase programs have become more popular among private companies in recent years, following the example of many public companies. Many private companies "recycle" shares by repurchasing from existing shareholders and later selling to new shareholders as the company matures. Further, many businesses currently experiencing slow growth (and an accompanying accumulation of excess equity) initiate repurchase programs to generate higher returns for the remaining shareholders.

■ *Sale to investor(s).* The shares may be sold to another investor desiring to invest in the company. While there is no market, it is occasionally possible to locate a purchaser for minority shares of a private company who will buy the shares on relatively favorable terms.

■ *Offers to company or shareholders.* The shares may be offered to the company or to the other shareholders, who may treat the offer with indifference (i.e., with unfavorable pricing).

■ *Buy-sell agreements.* Many companies and their shareholders enter into buy-sell agreements.[2] These agreements outline the obligations of the parties to buy or sell shares under specified circumstances, including when employees quit, are fired, die, or retire. Buy-sell agreements are often initiated with an agreed upon "buy-sell" price, with the parties agreeing to reset the price each year. Other agreements call for a periodic appraisal to reset the value, or when trigger events occur. Some buy-sell agreements are funded by life insurance. Other agreements provide for terms of repurchase.

There are other circumstances under which a minority investor's shares in a private company can be sold, but few of them are generally favorable to the investor. The point is that investors must accept uncertainty with respect to when (or even if) the subject investment will become marketable. They further expect that, because of this uncertainty, they may hold the investment for several or many years.

---

[2]For a detailed discussion of buy-sell agreements from business and valuation perspectives, see Z. Christopher Mercer, *Buy Sell Agreements: Ticking Time Bombs or Reasonable Resolutions?* (Memphis, TN, Peabody Publishing, L.P., 2007). Available at 1-800-769-0967.

Factors to Consider in Estimating the Expected Holding Period

Longer holding periods reduce the present value of the expected share-holder cash flows, resulting in higher marketability discounts. Investors develop holding period expectations by considering factors that may be more qualitative than quantitative. By considering the facts and circumstances of a particular valuation, appraisers may assess the likelihood that the expected holding period will be relatively short, relatively long, or somewhere in between. Although subjective, the holding period expectations are reasonably related to:

- *Historical ownership policies (insiders, outsiders, family, investors, and so on)*. If there is a history of insider ownership, whether within a family (or a group of families) or a small group of owners and/or managers, there may be little likelihood of a market developing for the subject shares. On the other hand, if the investor group includes venture capitalists or private equity groups, it is virtually certain that there will be pressure to liquidate their investments (and maybe everyone's) within a definable time frame (often three to seven years or so).

- *Buy-sell or other shareholder agreements.* Buy-sell agreements can define value from the perspective of a hypothetical willing investor, or they can significantly dampen expected future value, depending upon the nature of the agreement. Other shareholder agreements can also have an impact upon marketability, and must be examined to determine their significance. An adverse buy/sell agreement may, for example, effectively insure that there will be no favorable liquidity opportunities until the company is sold or there is an IPO. Agreements requiring new investors to be subject to terms limiting future liquidity options are an example of this type of adverse agreement.[3]

- *Management/ownership succession (age, health, competence, emerging liquidity needs, and so on)*. While we never know with certainty when favorable opportunities to achieve marketability may occur, certain conditions can increase the probability that a sale, IPO, or other favorable exit opportunity will arise. For example:
  - The prospects for marketability may increase if key management is in poor health. Note that while potentially favorable from a future

---

[3]See the further discussion of the impact of recent changes (2006) to the *Uniformed Standards of Professional Practice (USPAP)* on the required analysis and reporting regarding buy sell agreements in Chapter 9.

marketability standpoint, key person dependencies could dampen overall valuation at the enterprise level.

○ Aging owners may indicate that the shares may become marketable, particularly if the owners have no children or other successors in place to carry on the business.

○ Owners who are known to have near-term liquidity needs (e.g., personal financial problems) may also indicate a greater probability of a sale of the business or other opportunities for marketability.

■ *Business plans and likely exit strategies of the controlling owner(s).* If there is a specific plan calling for the sale of the business within a foreseeable time frame, the outer limits of an expected holding period may be reasonably defined.

■ *Emerging attractiveness for equity offering or acquisition.* A company may be at the stage in its life cycle where opportunities for favorable events are emerging. Attractive companies have a higher probability of being sold or engaging in an IPO than other companies, even if management and ownership aver that the company will remain private. Most businesses are sold quite unexpectedly, and attractive businesses have a much higher probability of unexpected offers.[4]

■ *History of transactions involving minority interests.* If a company or certain of its shareholders have a history of purchasing shares from shareholders who need liquidity at low relative valuations, the necessity of planning for a long holding period is obvious. Alternatively, a more favorable history can provide comfort that there will be a (reasonable) market, if needed.

Holding Period Areas of Investigation   In order to estimate the expected range of probable holding periods, we suggest that an analysis of certain facts regarding the subject interest will often provide credible evidence for the appraiser. Questions designed to elicit these important facts can be included in the management questionnaires used by appraisers. The key facts that might be considered by the appraiser (and hypothetical willing buyers and sellers) include:

■ The age(s) of the principal owners/managers and the availability of competent successor management.

---

[4]See *Is Your Business Ready for Sale?*, a booklet and teleseminar series published for business owners by Mercer Capital. Contact Mercer Capital at 1-800-769-0967 regarding availability.

- The age(s) of the principal shareholder(s), if different from management. The dynamic of age among the ownership group and the management group could lead to a reasonable impression of the need to sell the company.
- The financial condition of the principal owner(s) independent of the subject business. The greater the reliance of stakeholders on the value of the business, rather than on the current benefits derivable from it, the greater the probability of an earlier, rather than a later, sale or liquidation of the business. This information is sometimes available, although not always, but is certainly a justifiable area of inquiry for the hypothetical willing buyer (and the appraiser). The independent financial conditions of the partners in a family limited partnership can have a significant bearing on the pressures facing a successor general partner when a senior generation partner dies.
- The intentions of the principal owner or managers regarding the future of the business. If the current owner/manager has made it known that he plans to sell and retire in the next 3–5 years, there will be a period of increasing likelihood of a sale of the business. In the alternative, if the current owner/manager has plans to "die in the saddle," there may be a low likelihood of a near-term sale.
- Family or shareholder relationships. While tensions between existing shareholders can have a dampening effect on the interest of prospective investors in a company, those same tensions can increase the probability that a sale or other transaction will occur and provide future liquidity opportunities for minority shareholders.
- Conditions in the subject company's industry. Many industries are in early or later stages of consolidation. The very fact that a company is in one of the rapidly consolidating industries increases the probability that a sale or other disposition may occur. And this is true regardless of the present, stated intentions of management or ownership. Taken into consideration with other factors in a valuation situation, presence in a consolidating industry could lead to a reasonable expectation for a relatively shorter, rather than longer, holding period. At the other extreme, if an industry is dead or dying, opportunities for shareholder liquidity may be extremely rare.
- A history of recapitalizations (or sales of substantial portions of businesses) or the likelihood of a recapitalization in the foreseeable future. Substantial recapitalizations provide opportunities for minority shareholders to dissent to transactions and to receive the fair value of their shares. Depending on the state in which a corporation is domiciled, judicial interpretation of dissenters' rights statutes may call for

favorable valuations. Such circumstances may allow the subject interest to become marketable on relatively favorable terms.

Estimating Ranges for the Expected Holding Period

Investors and appraisers must develop holding period expectations.[5] While it is almost never possible to define a particular holding period with certainty, it is normally possible to make an informed judgment as to whether the holding period will be relatively short (five years or less), relatively long (more than ten years), or something in between. In practice, we tend to consider a reasonable range of expected holding periods, together with a range of required holding period returns before making a final decision about the marketability discount to be used in a specific case.

When the facts provide no indication of near-term marketability for the subject interest (for example, within the next five years), we often consider a base range of five to ten years at the outset. The reasonableness of this estimate can be tested based on the implied prospective returns assuming a particular marketability discount. This is not a universally appropriate assumption; however, it does allow the appraiser to establish a base against which to compare shorter and longer holding periods.

We are not aware of any academic studies investigating the duration of a given shareholder group for a private company. Family business experts suggest that only a small percentage of companies are successful in transitioning to the second generation of family management. This would imply that most businesses experience changes of control within at least 20 years or so.

Experience with private companies over nearly three decades has led Mercer to believe that the half-life of business control is probably in the range of eight-to-ten years, give or take a bit. Within this time frame many companies will sell, recapitalize, or merge with another entity in change of control transactions. Obviously some companies transact earlier, and some later.

In the final analysis, the appraiser must reach a conclusion regarding the expected holding period in the context of the facts and circumstances of each case. The tab labeled *Exhibit – Summary QMDM Analysis* in the *QMDM Companion* provides calculations for several different expected holding periods to assist the appraiser in assessing the reasonableness of the implied returns associated with those holding periods. These calculations

---

[5] See the further discussion in Chapter 9 of the impact of recent changes (2006) in *USPAP* on the required analysis and reporting regarding the impact of holding period, interim benefits, and the difficulty and cost of marketing a subject interest.

provide perspective for the appraiser and facilitate an understanding of the sensitivities of the resulting marketability discount to differing assumptions.

Business appraisers cannot be expected to know the unknowable. But appraisers can make decisions regarding the likelihood of a relatively short expected holding period versus a relatively long expected holding period. And, given the particular facts of a situation, those general assessments can often be more narrowly refined. In the final analysis, the appraiser must make an explicit assumption regarding the expected holding period. The appraiser's objective is to gain a sufficient understanding of the facts and circumstances regarding a particular investment to make a reasonable holding period assumption. When developing a shareholder level discounted cash flow model, appraisers must evaluate the expected holding period of the subject interest.

Assumption #2A: Expected Dividend Yield (*D*%)

Appraisers using a shareholder level discounted cash flow model must project interim shareholder cash flows during the expected holding period. Other things being equal, expected dividends mitigate the marketability discount relative to a similar investment with no dividend. In other words, interim cash flows offer direct access to at least a portion of enterprise cash flows.

C corporations pay *dividends*, S corporations and other tax pass-through entities make *distributions*. We use the terms almost interchangeably in this book because all dividends/distributions are adjusted to a comparable basis for the QMDM.

Determining Expected Dividend Yields

Appraisers estimate the expected interim cash flows for a particular subject interest (and the resulting marketable minority yield) on the basis of several considerations:

1. *The history of dividends/distributions.* If a company has a long history of paying dividends (or, for tax pass-through entities, economic distributions in excess of the level necessary for its owners to pay their personal taxes on the corporate earnings), then the appraiser may reasonably assume that policy will continue into the future. Often, management will state its intention of continuing the historical policy for the foreseeable future. In addition, cash flow and balance sheet circumstances may suggest that an enterprise would accumulate abnormally high levels of cash in the absence of shareholder distributions.

2. *Preferential dividend claims.* Occasionally one ownership class will have a preferential claim on distributions that will create a clear expectation of ongoing dividends (or reduce the cash flow available for distribution to other classes of securities).

3. *Other enterprise characteristics.* Sometimes a company has not paid dividends in the past because available cash flow has been used to repay accumulated debt of the enterprise. If the debt has been repaid at the valuation date, or is about to be repaid, or even if the debt has been paid down to relatively normal financing levels, shareholder distributions may reasonably be expected.

   Occasionally, a company may be expected to make a one-time distribution, either in addition to normal distributions or in their absence. If such a distribution is reasonably expected at the valuation date, the appraiser may separately estimate its impact on shareholder value.[6] Companies may also have periodic, but irregular distributions. The appraiser may need to estimate these separately, if significant, or estimate an average distribution yield based on historical, but irregular distributions.

4. *Controlling shareholder characteristics.* The circumstances of the controlling shareholders (or partners or managing members) or their families may indicate that there is a high likelihood of future distributions. High cash flow requirements or high lifestyle requirements may indicate the likelihood of regular future distributions. Likewise, if the subject enterprise is controlled by a holding company, debt-service requirements of the holding company may promote payment of dividends to the minority shareholders of the subsidiary.

5. *Enterprise tax characteristics.* With tax pass-through entities, the appraiser must convert the anticipated cash distribution to a C corporation equivalent yield. In some cases, the resulting C corporation equivalent yield may be negative, for example, when pass-through income tax liabilities exceed cash distributions.

Adjusting for the Tax Characteristics of the Enterprise

Enterprises organized as C corporations pay federal and state income taxes on their earnings before returns are available to their shareholders. When C corporations pay dividends to their shareholders, the dividend income is taxable to the recipients at their respective personal dividend income tax

---

[6]The appraiser would also, of course, take into account the effect of such a distribution on growth in value over the holding period.

EXHIBIT 8.1 Calculation of Expected Dividend Yield for a C Corporation

QUANTITATIVE MARKETABILITY DISCOUNT
    MODEL (QMDM)
QMDM ASSUMPTION #2a
Expected Dividend Yield for C Corporation

1 C CORPORATION DIVIDEND YIELD		Inputs/ Calculations		
2 Expected Dividends		$ 0.45	< >	Appraiser's estimate
3 Marketable Minority Interest Value	÷	$10.00	< >	Per the valuation
4 Implied Ongoing Dividend Yield	=	4.5 %		Rounded

rates. So dividend income received by shareholders of C corporations can be described as *after corporate taxes but before personal taxes.*

C Corporations For C corporations, the calculation of expected dividend yield is straightforward. The expected dividend is divided into current value at the marketable minority level to obtain the yield. The *QMDM Companion* provides a table for calculating the yield for a C corporation (at the tab labeled *Exhibit – Assumption #2 - D%*). In the example shown in Exhibit 8.1, a C corporation has an expected dividend of $0.45 per share (annual basis), and a marketable minority value of $10.00 per share. The C corporation's dividend yield is therefore 4.5%.

S Corporations and Other Tax Pass-Through Entities[7] Although many private companies are organized as S corporations, no public companies are. As a result, market evidence regarding publicly traded companies is derived from C corporations. Therefore, we recommend that distributions for S corporations and other tax pass-through entities be expressed on a C corporation equivalent basis. S corporation shareholder returns before personal taxes are then comparable to those of C corporation shareholder returns before personal taxes. Because the QMDM is an alternative returns model that compares the return potential of the subject interest to the expected returns available from the universe of alternative publicly traded and private investments, the appropriate benchmark for comparing yields is that of a C corporation equivalent dividend.[8]

---

[7]We apply the Integrated Theory to the valuation of S corporations in Chapter 10.
[8]Some might argue that if the interim cash distributions of pass-through entities are tax-effected, it necessarily follows that the QMDM analysis must also include consideration of the income tax status of the terminal value (or exit value). We

The income of S corporations (and other tax pass-through entities) is attributed to the owners pro rata to their ownership in the corporation (or other entity). Income "passes through" from S corporations to their shareholders who then pay taxes on that income at their personal income tax rates. For purposes of this discussion, references to S corporations are also applicable to other tax pass-through entities, including partnerships, limited partnerships, and limited liability companies.

Income distributed from S corporations to their shareholders is sometimes characterized as being *after corporate taxes (none) and before personal taxes.* This characterization ignores the economic reality that S corporations virtually always distribute sufficient income to their shareholders to enable them to pay the "corporate" tax liability that flows through to them personally. Otherwise, unhappy shareholders would likely take measures to break the S election.

Given the flow-through of "corporate" taxes to S corporation shareholders, there is no economic benefit to shareholders until distributions sufficient to pay the taxes are received. After that point, however, shareholder distributions are "tax-free." As a result, S corporation distributions are not comparable to C corporation dividends, which are taxable to shareholders.

EXHIBIT 8.2   Formula for C Corporation Equivalent Distribution

$$
\begin{aligned}
\text{C Corp Equivalent} \\
\text{Distribution (\$)} \\
\text{for an S Corp}
\end{aligned}
=
\frac{
\begin{aligned}
&\text{Pro Rata (Gross) Distribution} - (\text{Personal Income Tax} \\
&\qquad \times \text{Pro Rata Pass-Through Income})
\end{aligned}
}{
(1 - \text{Personal Income Tax Rate on Dividends})
}
$$

$$
=
\frac{\text{Net (After Personal/Corporate Taxes) S Corp Distribution}}{(1 - \text{Personal Income Tax Rate on Dividends})}
$$

---

disagree with this proposition. Interim cash distributions are restated to a fully taxable C corporation equivalent basis because the bulk of historical and current data on stock returns relates to returns (before personal taxes) on investments in C corporations, and dividends are generally fully taxable to the investor. Depending on a variety of factors, the proceeds from the sale of the stock of a C corporation or the proceeds from the liquidation of a C corporation may be less than fully taxable, or subject to an unusually high effective tax rate. Nevertheless, total return statistics are based on reported prices of securities, not on the net proceeds to individual investors. In most cases, any attempt to project special tax benefits or liabilities related to the exit value would involve speculation regarding potential buyers and sellers. In cases where special tax considerations have been identified, are readily quantifiable, and are appropriate for consideration, it may be necessary to incorporate these facts into the QMDM analysis.

EXHIBIT 8.3 Formula for C Corporation Equivalent Distribution Yield

$$\text{C Corp Equivalent Distribution Yield for an S Corp} = \frac{\text{C Corp Equivalent Distribution (\$) for an S Corp}}{\text{Marketable Minority Indication of Value for the S Corp}}$$

As shown on Exhibit 8.2, S corporation distributions can be made equivalent to C corporation dividends by "grossing up" the after corporate/personal tax distributions by the arithmetic inverse of the personal income tax rate on dividends from C corporations.

Applying the formula in Exhibit 8.3 to S corporation distributions yields a C corporation equivalent distribution. Exhibit 8.3 illustrates the derivation of the C corporation equivalent dividend yield.

A template for this calculation is provided in the tab labeled *Exhibit – Assumption #2a – D%* in the QMDM *Companion.*

- As shown in Exhibit 8.4, the template begins with total pre-tax earnings of the S corporation of $1.00 per share (Line 1).
- Pass-through taxes of $0.376 per share are estimated at the blended, marginal federal and state personal income tax rates (at Lines 2–5).
- The total distribution payout (80%) is then estimated at Line 6, to determine the expected total distribution per share (Line 7).
- The estimated pass-through taxes are subtracted from this total distribution, yielding the after pass-through tax S corporation dividend of $0.424 per share (Lines 8–9).

QUANTITATIVE MARKETABILITY DISCOUNT MODEL (QMDM)
QMDM ASSUMPTION #2a
C Corporation Equivalent Yield for Tax Pass-Through Entity

	C CORPORATION EQUIVALENT DIVIDEND YIELD FOR TAX PASS-THROUGH ENTITIES		Inputs / Calculations	
1	Expected Pre-Tax Earnings of Pass-Through Entity		$1.00	Per Share, appraiser's estimate
2	Personal Federal Ordinary Income Tax Rate	35.0%		
3	Personal State Ordinary Income Tax Rate	4.0%		Blended Federal/State Rate
4	Blended Marginal Tax Rate		37.6%	Federal Rate × (1 – State Rate) + State Rate
5	**Pass-Through Taxes**		$0.376	Line 1 × Line 4
6	**Expected Total Distribution Payout Percentage**	80.0%		Appraiser's estimate of annual distribution payout
7	Expected Total Distributions		$0.800	Line 1 times Line 6
8	– Pass-Through Taxes on Pre-Tax Earnings		($0.376)	From Line 3 above
9	= After-Tax Dividend		$0.424	
10	After Tax Dividend		$0.424	From Line 9 above
11	÷ Blended Tax Rate on C Corp Dividends	15.0%	85.0%	Federal/State corporate marginal rate (1 – personal blended tax rate)
12	= **C Corporation Equivalent Dividend**		$0.499	After-Tax dividend ÷ Blended Tax Rate on Dividends
13	C Corporation Equivalent Dividend		$0.499	From Line 12 above
14	÷ Marketable Minority Interest Value	÷	$10.00	Per Share, appraisers estimate (Exhibit x)
15	**Implied Ongoing Dividend Yield – C Corporation Basis**	=	5.00%	**C Corporation Equivalent Basis, Rounded**

EXHIBIT 8.4 Calculation of C Corporation Equivalent Dividend Yield

- The after pass-through tax distribution is then "grossed up" by dividing by (1 – Personal Tax Rate on Dividends) to obtain the C corporation equivalent dividend of $0.499 per share (Lines 10–12).
- Finally, the C corporation equivalent yield is divided by the appraiser's estimate of marketable minority value per share to obtain the C corporation equivalent yield of 5.0% (Lines 13–15).

Note that the C corporation equivalent dividend for a tax pass-through entity is positively related to the personal tax rate on dividend income. The personal dividend tax, rather than the corporate income tax, is what is ultimately avoided by the S corporation election. In other words, the relative benefit of S corporation status is greatest when the tax rate on C corporation dividend income is highest. As a result, the 2003 reduction of the personal tax rate on C corporation dividend income actually reduced the relative economic advantage of S corporation status.

S Corporation Distribution Yields Can Be Negative   Exhibit 8.5 illustrates the C corporation equivalent dividend yield calculation for an S corporation that fails to distribute any earnings to shareholders, despite the pass-through of taxable corporate income. As a result, the S corporation shareholder must fund the required tax payment independently, resulting in a negative C corporation equivalent dividend yield.[9] Such an expected circumstance

QUANTITATIVE MARKETABILITY DISCOUNT MODEL (QMDM)
QMDM ASSUMPTION #2a
C Corporation Equivalent Yield for Tax Pass-Through Entity

	C CORPORATION EQUIVALENT DIVIDEND YIELD FOR TAX PASS-THROUGH ENTITIES	Inputs / Calculations	
1	Expected Pre-Tax Earnings of Pass-Through Entity	$1.00	Per Share, appraiser's estimate
2	Personal Federal Ordinary Income Tax Rate	35.0%	
3	Personal State Ordinary Income Tax Rate	4.0%	Blended Federal/State Rate
4	Blended Marginal Tax Rate	37.6%	Federal Rate × (1 – State Rate) + State Rate
5	Pass-Through Taxes	$0.376	Line 1 × Line 4
6	Expected Total Distribution Payout Percentage	0.0%	Appraiser's estimate of annual distribution payout
7	Expected Total Distributions	$0.000	Line 1 times Line 6
8	– Pass-Through Taxes on Pre-Tax Earnings	($0.376)	From Line 3 above
9	= After-Tax Dividend	($0.376)	
10	After Tax Dividend	($0.376)	From Line 9 above
11	÷ Blended Tax Rate on C Corp Dividends	15.0%	Federal/State corporate marginal rate (1 – personal blended tax rate)
12	= C Corporation Equivalent Dividend	($0.442)	After-Tax dividend ÷ Blended Tax Rate on Dividends
13	C Corporation Equivalent Dividend	($0.442)	From Line 12 above
14	÷ Marketable Minority Interest Value ÷	$10.00	Per Share, appraisers estimate (Exhibit x)
15	Implied Ongoing Dividend Yield – C Corporation Basis =	–4.40%	C Corporation Equivalent Basis, Rounded

EXHIBIT 8.5   Calculation of C Corporation Equivalent Dividend Yield (No Distribution for Taxes)

[9] Given that the dividend yield for a C corporation cannot be negative, the analyst may choose not to "gross down" the resulting negative yield.

would have an adverse impact on the value of minority interests in the non-distributing S corporation.

The QMDM enables appraisers to consider both the positive impact of S corporation (and pass-through) earnings as well as the negative impact in those unusual circumstances where no or inadequate distributions are made to pay personal/corporate taxes. If the C corporation equivalent yield is negative, the present value of the expected cash outflows is subtracted from the present value of the terminal value at the end of the expected holding period (or range of holding periods).

Conclusion Regarding Tax Equivalent Yields Appraisers should be very deliberate when developing the yields for S corporations and other tax pass-through entities, and must consider the prevailing tax laws affecting S corporations and C corporations in the same manner as a hypothetical investor.

Hypothetical investors in tax pass-through entities with uncertain distribution policies must carefully weigh the implications of investing in nonmarketable securities, which could saddle them with a potential annual liability for taxes on corporate earnings without accompanying distributions to pay those taxes. This has valuation implications and should be treated carefully in the context of valuing minority interests in tax pass-through entities. The risk of adverse tax consequences from investments in tax pass-through entities is virtually always greater than zero, if only through a mismatching of the timing of distributions in a manner that is inconvenient (and potentially costly) to the investor/taxpayer.

The major point of this discussion of C corporation equivalent yields for tax pass-though entities, however, is that in using the QMDM, tax pass-through distributions must be converted to a C corporation equivalent basis for the dividend yield assumption of the QMDM. In so doing, appraisers will give appropriate consideration to the shareholder level tax benefits associated with the S election, and the pass-through status generally, for the duration of the expected holding period.

ASSUMPTION #2B: EXPECTED GROWTH OF DIVIDENDS (G_D)

For many business entities that pay a regular dividend or distribution to their owners, there is a reasonable probability that the dividend will grow as the enterprise grows. For this reason, the QMDM requires the business appraiser to make a reasonable assumption about the expected growth rate of dividends. The expected growth rate of dividends actually specifies the expected interim cash flows of the shareholder level discounted cash flow models over the expected holding period. While this assumption does not often have a major impact on the calculations of the QMDM, it is necessary to fully specify the model.

With respect to growth in dividends, appraisers make one of four potential assumptions, depending on the facts and circumstances pertaining to the subject interest:

1. *Dividends will grow at the same rate as the expected growth in value (a constant dividend yield).* In cases where earnings and value are expected to grow at approximately the same rate, it is appropriate to assume that dividends will grow at the same rate as the expected growth in value.

2. *Dividends will grow at the same rate as the expected growth of core earnings (a constant dividend payout ratio).* In such cases, it is appropriate to assume that dividend growth will mirror the expected growth of earnings of the subject enterprise. Many companies tie dividend growth to earnings growth.

3. *Dividends will not grow (a constant dollar dividend).* Quite a few companies have a history of paying the same dollar or per share dividend every year. If the expectation is that this policy is unlikely to change over the expected holding period, a 0% growth assumption for dividends may be appropriate. Alternatively, if a company has paid dividends that have varied, and the appraiser has used some average of historical dividends as the best available estimate of future dividends, a 0% growth assumption may be appropriate.

4. *Dividends will grow at some other rate.* Other special circumstances may dictate the appropriate dividend growth assumption. For example, if a company is on the verge of paying off a significant debt and its cash flow will be freed to pay increased dividends, it may be appropriate to estimate a blended future growth rate for dividends. In the alternative, financing arrangements may suggest that dividends will grow at a slower rate than either earnings or value.

As noted, the assumption regarding expected growth in dividends does not often have a material impact on QMDM marketability discount estimates. However, the analyst should make a specific estimate to develop a comprehensive shareholder level discounted cash flow model.

ASSUMPTION #2C: TIMING OF DIVIDEND RECEIPT

As with any discounted cash flow model, the appraiser must also make a decision regarding the timing of receipt of interim cash flows in the QMDM.

Appraisers familiar with the enterprise level discounted cash flow model understand the importance of this assumption.

Dividends can be assumed to be received at the end of each year, or at the middle of each year (simulating continuous, or quarterly, dividend payments). Given the importance of dividends or distributions to value for high-distribution entities, appraisers should be clear about this assumption and the reasons for the choice between end-of-year and mid-year receipt.

The *QMDM Companion* enables appraisers to make this assumption explicit. The appraiser can make the assumption "E" and the *QMDM Companion* will make calculations based on end-of-year receipt of interim cash flows. Similarly, if the appraiser selects "M", the model will calculate the present value of interim cash flows based on the assumption of mid-year receipt.

Assumption #3A: The Expected Growth Rate in Value (G_V)

The third assumption of the QMDM is the expected growth in value, or G_v. The expected growth in value defines the terminal value (TV) in the shareholder level discounted cash flow model. Prior to the application of the QMDM, the appraiser must develop an indication of value at the marketable minority level of value (V_{mm}) consistent with the expected earnings, cash flows, and risk of the enterprise. Recall from Chapter 7:

$$TV = V_{mm}x(1 + G_v)^{HP}$$

The QMDM assumes that marketability occurs at the marketable minority level of value although the model allows the appraiser to change this assumption if warranted.

Factors Influencing the Expected Growth Rate in Value

Several reference points can assist appraisers in estimating the expected growth in value. In most appraisals using the income approach, appraisers develop specific estimates of earnings or cash flow growth. If the discounted future benefits method is used, specific growth assumptions are made for a finite forecast period. If the Gordon Model is used to estimate the terminal value, an assumption is made regarding the expected long-term growth beyond the finite forecast period.

Public company investor returns consist of two components: current income (or dividend yield) and capital appreciation (or growth in value).

For public companies, the expected growth in value is the required return less the expected dividend yield. For private companies, various potential agency costs can disturb this relationship. We assign these agency costs to two categories, both of which increase the marketability discount applicable to the subject minority interest.

- *Non–pro rata distribution of enterprise cash flows.* Owner/managers of private companies occasionally divert a portion of the normalized enterprise cash flows to themselves on a non–pro rata basis through above-market compensation and perquisites or certain transactions with related parties. Such non–pro rata distribution of normalized enterprise cash flows reduces the interim shareholder cash flows, thereby increasing the appropriate marketability discount.
- *Suboptimal reinvestment of enterprise cash flows.* The enterprise valuation methods assume that cash flows are either distributed pro rata to the shareholders or reinvested at the discount rate of the enterprise. Whatever the source, suboptimal reinvestment diminishes the prospective terminal value of the shareholder level discounted cash flow model, thereby increasing the appropriate marketability discount. Managers of some private companies demonstrate a persistent inability or unwillingness to reinvest undistributed earnings at the required rate of return. This can be a result of undue risk aversion (accumulation of low-yielding excess assets) or empire building (chronic overpayment for acquisitions or new projects).

Note that the burden of expected suboptimal reinvestment is borne by all shareholders in the enterprise, whether owning a control or minority interest. From a controlling shareholder's viewpoint, the enterprise value is based on the normalized cash flows and efficient reinvestment of undistributed earnings, because the business could be sold for that value. However, the value of the *business plan* is reduced by the effect of the anticipated suboptimal reinvestment. The difference between the controlling shareholder and the minority shareholder of a private company is that the former has the power to eliminate the potential decrement in value by a change in reinvestment policy or through distributions. The latter does not, and the appraiser must consider this impact in determining the marketability discount applicable to minority interests.

Developing G_v

Estimating an appropriate terminal value is a critical step in applying the shareholder level discounted cash flow model. With the QMDM, the expected growth in value establishes the projected terminal value. Appraisers encounter a number of potential situations in which different assumptions regarding the expected growth in value are appropriate. We discuss several such situations here, together with suggestions regarding estimating G_v.

- *Dividend/distribution policies affect G_v.* Some closely held companies pay out all or a substantial portion of earnings to their shareholders. The core earnings growth in the enterprise valuation is that which could be achieved if the Company did not retain any earnings. If very high distributions are anticipated, it may be reasonable to assume that expected earnings and value growth will be approximately the same. For other companies that regularly distribute a portion of enterprise earnings, the expected growth in value may exceed the core earnings growth rate (G_e) because of the reinvestment of undistributed earnings.

  We have found that a reasonable expectation for growth in value often lies somewhere between the expected growth rate in core earnings and the internal growth rate (as measured by return on equity [ROE] times the earnings retention rate).

  For example, assuming that ROE equals 15%, expected growth in earnings is 7%, and the dividend payout ratio is expected to be 33.33%, the internal growth rate is calculated as follows:

$$\text{Internal Growth Rate (IGR)} = \text{Return on Equity (ROE)}$$
$$\times (1 - \text{Dividend Payout\%(DPO\%)})$$
$$\text{IGR} = 15\% \times (1 - 33.33\%)$$
$$\text{IGR} = 10\%$$

  Under these assumptions, the appraiser would likely estimate the expected growth rate in value to be in the range of 7% (the expected growth rate in earnings) and 10%, the internal growth rate. In the valuation of closely held business interests, the appraiser may need to make further assumptions about the likelihood of the hypothetical willing buyer being able to gain access to any excess assets that may accumulate by the end of the expected holding period. Doubts about future access could cause the appraiser to moderate the expected growth rate in value.

- *Enterprise level discounted cash flow analysis provides evidence of G_v.* An expected growth rate in value may be implied by an appraiser's discounted cash flow or discounted future earnings methodology. Appraisers using enterprise level DCF or DFE methods need to reconcile their assumptions regarding expected growth in value in the

QMDM analysis to the expected growth in value embedded in their DCF calculations.

■ *Underlying asset appraisals provide evidence of* G_v. The expected growth rate in value may be implied by the underlying real estate appraisal(s) for a real estate holding company. Many times, discussion with the appraiser of the underlying real estate (or a review of the real estate appraisal) will prove fruitful in developing a reasonable expectation for the growth in value of an asset holding entity.

■ *Changing leverage can affect* G_v. For leveraged companies, value can grow more rapidly than earnings as debt is repaid. This is the essence of the financial buyer's model for operating companies.[10] For an asset holding entity, for example, the real estate appraiser may have estimated that a particular property should grow in value at 5% to 6%. However, if the property is leveraged in a limited partnership, and the mortgage on the property is amortizing on the basis of a 15-year schedule, the pro rata value of a partnership interest will rise more rapidly than that of the underlying real estate. The expected growth in value over a range of potential holding periods can be estimated by making the appropriate calculations.

■ *Portfolio composition can affect* G_v. The portfolio composition of asset holding entities can provide evidence as to expected future growth in value. Consider a limited partnership holding $100 million of large capitalization, publicly traded securities. A diversified portfolio of such stocks might have an expected total return on the order of 10%, with the expected growth in value dependent upon the dividend payout policy of the partnership. Alternatively, a portfolio of fixed income securities may have a zero growth in value if all earnings are paid out, or a slower growth expectation than an equity portfolio if earnings are retained. The expected growth rate in value for an entity holding multiple asset classes will be a value-weighted average expectation for the various classes.[11]

Sensitivity and G_v

As with any discounted cash flow model, the value indicated by the QMDM is sensitive to the projected terminal value (as determined by the expected

---

[10]Note that such use of financial leverage may also have an impact on required return, which must also be considered.

[11]As an aside, this observation suggests that the expected management philosophy of a partnership (or a company) can influence the expected growth in value. Appraisers should ask appropriate questions of general partners (or key managers) to develop reasonable expectations of management intent.

Sensitivity of Marketability Discounts (G_v and HP)				
Expected Holding Period (HP) in Years				
3	**5**	**7**	**10**	**15**
Calculated Marketability Discounts (No Dividends)				

	3	5	7	10	15
4%	35%	51%	63%	76%	88%
8%	27%	41%	52%	65%	79%
10%	23%	35%	46%	58%	73%
12%	19%	29%	38%	50%	64%
15%	12%	19%	26%	35%	47%

Required Holding Period Return (R_{hp}) = 20%

EXHIBIT 8.6 Sensitivity of Marketability Discounts to Expected Growth in Value

growth in value). To illustrate that sensitivity, Exhibit 8.6 compares the resulting marketability discount over various levels of expected growth in value and expected holding periods at a constant required holding period return of 20% for interests paying no dividends.

Exhibit 8.6 indicates the marketability discounts calculated under the indicated assumptions. While the change in discount from one assumption to the next may appear large, it should be noted that changes in expected growth in value from 4% to 8% or from 12% to 15% and so forth are not trivial. Likewise, the illustrated changes in the expected holding period are also not trivial. So while the model is "sensitive" to changes, it should be clear that *significant changes* in the expected growth rate of value will create *significant changes* in value. Further, significant changes in the expected holding period (or other key assumptions) correspondingly create significant changes in value (and implied marketability discounts).

Appraisers and many users of appraisal reports are well-aware of the sensitivity of value indications based on the enterprise level DCF valuation method to changes in key assumptions such as projected margins (and interim earnings growth), the discount rate, the capital structure assumption, and the expected growth in earnings (or the multiple selection) for the terminal value estimate. Sensitivity to assumptions in valuation is simply a fact of life. What is important is to make reasonable assumptions given the pertinent facts and circumstances. Because the QMDM is a shareholder level discounted cash flow model, sensitivity to significant changes in assumptions is no surprise.

In the final analysis, the appraiser must make the same kind of judgments that hypothetical willing buyers (and real buyers) make about the expected growth rate in value, based on a full understanding of the facts and circumstances of the hypothetical (or real) investment.

ASSUMPTION #3B: ADJUSTMENTS TO THE TERMINAL VALUE

The expected growth in value establishes the terminal value at the marketable minority level of value. A related assumption specifies any premium or discount for the terminal value estimate relative to the marketable minority base. Sometimes, the facts of a particular valuation suggest that marketability may be achieved at the end of the expected holding period at a different level of value. For example, the enterprise may be sold to a strategic buyer. Alternatively, a minority interest discount may be relieved if a partnership is expected to liquidate within the relevant expected holding period. In such cases, the appraiser may indicate that a premium would be expected. Finally, the facts could indicate that a discount to marketable minority value is expected when marketability is achieved. This could occur, for example, through the operation of a buy-sell agreement. In the absence of a contrary assumption, the QMDM specifies the terminal value at the marketable minority level of value.

Assumption #4: Required Holding Period (Rate of) Return (R_{hp})

After estimating the interim shareholder cash flows and terminal value at the end of the holding period, application of the discounted cash flow model requires the appraiser to specify a discount rate. With respect to the QMDM, we refer to this discount rate as the required holding period return, or R_{hp}. Minority shareholders in private companies bear additional, unique risks associated with the nonmarketability of such investments in addition to the underlying risks of the enterprise. The appropriate discount rate for the QMDM is therefore the sum of the enterprise discount rate R_{mm} and the holding period premium (HPP) to compensate for the unique risks of nonmarketability.

$$R_{hp} = R_{mm} + \text{HPP}$$

In the following sections, we review the market evidence available to support not only the existence, but also the magnitude of the holding period premium. Before examining the available market evidence, we briefly consider a few conceptual questions:

- Can real-life buyers assess risks if they have the facts? Yes. After all, the parties to any transaction face a given set of unique facts and circumstances that affect the transaction price.
- Do transactions occur in which nonmarketable minority interests actually change hands at arm's length? Yes. The following discussion of available market evidence is derived from such transactions.
- In the context of financial, valuation, and economic theory, can business appraisers simulate the thinking of real-life sellers and buyers of minority interests in private companies? Yes. That is the essence of what appraisers do, regardless of the nature of the subject asset.

We have already described the cash flow attributes of investments in nonmarketable minority interests in private companies. We now turn our attention to the market evidence regarding the return expectations of investors in such interests.

Market Evidence Regarding Holding Period Premiums

Restricted Stock Discounts   First, we look to transactions involving the restricted securities of publicly traded companies to understand the existence and potential magnitude of the holding period premium. Consider a public company issuing securities that, because of various provisions of Rule 144 of the Securities Act of 1933, was subject to trading restrictions for two years.[12]

Assume that the market price of the public company on the date of the transaction is $1.00 per share. We can represent the current price of the public security in terms of the familiar Gordon Model as follows:

$$V_{mm} = \frac{CF_{mm}}{R_{mm} - G_e} = \$1.00$$

Publicly Traded Value

Now assume further that the restricted stock transaction occurred at a price of $0.75 per share, or a discount of 25%. In light of the preceding formula, there are a limited number of potential explanations for the $0.25 share diminution in price for the restricted stock transaction.

---

[12]The current restriction on marketability for restricted share purchases is generally one year. We use a two-year example because the majority of available restricted stock studies were conducted when this SEC restriction was two years.

- *A change in cash flows of the enterprise as a result of the transaction.* This is unlikely unless one assumes that the investment would augment enterprise cash flows, but that should increase, rather than decrease value.
- *A change in the expected growth rate in core earnings.* This is also unlikely unless one assumes that the investment would augment growth, which again would tend to increase, rather than to decrease value.
- *Incremental risks faced by the restricted stock investors in addition to those faced by holders of freely traded shares.* This is the most compelling explanation. Common sense suggests that an investment that cannot be sold for two years is riskier than one that is otherwise identical but may be freely traded at any time. This incremental risk is manifest in a premium to the base discount rate, R.

Assume that the enterprise discount rate of the public company is 10%. In the absence of dividends, the expected value of the stock at the end of the one year is $1.10 per share. At the end of two years, the expected value is $1.21 per share ($1.00 \times (1 + 10\%)^2$). Of course, no one knows exactly what the price of the subject security will be in two years, but investors have to make investment decisions on the basis of realistic expectations. The restricted stock investors must look at the investment in two stages:

- *Stage 1, the period of restriction on transfer.* During this two-year period, the restricted shares may not be traded, and the investors are "locked in" regardless of what happens with the company or with their own circumstances, which can also change.[13] During this period, the investors experience risks in addition to those of the enterprise, or shareholder level risks, as discussed in Chapter 3. The discount rate for this period consists of the enterprise discount rate plus specific holding period premiums.
- *Stage 2, the period of free transferability.* When the relevant restrictions lapse, the shares will be freely tradable with an expected value of $1.21. At this point, there would be no further *shareholder level risks* in addition to the risks of the enterprise, and the discount reverts to R_{mm}.

---

[13]Restricted stock investors may be able to sell their shares to other, qualified investors during the period of restriction. However, these new, qualified investors will be subject to any remaining period of restricted marketability. They will, in all likelihood, employ the same kind of logic to their investment as did the initial investor.

We can calculate R_{hp} with the known information in our example. Comparing the price of $0.75 per share paid for the restricted shares to the expected future value of $1.21 per share implies a required return of 27% after the expected two-year holding period. In other words, relative to the assumed enterprise discount rate of 10%, the effective holding period premium is 17%. The existence of restricted stock discounts demonstrates that holding period premiums exist and that they are not trivial.

Numerous empirical studies of observed restricted stock transactions have been published during the past few decades. The majority of these studies are based on transactions prior to 1997 involving the issuance of shares restricted under Rule 144 of the Securities and Exchange Act of 1934. The shares were sold to qualified investors, and there were legal restrictions on the transfer of the shares for at least two years. The studies reveal average discounts in the general range of 25% to 35%. Recall the summary of restricted stock studies in Appendix 7-A.

If, as was the case with many of the restricted stock investments, the investors acquired 5% or more of the public company, they would have been deemed affiliates at the end of the two-year period of restriction, and been subject to the dribble-out rules of Rule 144, thereby lengthening the effective holding period for the shares. Exhibit 8.7 summarizes an analysis of the effective rates of return for investments in restricted stocks assuming a range of realized returns on the corresponding freely traded shares over two- and three-year holding periods. To account for a wide range of possibilities, the model considers potential realized enterprise returns ranging from negative 10% per year up to positive 15% per year.

For purposes of illustration, we highlight the range of potential returns from 3% to 12% as the most likely potential outcome for the public companies whose shares were purchased by the restricted stock investors. Looking at both the two-year and three-year holding period assumptions, it is clear that annual return expectations typically associated with venture capitalists may have been common for at least some of the transactions in the restricted stock studies.

The Management Planning Study　　In this section, we focus on one particular restricted stock study for a more detailed consideration of the typical required returns and implied holding period premiums. The Management Planning, Inc. (MPI) study was first published as Chapter 12 of *Quantifying Marketability Discounts* in 1997. The MPI Study consisted of 49 restricted stock transactions taking place between 1980 and 1995. Exhibit 8.8 summarizes pertinent information from the MPI study and our analysis of the implications for the likely magnitude of the holding period premiums.

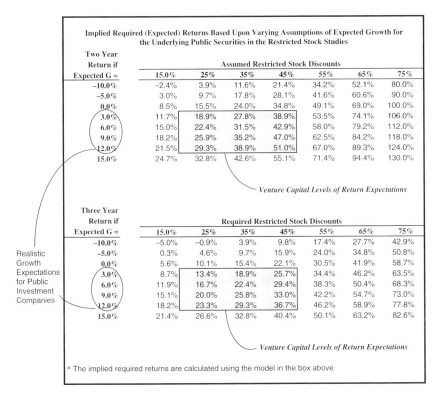

Implied Required (Expected) Returns Based Upon Varying Assumptions of Expected Growth for the Underlying Public Securities in the Restricted Stock Studies							
Two Year Return if		**Assumed Restricted Stock Discounts**					
Expected G =	**15.0%**	**25%**	**35%**	**45%**	**55%**	**65%**	**75%**
–10.0%	–2.4%	3.9%	11.6%	21.4%	34.2%	52.1%	80.0%
–5.0%	3.0%	9.7%	17.8%	28.1%	41.6%	60.6%	90.0%
0.0%	8.5%	15.5%	24.0%	34.8%	49.1%	69.0%	100.0%
3.0%	11.7%	18.9%	27.8%	38.9%	53.5%	74.1%	106.0%
6.0%	15.0%	22.4%	31.5%	42.9%	58.0%	79.2%	112.0%
9.0%	18.2%	25.9%	35.2%	47.0%	62.5%	84.2%	118.0%
12.0%	21.5%	29.3%	38.9%	51.0%	67.0%	89.3%	124.0%
15.0%	24.7%	32.8%	42.6%	55.1%	71.4%	94.4%	130.0%

Venture Capital Levels of Return Expectations

Three Year Return if		**Required Restricted Stock Discounts**					
Expected G =	**15.0%**	**25%**	**35%**	**45%**	**55%**	**65%**	**75%**
–10.0%	–5.0%	–0.9%	3.9%	9.8%	17.4%	27.7%	42.9%
–5.0%	0.3%	4.6%	9.7%	15.9%	24.0%	34.8%	50.8%
0.0%	5.6%	10.1%	15.4%	22.1%	30.5%	41.9%	58.7%
3.0%	8.7%	13.4%	18.9%	25.7%	34.4%	46.2%	63.5%
6.0%	11.9%	16.7%	22.4%	29.4%	38.3%	50.4%	68.3%
9.0%	15.1%	20.0%	25.8%	33.0%	42.2%	54.7%	73.0%
12.0%	18.2%	23.3%	29.3%	36.7%	46.2%	58.9%	77.8%
15.0%	21.4%	26.6%	32.8%	40.4%	50.1%	63.2%	82.6%

Realistic Growth Expectations for Public Investment Companies

Venture Capital Levels of Return Expectations

* The implied required returns are calculated using the model in the box above

EXHIBIT 8.7 Required Returns Implied by Restricted Stock Study Results

The average restricted stock discount in the MPI study was 27.7% (Line 1). The average revenues for the companies in the study were $80 million (Line 2), and the average transaction involved blocks of more than 19% of the outstanding shares (Line 3). So the typical transaction involved the sale of stock to a purchaser (or purchasers) who likely became an affiliate(s) of the company under the securities laws. As such, the applicable restrictions under Rule 144 included, at least generally, the following:

- Two-year restriction on marketability under the pre-1997 rules (Line 6).
- Additional restrictions on resale, because affiliates were subject to the dribble-out provisions of Rule 144. Based on MPI calculations, the average period to dribble out the purchased blocks was 14 quarters, or 3.5 years (Lines 4 and 5). If a purchaser of the average block began to dribble shares at the end of the two-year period of restriction, it would take an additional 3.5 years to sell the entire block. Assuming that the

shares could be sold evenly over that period, the average additional holding period is 1.75 years (3.5 / 2 on Line 7).

■ Adding the initial two-year period of restriction to the average additional holding period yields an average expected holding period of 3.75 years (Line 8).

Given specific evidence of an average expected holding period and an average discount, we need only make a reasonable assumption about the enterprise discount rate of the issuing public companies. In Exhibit 8.8, we assumed an enterprise discount rate of 15% (Line 9). The expected future value (at the end of the calculated holding period) is $1.69 per share. Relative to an average purchase price of $0.72 per share, the expected return over the holding period was 25.4% (Line 13), suggesting that the typical holding period premium in the transactions was on the order of 10% (25.4% − 15.0%).

Publicly Traded Partnership Returns Partnership Profiles, Inc. (PPI) of Dallas, Texas publishes an annual study focusing on rates of return expected by secondary market buyers of limited partner interests.[14] The information

Line	Per Management Planning Study	Average	Comment/Explanation
1	**Restricted Stock Discounts**	**27.7%**	Per the MPI Study (Chapter 12, *QMD*)
2	Market Capitalization ($mm)	$80.4	Primarily small capitalization companies
3	Block Size / Shares Outstanding (affiliates?)	19.2%	Large blocks on average (likely Rule 144 affiliates)
4	# Quarters to Dribble Out	14	Per MPI calculation
5	# Years to Dribble Out	3.5	Line 4 / 4 Quarters
	Additional Considerations		
6	Rule 144 Period of Restriction (in Years)	2.0	Per Rule 144 prior to April 1997
7	Years to Dribble Out	3.5	Per Line 5 above
8	**Effective Holding Period if Dribble (HP)**	**3.75**	Line 6 + Line 7 / 2 (assuming even dribble out)
9	Assumed Discount Rate = G_v	15.0%	Reasonable assumption*
10	Indexed Price Per Share	$1.000	
11	Purchase Price	$0.723	Line 10 less the Line 1 discount
12	Expected Future Value (to Effective HP)	$1.689	(Line 10) * (1 + Line 9)^Line 8
13	**Implied Return for HP**	**25.4%**	(Line 10 / Line 11)^(1 / Line 8) minus 1.0
14	Implied Holding Period Premium (HPP)	10.4%	Line 13 less Line 9

* The calculated HPP varies less than 1% over assumed discount rates (Line 9) raging from 10% to 20%

EXHIBIT 8.8 Analysis of Management Planning Restricted Stock Study

[14]2006 Rate of Return Study: Publicly-Held Real Estate Limited Partnerships and Real Estate Investment Trusts, Published by Partnership Profiles. http://www.partnershipprofiles.com.

conveyed in the most recent survey is based on data for publicly traded limited partnerships from 1994 to 2005. The assumptions related to the survey's derivation of expected rates of return include the following:

- Expected future distributions are based on historical levels and are projected to increase 3% per year until the forecasted liquidation of the partnership;
- Debt amortization for leveraged partnerships was forecast through the expected liquidation date, upon which all residual debt is projected to be paid;
- The underlying value of the partnerships' assets is projected to increase at an average annual rate of 3%; and,
- The liquidation horizon forecast by PPI is based on investor expectations as of the April/May time frame of each year. Many partnerships publicly announced their intent to liquidate beginning in 1995.

These assumptions are, in fact, the same assumptions used in the QMDM. With the QMDM, the appraiser makes assumptions about risk, expected cash flows, the expected holding period, and growth in value to solve for price, thereby determining the marketability discount. The Partnership Profiles study observes price in the market for limited partnership interests and uses assumptions about expected cash flows, growth in value, and the expected holding period to solve for the implied required return.

As shown in the table in Exhibit 8.9, time horizons for nonliquidating partnerships used in each year of the survey declined from 10 years in 1994 to 4 years in 2005.

EXHIBIT 8.9 Estimated
Time Horizons

1994	10 years
1995	8 years
1996	6 years
1997	5 years
1998	5 years
1999	5 years
2000	4 years
2001	4 years
2002	4 years
2003	4 years
2004	4 years
2005	4 years

	Distributing Partnerships		
Year	Overall	No / Low Debt	Mod / High Debt
1994	19.4%	19.1%	22.0%
1995	19.3%	18.2%	24.7%
1996	21.1%	19.5%	27.2%
1997	19.5%	18.1%	23.2%
1998	19.5%	19.0%	21.4%
1999	18.7%	17.7%	22.5%
2000	21.0%	20.5%	23.5%
2001	21.6%	21.0%	24.0%
2002	19.3%	18.9%	21.2%
2003	17.4%	17.3%	19.3%
2004	17.5%	16.3%	23.8%
2005	17.7%	17.6%	18.3%
Average	19.3%	18.6%	22.6%

EXHIBIT 8.10   Expected Returns for Distributing Partnerships

Based on these assumptions, the expected rates of return for nonliquidating partnerships making distributions were calculated from 1994 to 2005 (summarized in Exhibit 8.10).

Exhibit 8.10 illustrates a general decline in expected returns for partnership interests over the past ten years. This information suggests that expected returns for investments in distributing limited partnership interests typically range from the high teens to the low twenties, depending on debt levels.

The expected rates of return for nonliquidating partnerships not currently providing distributions were also calculated from 1994 to 2005 (summarized in Exhibit 8.11).

As shown in the preceding table, partnerships that have not historically paid distributions are priced to achieve higher expected returns overall than distributing partnerships. Among the nondistributing partnership interests, those with higher levels of debt had higher expected returns than those with less financial leverage, consistent with the expected returns data for distributing partnerships.

The data derived from the PPI study can help support the overall reasonableness of an appraiser's estimate of the range of expected required holding period returns applied in the QMDM.

| | Nondistributing Partnerships | | |
Year	Overall	No / Low Debt	Mod / High Debt
1994	24.5%	20.2%	25.5%
1995	26.7%	16.7%	28.7%
1996	27.7%	21.3%	28.9%
1997	25.7%	24.2%	25.8%
1998	23.9%	22.7%	24.0%
1999	24.3%	16.7%	27.4%
2000	18.3%	16.4%	22.1%
2001	19.6%	18.3%	22.3%
2002	14.9%	14.7%	16.7%
2003	16.1%	12.5%	21.4%
2004	20.2%	14.1%	29.0%
2005	22.3%	13.6%	26.3%
Average	**22.0%**	**17.6%**	**24.8%**

EXHIBIT 8.11   Expected Returns for Nondistributing Partnerships

Venture Capital and Private Equity Returns

While some may think of "venture capital" as relating only to investments in start-up companies, the industry is much broader and well developed. Some venture capital investments fall into the early-stage or seed stage investment category; however, other investments are made in later stage enterprises. Some venture capital businesses require multiple rounds of investments as they develop over time. Other funds participate in leveraged buyouts, management buyouts, and direct investments in well-developed private companies. Still others invest in mezzanine financing, providing capital in between venture capital investors and traditional suppliers of debt capital, often requiring an "equity kicker" component to such financing. Finally, some funds invest in a combination of investment categories.

Thompson Venture Economics, in conjunction with the National Venture Capital Association, provides historical return data for a variety of venture capital investment categories. Exhibit 8.12 summarizes returns for various historical periods as of June 30, 2006.[15]

These statistics represent average realized returns. These averages are the result of many investments, all of which were made based on expected

---

[15]The data for this table was downloaded on December 27, 2006. The cited information was located at: http://www.thomson.com/pdf/financial/news_release_pdfs/2006_10_30_Q206_PE_Performance.

EXHIBIT 8.12 Venture Economics' U.S. Private Equity Performance Index (PEPI)[*]

Fund Type	Investment Horizon Performance through June 30, 2006				
	1 Yr	3 Yr	5 Yr	10 Yr	20 Yr
Early/Seed VC	11.2%	5.4%	−7.6%	36.9%	20.5%
Balanced VC	20.5%	12.5%	−0.2%	17.0%	14.5%
Later Stage VC	16.4%	9.4%	−1.1%	9.5%	13.7%
All Venture	**16.2%**	**9.0%**	**−3.5%**	**20.8%**	**16.5%**
Small Buyouts	12.1%	9.6%	3.7%	7.1%	25.9%
Medium Buyouts	21.5%	11.8%	5.0%	11.1%	16.1%
Large Buyouts	26.8%	15.8%	6.3%	8.6%	12.5%
Mega Buyouts	28.5%	17.5%	7.2%	8.9%	11.6%
All Buyouts	**27.3%**	**16.3%**	**6.6%**	**8.9%**	**13.4%**
Mezzanine	9.7%	5.3%	2.6%	6.2%	8.7%
All Private Equity	**22.5%**	**13.4%**	**3.6%**	**11.4%**	**14.2%**
NASDAQ	5.6%	10.2%	0.0%	6.2%	11.7%
S & P 500	6.6%	9.2%	0.7%	6.6%	9.8%
All Venture Premiums[**]					
Over NASDAQ	10.6%	−1.2%	−3.5%	14.6%	4.8%
Over S & P 500	9.6%	−0.2%	−4.2%	14.2%	6.7%
All Private Equity Premiums[**]					
Over NASDAQ	16.9%	3.2%	3.6%	5.2%	2.5%
Over S & P 500	15.9%	4.2%	2.9%	4.8%	4.4%

[*]*Source: Thompson Venture Economics / National Venture Capital Association* The Private Equity Performance Index is based on the latest quarterly statistics from Thompson Venture Economics' Private Equity Performance Database analyzing cash flows and returns for over 1,862 U.S. venture capital and private equity partnerships with a capitalization of $679 billion. Returns are net to investors after management fees and carried interests.
[**]*Premium calculations by author*

returns. Because many venture capital investments fail completely and represent total losses for investors, the expected returns at the initial time of investment likely exceeded the average realized returns.

Note the caption "All Private Equity Premiums" at the bottom of Exhibit 8.12. Private equity performance has exceeded that of the NASDAQ and the S&P 500 over the past one, three, five, ten, and twenty years. The premiums in terms of rates of return have been on the order of 3% to 5% in all but the most recent year, when private equity returns were outstanding.

This venture capital data should provide comfort that expected returns for illiquid investments in privately owned business enterprises generally should be in the range from the high teens to the low-to-mid twenties, or possibly higher in appropriate circumstances.

Estimating the Required Holding Period Return

In this section, we review several of the specific shareholder level risks that contribute to the estimated holding period premium. Interestingly, nearly all of them are discussed in the various restricted stock studies. The specific shareholder level risks include:

- *Uncertainty of holding period*. Investors demand additional compensation for bearing the risk of a long and indeterminate probable holding period. To the extent that the holding period can be fixed, or its uncertainty reduced, there is some mitigation of risk. Long expected holding periods without marketability leave investors exposed to adverse changes in either the subject company or their own circumstances. Rational investors desire a premium return relative to alternative investments that are readily marketable.[16]
- *Likelihood of interim cash flows*. The dividend yield can be a powerful influence on the size of the appropriate marketability discount. Although

---

[16]In a 2001 paper, "Firm Value and Marketability Discounts," (Fall 2001, *Journal of Corporation Law*, Volume 27, Issue 1, pp. 89–115) Mukesh Bajaj (and his co-authors David J. Dennis, Stephen P. Ferris, and Atulya Sarin) suggest that there may be a "clientele effect" at work that minimizes the impact of the expected holding period on value. "... Because buyers of the restricted shares tend to be institutional investors that do not value liquidity highly (e.g., life insurance companies and pension funds), it seems unlikely that such investors would require substantial marketability discounts for the commitments not to resell quickly." The discussion in the Bajaj article was actually referencing another article. See Hertzel, Michael, and Smith, Richard L., "Market Discounts and Shareholder Gains for Placing Equity Privately," 48 *Journal of Finance* 459, 459–469 (1993). In both of these papers, regression analyses were performed that isolated the impact of registration among other factors (13.2% in the case of Hertzel & Smith and 7.2% in the case of Bajaj, et al.). Readers should be aware that the average total restricted stock discounts in the studies were 20.1% and 22.2%, respectively. Factors discussed that account for differences between the "liquidity" portion and the total discounts include information costs, monitoring costs, and financial distress (i.e., creating additional risk over a period of illiquidity). These are the kinds of factors we are attempting to capture with the QMDM in order to estimate appropriate *total marketability discounts* from freely traded valuation indications.

some companies have long track records of regular and predictable dividends, those that do not add a particular element of risk to the (total) return to be expected by the hypothetical willing investor. In other words, the total return is deferred until a liquidity event that will occur at an indeterminate time in the future. As a result, we believe it is appropriate to add an increment of required return if there are limited or no prospects for regular dividends from an investment. Two additional comments are necessary here:

1. There is commonly some incremental uncertainty regarding interim cash flows with tax pass-through entities (such as S corporations, limited partnerships, and limited liability corporations). The possibility that there are taxable earnings at the business level and cash distributions insufficient to enable the holders to fully cover their personal tax liabilities is real.[17]

2. The appraiser should consider the actual historical record of shareholder dividends as well as the outlook for future dividends in assessing these risks, while acknowledging that minority shareholders do not determine dividend policy.

- *Prospects for marketability.* Is the subject company a likely IPO candidate? Is it likely to be attractive as an acquisition candidate? And what is happening in the industry that could encourage a sale of the entire business? Does management have any plans to sell the company? Considering the history of the business, what is the likelihood it will be sold? If the prospects for marketability look poor, it may be necessary to provide an enhancement to the required holding period return.

- *Uncertainty regarding a favorable exit.* If and when the subject interest becomes marketable, what is the likelihood of being "squeezed" or discounted? If the past practices of the company suggest that minority shareholders have been disadvantaged, there is a greater likelihood that such behavior will occur in the future. It is important to consider the actual history of transactions at the minority level in assessing the probability of an unfavorable exit. Further, minority shareholders are seldom in a position to assure that optimal pricing is obtained when entire companies are sold.

- *Restrictive agreements.* Many private companies have shareholder agreements or charter provisions that restrict (or enhance) the transfer of their shares. This is an important source of risk (or risk reduction) for hypothetical and real buyers of those interests. Many restrictive

---

[17]Agreements requiring tax liability distributions can, of course, minimize the risks associated with mismatches between personal liability for entity taxes and actual distributions.

agreements, even the fairly common "right of first refusal" clauses, which normally provide an option for shareholders or a company to acquire shares at an offered price before they are free for transfer, can have a chilling effect on the prospects for marketability.

Why? Simply put, it takes a lot of work and analysis to understand a private company. The due diligence undertaken by sophisticated investors is time-consuming and costly. Why go to the effort to evaluate an investment when, if the proposed price is favorable to you, the shares will likely be acquired by insiders? If the price is not going to be favorable, one would not buy it anyway. Such restrictions can have a significant impact on the required holding period return.[18]

■ *Information costs and monitoring costs.* As noted in the discussion of restrictive agreements, there are very real costs involved in preparing to invest in business enterprises. In many cases, there is no future opportunity to recoup either the real costs of investigation for the investment or the expected ongoing costs of monitoring the investment. As result, investors require an element of premium return that is manifest in a larger discount to the enterprise value.[19]

This list is not exhaustive, and is expanded upon in the *QMDM Companion.* If other facts and circumstances indicate any other specific shareholder level risks, they should be considered by appraisers when developing the required holding period return.

The Framework for Estimating the Required Holding Period Returns

The challenge facing appraisers using a shareholder level discounted cash flow model is translating the identified shareholder risks into a range of holding period premiums. In our experience, there are no simple shortcuts.

■ *Appraiser experience and judgment.* Experience in seeing a variety of valuation facts and circumstances and in seeing how conclusions of value relate to each other can be very helpful. However, the term "in my professional judgment" lacks significance unless it can be supported based on facts and circumstances and external evidence. Practice does not make perfect if the practice techniques are flawed.

---

[18]See the discussion in Chapter 9 regarding recent changes in *USPAP* requiring analysis of the effect on value, if any, of restrictions on transfer.
[19]Ibid.

- *Common sense.* Appraisers must employ basic common sense in the judgments that they make. For example, common sense will dictate that two investments, one growing in value at 6% with no dividends, and the other growing in value at 6% and with a 6% annual dividend yield, should have materially different marketability discounts over similar expected holding periods. The fact that traditional benchmark analysis did not provide any basis to draw such distinctions and we knew that such differences had to exist led us to develop the Quantitative Marketability Discount Model.

- *Reasonableness.* Common sense and reasonableness often go hand in hand. Revenue Ruling 59–60 admonishes appraisers to employ the "critical three" factors of common sense, informed judgment, and reasonableness. When marketability discounts are developed using the QMDM, the reasonableness of the concluded value can be assessed by calculating implied dividend yields, by calculating implied returns over a range of holding periods, or by making other relevant comparisons.

- *Comparisons with returns implied by the various restricted stock studies.* While the average discounts in any restricted stock study are irrelevant for purposes of assessing marketability discounts (because of lack of comparability of businesses, time, expected holding periods, and other factors), we have previously discussed how the implied required returns (and expected holding periods) can be inferred from the average discounts in the studies.

- *Comparisons with other market evidence.* Current and historical market return data are available for transactions in publicly traded real estate limited partnerships in publications of *Partnership Profiles*. In addition, market evidence is available regarding venture capital and private equity funds. The expected returns from these sources provide another reference point to test the validity of assumed shareholder-specific risk premia and, therefore, required holding period returns.

Ultimately, holding period premiums are analogous to the company-specific risk premiums used to derive enterprise discount rates. Most appraisers are comfortable estimating such company-specific risk premiums. There are no studies to help appraisers make such estimates. Nevertheless, appraisers make reasonable assumptions in the context of their experience, judgment, common sense, reasonableness, and comparisons with alternative returns available in the marketplace.

Methodology for Developing the Required Holding Period Return

Exhibit 8.13 is developed from the template tab in the *QMDM Companion* labeled *Exhibit – Assumption #4 - R_{hp}*. More than twenty potential risk

QUANTITATIVE MARKETABILITY DISCOUNT MODEL (QMDM)
QMDM ASSUMPTION #4
Required Holding Period Return (Shareholder-Level Discount Rate)
(Using the Adjusted Capital Asset Pricing Model)

	Components of the Required Holding Period Return		Estimated Range Lower	Estimated Range Higher	Source/Brief Rationale
1	Long-Term Government Bond Yield-to-Maturity		5.50%	5.50%	
2	Ibbotson Common Stock Premium	6.00%			
3	× Market Beta	1.00			
4	= Beta Adjusted Common Stock Premium	6.00%			As developed in text
5	+ Small Cap Stock Premium	3.00%			
6	'+ Specific Company Risk	2.00%			
7	= Total Equity Premium		11.00%	11.00%	
8	**Base Holding Period Required Return**		16.50%	16.50%	<> Base equity discount rate

Investor-Specific Risk Premium(s) for This Investment:

		Lower	Higher	
9	+ Uncertainties of Expected Holding Period	1.00%	2.00%	Per Text
10	+ Information Acquisition Cost Premium	1.00%	1.00%	Per Text
11	+ Premium for Expected Holding Period Monitoring Costs	0.50%	0.50%	Per Text
12	+ Adjustment for Large Size of the Interest	0.50%	1.00%	Per Text
13	+ Rights of First Refusal Limiting Transferability (ROFR)	0.50%	1.00%	Per Text
14	+ Uncertainties due to Potential for Unfavorable Exit	0.00%	0.00%	
15	+ Potential for Adverse Cash Flow	0.00%	0.00%	
16	+ More Onerous Restrictions on Transfer	0.00%	0.00%	
17	+ Lack of Diversification of Assets	0.00%	0.00%	
18	+ Unattractive Asset Mix	0.00%	0.00%	
19	+ Uncertainties Due to Risks of Future Investment Strategies	0.00%	0.00%	
20	+ Unlikely Candidate for Merger/Sale/Acquisition/IPO	0.00%	0.00%	Other potential investor risks
21	− Likely Candidate for Merger/Sale/Acquisition	0.00%	0.00%	
22	+ Uncertainties Related to Buy-Sell Agreement	0.00%	0.00%	
23	+ Restrictions on Use as Loan Collateral	0.00%	0.00%	
24	+ Small Shareholder Base	0.00%	0.00%	
25	+ Lack of Expected Interim Cash Flows	0.00%	0.00%	
26	+ General Illiquidity of the Investment	0.00%	0.00%	
27	+ Other	0.00%	0.00%	
28	**Total Investor-Specific Risk Premium for This Entity**	3.50%	5.50%	Sum of above
29	Estimated Range of Required Holding Period Returns	20.00%	22.00%	Enterprise discount rate plus shareholder risks
30	Rounded Range	20.00%	22.00%	To Nearest 0.5%
31	**Mid-Point of Estimated Required Holding Period Return Range**		21.0%	Assumption #4 of the QMDM

EXHIBIT 8.13 Calculation of Required Holding Period Return

factors are shown in the Exhibit, together with some general comments about the factors. The list (with analytical and practical comments) is provided in the QMDM *Companion* as a beginning checklist for appraisers as they consider the specific facts and circumstances of valuation situations.

The beginning point for the development of the required holding period return is the enterprise discount rate. An equity discount rate of 16.5% is developed on Exhibit 8.13 (Lines 1–8) as described in Chapter 6 using the Adjusted Capital Asset Pricing Model. To this base enterprise discount rate we add increments of risk (holding period premiums) based on specific risks associated with the subject investment.

The Exhibit provides an example of the required holding period return build-up for the QMDM. In the example, five specific factors have been considered (Lines 9 to 13). These include uncertainties related to a holding period of unknown length, information and expected monitoring costs, the fact that no distributions are expected from the investment, and a premium because the right of first refusal applicable to the shares has a dampening impact on their marketability. In an appraisal report, the rows showing the factors not selected would likely not be shown.

Note that we have developed a range of holding period returns based upon the specific risk factors noted in the Exhibit. This is intentional, reflecting the uncertainties facing our hypothetical buyer regarding liquidity and other issues. Note further that specific risk factors were picked for each of the five shareholder risks. There are no studies to provide guidance or market evidence for the shareholder-specific risk factors, so appraisers must estimate them exercising common sense, judgment, and reasonableness. We have previously considered the magnitude of returns suggested by the restricted stock studies, which is also helpful. But it is important to reiterate that these judgments are analogous to those made by appraisers every day in the development of enterprise discount rates.

Exhibit 8.13 anticipates an example used in Chapter 9. The example corporation is a C corporation and the subject interest is a 20% minority interest. The company has been valued at $10 million. The specific investor-specific risk factors used in the example include the following:

- *Uncertainties of the expected holding period.* This is a general risk factor that takes into account that the expected holding period is of uncertain length. We often consider this factor as adding 1% to 3% or so of required return to the base discount rate.
- *Information acquisition cost premium.* It takes a lot of work to develop an understanding of a closely held business enterprise and the facts and circumstances surrounding an investment in it. With nonmarketable investments there is normally no other source of recovery of information costs than through an increase in the required return.
- *Expected holding period monitoring costs.* A related cost to that of information access is the cost of monitoring the investment on an ongoing basis. Again, the only opportunity to recover costs is through an increase in the required return.
- *Large size of the interest.* Fair market value presumes agreement between a willing buyer and a willing seller. It is necessary for the appraiser to consider the relevant pool of buyers and sellers in this context. This subject interest has a marketable minority value of $2.0 million (20% interest times $10 million enterprise value), which means that, after the application of a marketability discount, it is likely to have a value in excess of $1.0 million. This large size (value) of the interest limits the available pool of buyers to individuals or institutions who can commit such amounts of their portfolio to nonmarketable investments for potentially long holding periods.

■ *Right of first refusal limits transferability.* The subject company has a right of first refusal, which further limits the marketability of the subject interest. This component of return provides compensation for this fact.

Note that specific judgments are reflected in the estimation of investor-specific risk premiums. In this example, we have developed a range of holding period premiums of 3.5% to 5.5%, yielding a range of required holding period returns of 20% to 22%, with a midpoint of 21%. Recall the formula discussed earlier: $R_{hp} = R + HPP$. So where did the components of 3.5% to 5.5% come from? They are developed in the context of the facts and circumstances of the subject valuation and in the context of alternative rates of return that we have been discussing in this chapter.

To put these risk assessments into perspective, we note what two valuation texts have to say about the similar risk assessments made by appraisers when adding company-specific risk components to their enterprise discount rates:

> To the extent that the subject company's risk characteristics are greater or less than the typical risk characteristics of the companies from which the equity risk premium and the size premium were drawn, a further adjustment may be necessary to estimate the cost of capital for the specific company. Such adjustments may be based on (but not necessarily limited to) analysis of five factors:
>
> 1. *Size smaller than the smallest size premium group*
> 2. *Industry risk*
> 3. *Volatility of returns*
> 4. *Leverage*
> 5. *Other company-specific factors . . .*
>
> Because the size premium tends to reflect some factors of this type, the analyst should adjust further only for specific items that are truly unique to the subject company. Unfortunately, despite the widespread use by analysts and appraisers of a company-specific premium in a build-up (or CAPM) model, I am not aware of any academic research on the subject, and it remains in the realm of the analyst's judgment.[20]

---

[20]Shannon P. Pratt, *Cost of Capital: Estimation and Applications, Second Edition* (Hoboken, New Jersey, Wiley & Sons, Inc., 2002), p. 65, 67.

Another text states the following:

> ... *It must be emphasized, however, that the use of such tools [referring to a build-up including several enterprise components like the investor components in Exhibit 8.9 and a less quantitative table] is subjective in nature without a direct formula or correlation table to quantify the required adjustment to capture the additional returns required for such risks* ...

> *Such an analytical framework is only a diagnostic tool to assist the practitioner in the exercise of professional judgment. No formulas, guidelines, or rules of thumb can be relied on consistently to derive indications of unsystematic risk for a specific enterprise.*[21]

The point of this digression to discuss company-specific risk factors in developing enterprise discount rates is simply this: SCR Premiums in enterprise valuations are analogous to investor-specific risk premiums that must be estimated when valuing shareholder-level cash flows. It would be inconsistent to accept appraiser judgments in enterprise discount rate development but to criticize them in shareholder-level discount rate development.

In the example in Exhibit 8.13, the concluded range of required holding period returns is from 20.0% to 22.0% (rounded). The midpoint of this range is 21.0%. In our experience in applying the QMDM several thousand times over more than a decade now, the required holding period returns have ranged from lows in the middle-to-upper teens (relatively low perceived shareholder risks) for attractive, asset-oriented holding companies, to around 30% for operating companies with particularly unattractive shareholder characteristics.

The midpoint estimate of the required holding period return can be carried forward to the template/tab labeled *Exhibit – Summary QMDM Analysis* in the *QMDM Companion* as the fourth of the basic assumptions of the QMDM.

Review of QMDM Assumptions

The QMDM is a standardized shareholder level discounted cash flow model applicable to the valuation of minority interests in private companies. The required assumptions for using the model correspond to those required

---

[21]James A. Hitchner, Editor, *Financial Valuation: Applications and Models* (Hoboken, New Jersey, John Wiley & Sons, Inc., 2003), p. 146.

to develop an enterprise level discounted cash flow model. Moreover, the sensitivity of the conclusion of value developed using the QMDM is subject to the same sensitivities as the enterprise level discounted cash flow model.

The following table outlines the sensitivity of the QMDM to changes in the various assumptions. Note that the sensitivities are discussed relative to the nonmarketable minority interest value, not the marketability discount.

Shareholder Level DCF (QMDM) Inputs	Sensitivity
1. Range of Expected Holding Periods	Longer holding periods without marketability lead to lower nonmarketable minority values
2a. Expected Distribution/ Dividend Yield	The value of the subject interest is positively related to the expected level of interim cash flows
2b. Expected Growth in Distributions/Dividends	The value of the subject interest is positively related to the expected growth in interim cash flows
2c. Timing (Mid-Year or End of Year)	The value of the subject interest is higher under the mid-year convention
3a. Growth in Value over Holding Period	Higher growth in value leads to higher terminal values and a higher present value for the subject interest
3b. Premium or Discount to Projected Enterprise Value	Premiums increase the value of the subject interest; discounts decrease the value
4. Range of Required Holding Period Returns	The value of the subject interest is inversely related to the discount rate

We recommend that users of the QMDM experiment with different combinations of assumptions to develop greater insight into the sensitivity of the concluded value of the subject interest.

CHAPTER 9

Applying the QMDM

INTRODUCTION

The assumptions of the shareholder level discounted cash flow model are applicable to all valuation scenarios. Specifying them forces the appraiser (and the reader of the appraisal report) to address the underlying economic factors giving rise to the marketability discount. Differences of opinion are likely to exist with respect to the estimation of one or more of the parameters, but the QMDM framework pushes the parties to analyze the specific facts and circumstances of the subject interest and carefully support their assumptions.

This chapter is comprised of three sections. The first is a comprehensive example of applying the QMDM to the valuation of a subject nonmarketable minority interest using the *QMDM Companion*. The second section provides five condensed examples of the QMDM applied to nonmarketable minority shareholder interests with markedly different economic characteristics. The third section discusses the QMDM in the context of recent changes to the *Uniform Standards of Professional Appraisal Practice*.

COMPREHENSIVE EXAMPLE OF THE QMDM IN USE

In this section, we walk through using the QMDM to estimate the marketability discount for a hypothetical nonmarketable minority interest. First, recall the seven inputs to the shareholder level discounted cash flow model, as shown in Exhibit 9.1.

With these general inputs in mind, we can review an example appraisal situation and develop appropriate assumptions for the QMDM based on the specific facts and circumstances related to the subject company and to the particular subject interest. Assume the following background:

- The appraiser has just completed an appraisal of a C corporation operating company that values the enterprise at $10.0 million, or $1.00 per share at the marketable minority level of value. The company expects

Enterprise Level DCF Assumptions	Shareholder Level DCF (QMDM) Assumptions
1. Forecast Period	1. Range of Expected Holding Periods
2. Projected Interim Cash Flows (during forecast period)	2a. Expected Distribution / Dividend Yield 2b. Expected Growth in Distributions / Dividends 2c. Timing (Mid-Year or End of Year)
3. Projected Terminal Value (at end of forecast period)	3a. Growth in Value over Holding Period 3b. Premium or Discount to Projected Enterprise Value
4. Discount Rate	4. Range of Required Holding Period Returns

EXHIBIT 9.1   Enterprise and Shareholder Level DCF Assumptions

net earnings of $1.0 million for the next year. It was valued based on an enterprise discount rate of 16% and expected growth in earnings of 6%($1.0 million/(16% − 10%) = $10.0 million). The company has equity of $6.7 million (and a return on equity of 15%). The valuation represents 10x net income, and 6x pre-tax income.

- The company makes quarterly distribution to its shareholders equal to 40% of annual net earnings (Assumption #2a). This policy was established years ago and is expected to continue. The particular company has historically not been aggressive with its reinvestment for growth and has accumulated excess assets (which were paid out in a special dividend in the year of the appraisal). No special dividends are anticipated for a number of years.
- Given the expectation that the company will be accumulating excess assets, the expected growth in value (Assumption #3a) has been estimated to be 10% (greater than the 6% expected growth in earnings but less than the 16% discount rate adjusted for the 4% dividend yield).
- Dividends are expected to grow with earnings at about 6% per year (Assumption #2b).
- The company provides annual financial statements to its minority shareholders, but that is the extent of financial disclosure. The audited financial statements are provided in about April of each year following the company's December 31 year-end. No explanations of results are provided, and there is no discussion of the outlook for the future. The interest being valued represents 20% of the ownership of the company. The pro rata share of enterprise value is $2.0 million, so this is a large block of stock that may be difficult to market (Assumption #4). It is the company's largest minority block of stock. The controlling shareholder owns 67% of the stock, and there are some forty other shareholders. There is a right of first refusal that provides opportunities for both the company and the other shareholders to purchase the block at the same

price available from a bona fide offer from outside the shareholder base. These rights tie up the shares for a period of 120 days while the company and the other shareholders review their options (Assumption #4).

■ The company is in a consolidating industry and it could be sold easily (Assumption #1). The controlling shareholder is 55 years old and he has indicated that he will retire (and sell the company) by the time he is 65 or so (Assumption #1). However, those who know him find it difficult to believe that he could ever let go of the company while he is still alive (Assumption #1).

The Specific QMDM Assumptions for the Example

Based on these assumed facts and circumstances, we will develop a valuation at the nonmarketable minority level of value using the QMDM. The specific assumptions of the QMDM for this example are summarized in Exhibit 9.2.

Assumption #1 — Range of Expected Holding Periods. Based on all the facts and circumstances, the appraiser estimated the expected holding period to be a broad range of five to ten years. This assumption was based on the fact that the controlling shareholder says he will retire in that time frame, but considers that no one in the management group believes that he will do so. It further considers that the company's industry is consolidating and that the company is an attractive consolidation candidate.

Assumption #2a — Expected Distribution / Dividend Yield. Based on the current dividend policy of distributing 40% of earnings, net earnings of $1.0 million, and a dividend payout ratio of 40%, the expected dividend is $400 thousand. Dividing this by the marketable minority value of $10 million yields the expected dividend yield of 4.0%.

Assumption #2b — Expected Growth in Distributions / Dividends. Based on history and discussions with management, the company is likely

Enterprise Level DCF Assumptions	Shareholder Level DCF (QMDM) Inputs	Model Inputs	
1. Forecast Period	1. Range of Expected Holding Periods (Years)	Low	5
		High	10
2. Projected Interim Cash Flows (during forecast period)	2a. Expected Distribution / Dividend Yield	Yield	4.0%
	2b. Expected Growth in Distributions / Dividend Yield	Growth	6.0%
	2c. Timing (Mid-Year or End of Year)	Timing	M
3. Projected Terminal Value (at end of forecast period)	3a. Growth in Value over Holding Period	G_V	10.0%
	3b. Premium or Discount to Marketable Value	Prem/Disc	0.0%
4. Discount Rate	4. Range of Required Holding Period Returns	Low	20.0%
		High	22.0%

EXHIBIT 9.2 QMDM Model Inputs

to maintain the current dividend payout ratio, suggesting that dividends are likely to grow at the same rate as earnings, or about 6.0% per year.

Assumption #2c — Timing (Mid-Year or End of Year). Dividends are projected using the mid-year convention because the company declares and distributes dividends on a quarterly basis.

Assumption #3a — Growth in Value over Holding Period. The expected growth rate in value is 10%, which was estimated to lie between the expected growth rate in earnings (from the enterprise appraisal) and the enterprise discount rate, adjusted for dividends. Note that this is a situation where the value of the business plan will be less than the value of the business because the controlling shareholder expects to reinvest retained earnings at less than the discount rate. While the controlling shareholder could sell the company today, he chooses instead to operate it in a somewhat comfortable fashion and he, too, will experience the (future) value detriment of slower than optimal value growth until he sells the company or changes operating philosophy. In other words, the controlling shareholder will experience the same expected return as the minority shareholder (10% growth in value plus 4% yield, rather than the 16% discount rate).

Assumption #3b — Premium or Discount to Marketable Minority Value. Because the appraiser made appropriate normalizing adjustments in assessing the company's marketable minority value, he believes that there would be little room for a significant control premium above the marketable minority value. No premium or discount to the marketable minority value is projected in this case.

Assumption #4 — Range of Required Holding Period Returns. We developed this required return as the example in Exhibit 8.13. The base holding period required return was 16.5%, which was developed as the equity discount rate in the enterprise appraisal. As detailed in Exhibit 9.3, the required holding period return is estimated to be 21%, which is the midpoint of a range of 20% to 22%. Specific shareholder level risk premiums were estimated based on the appraiser's analysis of the situation.

- *Uncertainties of expected holding period.* The assumed facts reflect considerable uncertainties regarding the duration of the expected holding period. A premium of 1% to 2% was added for this factor.
- *Information acquisition cost premium.* It is difficult to learn about investment situations like this example and costly to acquire the needed information. Hypothetical investors have no other means of recouping these costs other than through a premium return expectation. A premium of 1.0% is added for this factor.
- *Expected holding period monitoring costs.* This company provides only its annual report each year. Nevertheless, investors would attempt to

talk with management and to learn as much about the company's ongoing performance as possible. There is no other means of recouping these costs other than through a premium return expectation. A premium of 0.5% is added for this factor.

- *Adjustment for large size of the interest.* The interest is relatively large in dollar terms. This fact will limit the pool of prospective hypothetical buyers to those of considerable capacity. These investors tend to recognize this fact and to charge a premium return component. A premium of 0.50% to 1.00% is added for this factor.
- *Rights of first refusal limiting transferability (ROFR).* This company has a right of first refusal that taints the marketability of the subject interest. The restrictions on transfer increase the difficulty of finding future buyers of the interest. A premium of 0.50% to 1.00% is added for this factor.
- The combined investor-specific risk factors range from 3.5% to 5.5%, providing a range of required returns of 20% to 22%, and a midpoint of 21%. Recall from the discussion in Chapter 8 that this required return range and the estimated premiums lie comfortably within the range of available market evidence. We use the specified range and the midpoint in the QMDM analysis.

Exhibit 9.3 summarizes the development of the required holding period return for this example.

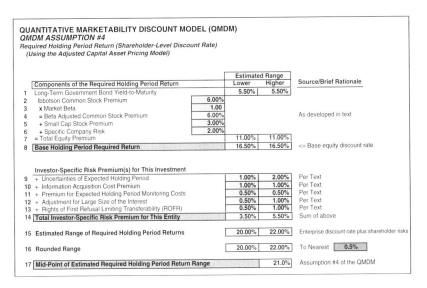

QUANTITATIVE MARKETABILITY DISCOUNT MODEL (QMDM)
QMDM ASSUMPTION #4
Required Holding Period Return (Shareholder-Level Discount Rate)
  (Using the Adjusted Capital Asset Pricing Model)

	Components of the Required Holding Period Return		Estimated Range Lower	Estimated Range Higher	Source/Brief Rationale
1	Long-Term Government Bond Yield-to-Maturity		5.50%	5.50%	
2	Ibbotson Common Stock Premium	6.00%			
3	x Market Beta	1.00			
4	= Beta Adjusted Common Stock Premium	6.00%			As developed in text
5	+ Small Cap Stock Premium	3.00%			
6	+ Specific Company Risk	2.00%			
7	= Total Equity Premium		11.00%	11.00%	
8	**Base Holding Period Required Return**		16.50%	16.50%	<> Base equity discount rate
	Investor-Specific Risk Premium(s) for This Investment				
9	+ Uncertainies of Expected Holding Period		1.00%	2.00%	Per Text
10	+ Information Acquisition Cost Premium		1.00%	1.00%	Per Text
11	+ Premium for Expected Holding Period Monitoring Costs		0.50%	0.50%	Per Text
12	+ Adjustment for Large Size of the Interest		0.50%	1.00%	Per Text
13	+ Rights of First Refusal Limiting Transferability (ROFR)		0.50%	1.00%	Per Text
14	**Total Investor-Specific Risk Premium for This Entity**		3.50%	5.50%	Sum of above
15	Estimated Range of Required Holding Period Returns		20.00%	22.00%	Enterprise discount rate plus shareholder risks
16	Rounded Range		20.00%	22.00%	To Nearest 0.5%
17	**Mid-Point of Estimated Required Holding Period Return Range**			21.0%	Assumption #4 of the QMDM

EXHIBIT 9.3 Calculation of Required Holding Period Return

The QMDM Results

Exhibit 9.4 is a portion of the full-page exhibit from the tab in the *QMDM Companion* labeled "Exhibit – Conclusion of QMDM." The appraiser's assumptions are input at the top. Implied marketability discounts are calculated for alternative holding periods. The implied range of marketability discounts for the range of discounts rates (20% to 22%) and the range of expected holding periods (five to ten years) is highlighted for reference. The appraiser's concluded marketability discount of 35% is highlighted.

The appraiser applied the 35% marketability discount and reached a conclusion of $0.65 per share ($1.00 – 35%) on a nonmarketable minority interest basis. Applying this per-share value to the enterprise, the overall value is $6.5 million at the nonmarketable minority level of value. So the nonmarketable minority conclusion represents 3.9x pre-tax earnings and 6.5x net income. The 40% dividend payout provides a total dividend of $400 thousand ($1.0 million × 40%), which further implies a dividend yield for the nonmarketable minority investor of 6.2% ($400 thousand / $6.5 million). Based on these facts and other comparisons to relevant returns in

QUANTITATIVE MARKETABILITY DISCOUNT MODEL (QMDM)
Conclusion of the Analysis

Enterprise Level DCF Assumptions	Shareholder Level DCF (QMDM) Inputs	Model Inputs	
1. Forecast Period	1. Range of Expected Holding Periods (Years)	Low	5
		High	10
2. Projected Interim Cash Flows (during forecast period)	2a. Expected Distribution / Dividend Yield	Yield	4.0%
	2b. Expected Growth in Distribution / Div. Yield	Growth	6.0%
	2c. Timing (Mid-Year or End of Year)	Timing	M
3. Projected Terminal Value (at end of forecast period)	3a. Growth in Value over Holding Period	G_v	10.0%
	3b. Premium or Discount to Marketable Value	Prem/Disc.	0.0%
4. Discount Rate	4. Range of Required Holding Period Returns	Low	20.0%
		High	22.0%
		Base Value (Marketable Minority Interest)	$1.00

Average Indicated Discounts for Selected Holding Periods (Mid-Point Return +/– 1%)

Average of 2–4 Year HP	15%	Average of 5–10 Year HP	32%
Average of 5–7 Year HP	27%	Average of 10–15 Year HP	45%
Average of 8–10 Year HP	37%	Average of 15–20 Year HP	54%
Average of 10–20 Year HP	49%		
		Concluded Marketability Discount	35%

	Assumed Holding Periods in Years													
	1	2	3	4	5	6	7	8	9	10	15	20	25	30
	Implied Marketability Discounts													
17.0%	2%	5%	7%	9%	11%	13%	15%	17%	19%	21%	30%	37%	43%	47%
18.0%	3%	6%	9%	12%	15%	17%	20%	22%	24%	27%	36%	43%	49%	53%
19.0%	4%	8%	11%	15%	18%	21%	24%	26%	29%	31%	42%	49%	54%	58%
20.0%	5%	9%	13%	17%	21%	24%	27%	30%	33%	36%	46%	54%	59%	62%
21.0%	5%	11%	15%	20%	24%	27%	31%	34%	37%	40%	51%	58%	63%	65%
22.0%	6%	12%	17%	22%	26%	31%	34%	38%	41%	44%	55%	61%	66%	68%
23.0%	7%	13%	19%	24%	29%	33%	37%	41%	44%	47%	58%	65%	68%	71%
24.0%	8%	15%	21%	27%	32%	36%	40%	44%	47%	50%	61%	67%	71%	73%
25.0%	8%	16%	23%	29%	34%	39%	43%	47%	50%	53%	64%	70%	73%	74%

Required Holding Period Return (Annual %)

PV = 100%

EXHIBIT 9.4 Example QMDM Results

his appraisal report, the appraiser concluded that his 35% marketability discount and the resulting $0.65 per share result were reasonable.

Application of the QMDM in this example resulted in the ever-popular 35% marketability discount. The differences between the QMDM example and benchmark analysis include:

- Every assumption is developed from and supported by the particular facts and circumstances of the example appraisal.
- By employing the QMDM, the appraiser is able to model the expected economics of the investment from the viewpoint of the hypothetical (or a real) buyer.
- If the facts and circumstances change at a later time when a reappraisal is needed, the appraiser has the tools to reflect those changes in his conclusion of value at the nonmarketable minority level of value.

The importance of using a shareholder level discounted cash flow model like the QMDM to develop marketability discounts can be easily illustrated by changing one assumption. In this modified case, the controlling shareholder is 62 years old and expects to sell the company or create liquidity opportunities around the age of 65. Assume now that every other aspect regarding this subject interest remains the same except that the expected holding period is reduced from five-to-ten years to two-to-four years.

Examining Exhibit 9.4, the appropriate range of marketability discounts for consideration would be 9% to 22%. The average discount in that range is 15%, which might be a reasonable conclusion under these circumstances. Absent a tool like the QMDM, the appraiser would be unable to make the distinction between the first example and the second with any objectivity or confidence.

The Conclusion Is Selected from Within a Range

Some appraisers are uncomfortable selecting the marketability discount from within a range determined by the required holding period return range and the expected holding period range. In the example, the highlighted range of marketability discounts is from 21% to 44%. Several comments are appropriate:

- *Valuation is a range concept.* The concept of negotiation implies a relevant range of negotiation. Transactions do not occur when one party or the other makes offers outside the relevant price range for consideration (unless the buyer is irrational on the high side or the seller is irrational on the low side).

- *The specified range is the relevant range for consideration.* The discount range was developed based on the best available information and considers the expected cash flows to the shareholder for the relevant expected holding period and values those cash flows at an appropriate range of required returns. The range of 21% to 44% is narrower than the alternate range of 0% to 100%.
- *The conclusion is selected from within the relevant range.* Within the specified range, a marketability discount of 35% is selected. The selection of 35% is based on the specific analysis of the facts and circumstances of the example valuation situation. There is little evidence to suggest early opportunities for marketability, so a conclusion weighted slightly above the midpoint of the five-to-ten-year range of discounts is appropriate.

At this point, we have selected a marketability discount of 35% for the initial set of assumptions. We have made this selection after carefully developing each of the seven assumptions of the QMDM. What more can we do to help assess the reasonableness of this conclusion?

Recall that the discounted cash flow model is a rate of return model. We forecast expected cash flows (and their growth) and assess the risk of achieving those cash flows, whether at the enterprise or the shareholder levels. Discounting the expected cash flows to the present at an appropriate discount rate yields present value.

If we turn the model around and begin with present value, while knowing the expected cash flows, we can derive the implied rate of return from those cash flows. This type of analysis is referred to as internal rate of return ("IRR") analysis. The question in capital budgeting, of course, is whether a project's expected cash flows will justify the cost of investing in it. So companies derive expected IRRs for projects and compare them to their required rates of return, i.e., their costs of capital.

We can perform IRR analysis to assess the reasonableness of the concluded discount. The concluded marketability discount specifies the price at the nonmarketable minority level of value. Given the price and the expected cash flows, we can examine the rates of return that would be achieved by investors purchasing an interest at the concluded price over a range of expected holding periods. In addition, we can observe prospective returns given different marketability discounts.

Exhibit 9.5, which is a portion of the tab in the *QMDM Companion* called "Exhibit – Conclusion of the Analysis" summarizes the results of this analysis.

The shaded area of Exhibit 9.5 reflects the rates of return that would be (expected to be) achieved by an investor acquiring the subject interest at the

RETURNS EXPECTED TO BE REALIZED OVER VARIOUS HOLDING PERIODS GIVEN MARKETABILITY DISCOUNT SELECTED													
1.25% *Selected Discount Increment*													
				Subsequent Holding Period in Years									
1	2	3	4	5	6	7	8	9	10	15	20	25	30
30.0% 64%	38%	30%	26%	23%	22%	21%	20%	19%	19%	17%	16%	15%	15%
31.3% 68%	39%	30%	26%	24%	22%	21%	20%	20%	19%	17%	16%	16%	15%
32.5% 71%	40%	31%	27%	24%	23%	21%	21%	20%	19%	17%	16%	16%	15%
33.8% 74%	42%	32%	28%	25%	23%	22%	21%	20%	20%	18%	17%	16%	15%
35.0% 77%	43%	33%	28%	25%	24%	22%	21%	20%	20%	18%	17%	16%	15%
36.3% 81%	44%	34%	29%	26%	24%	23%	22%	21%	20%	18%	17%	16%	16%
37.5% 85%	46%	35%	30%	27%	25%	23%	22%	21%	20%	18%	17%	16%	16%
38.8% 89%	48%	36%	30%	27%	25%	23%	22%	21%	21%	18%	17%	16%	16%
40.0% 93%	49%	37%	31%	28%	25%	24%	23%	22%	21%	19%	17%	17%	16%

(Left axis label: Discount Applied)

EXHIBIT 9.5 Expected Rates of Return

concluded nonmarketable minority value over the expected holding period of five to ten years. Are these expected results reasonable in the context of fair market value (or for a specific investor's investment value)?

- The required return range of 20% to 22% would be achieved over a span of from seven to ten years. This seems reasonable given the fact that there is little evidence to suggest that marketability would be achieved earlier that that.
- An expected return of 24% to 25% would be achieved if the actual holding period were five to six years. This is higher than the required return, but there is little expectation of achieving marketability within the early portion of the expected holding period.
- If marketability were achieved in say, years two or three, very high rates of return would be achieved. However, there is little evidence suggesting that this would occur. If marketability were expected at this early stage, hypothetical willing sellers would demand a higher price (and a lower marketability discount) than 35%.
- What about longer holding periods? The pricing at the 35% marketability discount assures that investors would achieve 15% to 18% returns even if the expected holding period stretched to twenty or even thirty years. While this return range is shy of the required (going in) return, it nevertheless provides downside risk protection for the hypothetical willing buyer.
- Finally, we note the sensitivity of expected returns to changes in the price (i.e., the marketability discount).
  - If we assume a lower marketability discount, say 30%, the expected returns over the five-to-ten-year expected holding period are only 19% to 23%. The only way that the hypothetical investor could achieve the required return range of 20% to 22% would be to hope for a relatively short holding period, which the facts and circumstances do not support.

○ Now assume a higher marketability discount of, say, 40%. The expected returns over the five-to-ten-year period are 21% to 28%. While this expectation would be fine for the hypothetical buyers of the interest, it is likely a bit rich for the hypothetical sellers.

The QMDM is a shareholder level discounted cash flow method. The calculated range of marketability discounts in Exhibit 9.4 is nothing more than a sensitivity table enabling the appraiser or reader of appraisal reports to understand the sensitivity of the conclusion to relevant changes in key assumptions. And the calculated range of implied returns in Exhibit 9.5 is another sensitivity table relating the concluded marketability discount (price) with prospective returns across a range of expected holding periods. Both of these tools are part of the *QMDM Companion* included with this book.

In the final analysis, the use of the QMDM enables appraisers to make important valuation judgments regarding nonmarketable minority investments based on facts and circumstances pertinent to each valuation situation. If the assumptions are reasonable and the tests of reasonableness are confirming, the conclusions reached should also be reasonable.

CONDENSED QMDM EXAMPLES

Five condensed examples of the QMDM in use are provided for perspective and to illustrate the ability of appraisers using the model to consistently and logically address different fact patterns. We make no effort in these examples to develop the assumptions fully, but they are reasonable based on the facts and assumptions underlying each example. The examples include:

1. An unleveraged family limited partnership holding land.
2. An unleveraged family limited partnership holding commercial real estate and providing high distributions.
3. A leveraged family limited partnership holding commercial real estate.
4. A rapidly growing C corporation paying no dividends.
5. A mature C corporation with potential for near-term sale.

Example #1: An Unleveraged Family Limited Partnership Holding Land

In our first example, a real estate limited partnership owns raw land that is expected to grow in value at about 6% per year according to the real estate appraiser. The expected holding period is fairly lengthy, eight to ten

QUANTITATIVE MARKETABILITY DISCOUNT MODEL (QMDM)
Conclusion of the Analysis
Nonleveraged Family Limited Partnership
Principal Asset: Real Estate

Enterprise Level DCF Assumptions	Shareholder Level DCF (QMDM) Inputs	Model Inputs	
1. Forecast Period	1. Range of Expected Holding Periods (Years)	Low	8
		High	10
2. Projected Interim Cash Flows (during forecast period)	2a. Expected Distribution / Dividend Yield	Yield	0.0%
	2b. Expected Growth in Distribution / Div. Yield	Growth	0.0%
	2c. Timing (Mid-Year or End of Year)	Timing	E
3. Projected Terminal Value (at end of forecast period)	3a. Growth in Value over Holding Period	G_v	6.0%
	3b. Premium or Discount to Marketable Value	Prem/Disc.	11.1%
4. Discount Rate	4. Range of Required Holding Period Returns	Low	19.0%
		High	21.0%
		Base Value (Marketable Minority Interest)	$1.00

Average Indicated Discounts for Selected Holding Periods (Mid-Point Return +/– 1%)

Average of 2–4 Year HP	23%	Average of 5–10 Year HP	55%
Average of 5–7 Year HP	47%	Average of 10–15 Year HP	75%
Average of 8–10 Year HP	63%	Average of 15–20 Year HP	87%
Average of 10–20 Year HP	80%		
		Concluded Marketability Discount	65%

				Assumed Holding Periods in Years										
Required Holding Period Return (Annual %)	1	2	3	4	5	6	7	8	9	10	15	20	25	30
	Implied Marketability Discounts													
16.0%	-	7%	15%	23%	29%	35%	41%	46%	51%	55%	71%	82%	88%	93%
17.0%	-	9%	17%	25%	32%	39%	44%	50%	54%	59%	75%	85%	91%	94%
18.0%	0%	10%	19%	28%	35%	42%	48%	53%	58%	62%	78%	87%	92%	96%
19.0%	1%	12%	21%	30%	38%	44%	51%	56%	61%	65%	80%	89%	94%	97%
20.0%	2%	13%	23%	32%	40%	47%	53%	59%	64%	68%	83%	91%	95%	97%
21.0%	3%	15%	25%	35%	43%	50%	56%	61%	66%	70%	85%	92%	96%	98%
22.0%	3%	16%	27%	37%	45%	52%	58%	64%	69%	73%	87%	93%	97%	98%
23.0%	4%	17%	29%	39%	47%	54%	61%	66%	71%	75%	88%	94%	97%	99%
24.0%	5%	19%	31%	41%	49%	57%	63%	68%	73%	77%	89%	95%	98%	99%

PV = 100%

EXHIBIT 9.6   QMDM Results: Example #1

years. Liquidity will likely come as development approaches the properties. The appraiser has determined that a required holding period return of 20% is appropriate, partially because of burdensome features of the limited partnership agreement. There are no dividends, with the property generating just enough cash flow to pay expected expenses. The results of the QMDM calculations for this example are shown in Exhibit 9.6.

Under the indicated assumptions, the midpoint marketability discount for the eight-to-ten-year expected holding period is 64%. The appraiser concluded that the appropriate marketability discount was 65%. Such a discount would be appropriate for an investment with the described characteristics. This is a very large marketability discount in relationship to the means and medians of restricted stock studies (although well within the range of discounts found in the studies).

The concluded marketability discount of 65% in this example is large, for specific reasons however. Prospective investors are faced with a quite long (eight to ten years) expected holding period with no interim cash flows. Relative to more attractive investments with interim cash flows, the discount should be larger.

For perspective, we can consider an alternate set of assumptions. Examining Exhibit 9.6, the appropriate marketability discount for a two to four year holding period would have been about 25%. As this simple illustration demonstrates, appraisers cannot ignore the outlook for the expected holding period or the growth potential of the underlying assets when valuing nonmarketable minority interests in asset-holding entities.

Example #2: An Unleveraged Family Limited Partnership Holding Commercial Real Estate and Providing High Distributions

In our second example, a family limited partnership holds an attractive, well-maintained, high-occupancy apartment building. The property value is expected to grow at about 3% to 4% per year per the real estate appraisers. The partners receive distributions of 10% (of pro rata value) per year, and rent increases suggest that distributions will grow at 3% to 4% per year. There is a long history of distributions, which are expected to continue. The expected holding period is 10 to 15 years based on current family ownership and long-term plans. The required holding period return of 17% is mitigated by the high level and predictability of distributions. The results of the QMDM calculations for this example are shown in Exhibit 9.7.

Under the indicated assumptions, the highlighted range of marketability discounts reflects required holding period return range of 16% to 18% and a 10-to-15-year expected holding period. The calculated range is 9% to 22%. Within that range, the appraiser selected the average, or 15% as the appropriate marketability discount. Relative to Example #1, the substantial impact of the interim cash flows on the value of the subject interest is evident.

Interestingly, Example #2 reflects the assumptions made and the conclusion reached by one appraiser using the QMDM for the partnership valued in *Weinberg*.[1] The Court concluded that a 20% discount was warranted. In that decision, the Court commented that small changes in assumptions using

---

[1] *Estate of Etta H. Weinberg, et al., v. Commissioner*, T.C. Memo. 2000-51. In *Weinberg*, the Court made a hypothetical calculation and increased the expected holding period by five years from 10-to-15 years to 15-to-20 years, and increased the discount rate by 3%. The combination of these changes would have increased the calculated marketability discount from 15% (used by one appraiser) to 30%. Big changes in DCF assumptions create big changes in results. See also Mercer Capital's *E-Law Newsletter* 2000-03 & 04, "*Weinberg et al. v. Commissioner* - It's Not About the Marketability Discount," March 13, 2000 (www.mercercapital.com) and "It's Not About Marketability, It's About Minority Interest," *Valuation Strategies*, July/August 2000.

QUANTITATIVE MARKETABILITY DISCOUNT MODEL (QMDM)
Conclusion of the Analysis
Unleveraged Family Limited Partnership
Principal Asset: Cash Flowing Commercial Real Estate

Enterprise Level DCF Assumptions	Shareholder Level DCF (QMDM) Inputs	Model Inputs	
1. Forecast Period	1. Range of Expected Holding Periods (Years)	Low	10
		High	15
2. Projected Interim Cash Flows (during forecast period)	2a. Expected Distribution / Dividend Yield	Yield	10.0%
	2b. Expected Growth in Distribution / Div. Yield	Growth	3.5%
	2c. Timing (Mid-Year or End of Year)	Timing	M
3. Projected Terminal Value (at end of forecast period)	3a. Growth in Value over Holding Period	G_v	3.5%
	3b. Premium or Discount to Marketable Value	Prem/Disc.	0.0%
4. Discount Rate	4. Range of Required Holding Period Returns	Low	16.0%
		High	18.0%
		Base Value (Marketable Minority Interest)	$1.00

Average Indicated Discounts for Selected Holding Periods (Mid-Point Return +/– 1%)

Average of 2–4 Year HP	6%	Average of 5–10 Year HP	12%
Average of 5–7 Year HP	10%	Average of 10–15 Year HP	15%
Average of 8–10 Year HP	13%	Average of 15–20 Year HP	17%
Average of 10–20 Year HP	16%		
		Concluded Marketability Discount	15%

Required Holding Period Return (Annual %)	Assumed Holding Periods in Years													
	1	2	3	4	5	6	7	8	9	10	15	20	25	30
	Implied Marketability Discounts													
13.0%	-	-	-	-	-	-	-	-	-	-	-	-	-	-
14.0%	-	-	-	-	-	-	-	-	-	-	-	-	-	-
15.0%	1%	1%	2%	2%	3%	3%	4%	4%	4%	4%	5%	6%	6%	6%
16.0%	1%	3%	4%	5%	6%	7%	8%	8%	9%	9%	11%	12%	13%	13%
17.0%	2%	4%	6%	8%	9%	10%	11%	12%	13%	14%	17%	18%	19%	19%
18.0%	3%	6%	8%	10%	12%	14%	15%	16%	17%	18%	22%	23%	24%	25%
19.0%	4%	7%	10%	13%	15%	17%	18%	20%	21%	22%	26%	28%	29%	29%
20.0%	5%	9%	12%	15%	18%	20%	22%	23%	25%	26%	30%	32%	33%	33%
21.0%	5%	10%	14%	17%	20%	23%	25%	26%	28%	29%	34%	36%	36%	37%

PV = 100%

EXHIBIT 9.7 QMDM Results: Example #2

the QMDM can yield large changes in results, which some have viewed as a criticism of the model. This comment should instead be interpreted as a caution against the use of inadequately supported assumptions in any discounted cash flow model (whether at the shareholder or enterprise level of value).

Example #3: A Leveraged Family Limited Partnership Holding Commercial Real Estate

The family limited partnership in this example owns the same attractive, well-maintained, high-occupancy apartment building as in the prior example. In this case, however, there is a ten-year mortgage against the property with a current principal balance equal to 50% of the property value. After debt service payments, the remaining cash flow available for distribution to the partners represents a 3.5% yield on the marketable minority value of the partnership. The anticipated growth in cash flows from the property, when compared to the fixed debt service payment, results in significant expected growth in the net cash flows available for distribution, on the order of 16.5%. The end result is rapid expected growth

QUANTITATIVE MARKETABILITY DISCOUNT MODEL (QMDM)
Conclusion of the Analysis
Leveraged Family Limited Partnership
Principal Asset: Cash Flowing Commercial Real Estate

Enterprise Level DCF Assumptions	Shareholder Level DCF (QMDM) Inputs	Model Inputs	
1. Forecast Period	1. Range of Expected Holding Periods (Years)	Low	10
		High	15
2. Projected Interim Cash Flows (during forecast period)	2a. Expected Distribution / Dividend Yield	Yield	3.5%
	2b. Expected Growth in Distribution / Div. Yield	Growth	16.5%
	2c. Timing (Mid-Year or End of Year)	Timing	M
3. Projected Terminal Value (at end of forecast period)	3a. Growth in Value over Holding Period	G_v	10.0%
	3b. Premium or Discount to Marketable Value	Prem/Disc.	0.0%
4. Discount Rate	4. Range of Required Holding Period Returns	Low	18.0%
		High	20.0%
		Base Value (Marketable Minority Interest)	$1.00

Average Indicated Discounts for Selected Holding Periods (Mid-Point Return +/– 1%)

Average of 2–4 Year HP	11%	Average of 5–10 Year HP	22%
Average of 5–7 Year HP	19%	Average of 10–15 Year HP	26%
Average of 8–10 Year HP	24%	Average of 15–20 Year HP	27%
Average of 10–20 Year HP	26%		
		Concluded Marketability Discount	**25%**

					Assumed Holding Periods in Years									
	1	2	3	4	5	6	7	8	9	10	15	20	25	30
						Implied Marketability Discounts								
15.0%	1%	2%	3%	3%	3%	3%	3%	3%	2%	1%	-	-	-	-
16.0%	2%	4%	5%	6%	7%	8%	8%	8%	8%	8%	5%	-	-	-
17.0%	3%	5%	7%	9%	11%	12%	13%	13%	14%	14%	13%	9%	2%	-
18.0%	4%	7%	9%	12%	14%	16%	17%	18%	19%	20%	21%	18%	13%	7%
19.0%	4%	8%	12%	15%	17%	19%	21%	23%	24%	25%	28%	26%	23%	19%
20.0%	5%	10%	14%	17%	20%	23%	25%	27%	29%	30%	34%	34%	31%	28%
21.0%	6%	11%	16%	20%	23%	26%	29%	31%	33%	34%	39%	40%	38%	36%
22.0%	7%	13%	18%	22%	26%	29%	32%	35%	37%	39%	44%	45%	44%	43%
23.0%	7%	14%	19%	24%	29%	32%	35%	38%	40%	42%	48%	50%	50%	48%

Required Holding Period Return (Annual %)

PV = 100%

EXHIBIT 9.8   QMDM Results: Example #3

in distributions. The leverage also increases the expected growth in value to 10%, compared to the expected appreciation of the underlying property of 3.5%. Financial leverage increases risk, such that the required holding period return is assumed to range from 18.0% to 20.0%. The results of the QMDM calculations for this example are shown in Exhibit 9.8.

With these assumptions, the appropriate marketability discount is on the order of 25% for the 10-to-15-year holding period. Compared to Example #2, the return to minority investors is realized primarily through capital appreciation rather than interim distributions, warranting a larger discount. This result is consistent with the market evidence from the *Partnership Profiles* data discussed in Chapter 8.

Example #4: A Rapidly Growing C Corporation Paying No Dividends

In our next example, the subject enterprise is a rapidly growing C corporation with revenues of $50 million and a net income margin of 10%. The company is well-run, operating in an expanding service industry. Management expects to be able to maintain margins as revenue grows.

All earnings are being reinvested into the company to finance its growth, and there are realistic expectations for 15% compound growth in value for the next ten years or more. Management intends to continue to build the company, but a sale or even an IPO could be possible over the next decade should the controlling shareholders desire liquidity. There are no expectations, however, for any near-term sale. The required holding period return of 20% represents a premium to the enterprise's discount rate to reflect the numerous uncertainties and risks of illiquid minority ownership over and above the risks of the company. The appraiser estimated the holding period to be within the range of five to ten years. The results of the QMDM calculations are shown in Exhibit 9.9.

Under the indicated assumptions for Example #4, the appraiser determined the appropriate marketability discount to be 27%, which is the midpoint of the calculated discounts for the five-to-ten-year expected holding period. While the subject company is not expected to pay dividends, the minority shareholder can expect significant capital appreciation and reasonable prospects for eventual marketability. The highlighted range of discounts

QUANTITATIVE MARKETABILITY DISCOUNT MODEL (QMDM)
Conclusion of the Analysis
C Corporation
Rapid Growth and No Distributions

Enterprise Level DCF Assumptions	Shareholder Level DCF (QMDM) Inputs	Model Inputs	
1. Forecast Period	1. Range of Expected Holding Periods (Years)	Low	5
		High	10
2. Projected Interim Cash Flows (during forecast period)	2a. Expected Distribution / Dividend Yield	Yield	0.0%
	2b. Expected Growth in Distribution / Div. Yield	Growth	0.0%
	2c. Timing (Mid-Year or End of Year)	Timing	E
3. Projected Terminal Value (at end of forecast period)	3a. Growth in Value over Holding Period	G_V	15.0%
	3b. Premium or Discount to Marketable Value	Prem./Disc.	0.0%
4. Discount Rate	4. Range of Required Holding Period Returns	Low	19.0%
		High	21.0%
		Base Value (Marketable Minority Interest)	$1.00

Average Indicated Discounts for Selected Holding Periods (Mid-Point Return +/– 1%)

Average of 2–4 Year HP	12%	Average of 5–10 Year HP	27%
Average of 5–7 Year HP	22%	Average of 10–15 Year HP	41%
Average of 8–10 Year HP	32%	Average of 15–20 Year HP	52%
Average of 10–20 Year HP	46%		
		Concluded Marketability Discount	27%

Required Holding Period Return (Annual %)	Assumed Holding Periods in Years													
	1	2	3	4	5	6	7	8	9	10	15	20	25	30
	Implied Marketability Discounts													
16.0%	1%	2%	3%	3%	4%	5%	6%	7%	7%	8%	12%	16%	19%	23%
17.0%	2%	3%	5%	7%	8%	10%	11%	13%	14%	16%	23%	29%	35%	40%
18.0%	3%	5%	7%	10%	12%	14%	16%	19%	21%	23%	32%	40%	47%	54%
19.0%	3%	7%	10%	13%	16%	19%	21%	24%	26%	29%	40%	50%	57%	64%
20.0%	4%	8%	12%	16%	19%	23%	26%	29%	32%	35%	47%	57%	65%	72%
21.0%	5%	10%	14%	18%	22%	26%	30%	33%	37%	40%	53%	64%	72%	78%
22.0%	6%	11%	16%	21%	26%	30%	34%	38%	41%	45%	59%	69%	77%	83%
23.0%	7%	13%	18%	24%	29%	33%	38%	42%	45%	49%	64%	74%	81%	87%
24.0%	7%	14%	20%	26%	31%	36%	41%	45%	49%	53%	68%	78%	85%	90%

PV = 100%

EXHIBIT 9.9 QMDM Results: Example #4

is broad, but it is the relevant range. Within that range, the appraiser must assess the appropriate discount, just as a real-life investor would assess the price he would pay based on the overall facts and circumstances.

Example #5: Mature C Corporation with Potential for Near-Term Sale

Our final example features a mature C corporation operating in a cyclical industry. This example is summarized in Exhibit 9.10. The company pays a dividend equal to 5.0% of its marketable minority value and has an expected growth in value of 7.5%. Dividends are expected to grow at the same rate.

Industry fundamentals are likely to peak in the next two years or so, and the majority shareholder has committed to a sale of the company during that time *if* the right buyer comes forward with sufficiently attractive pricing and terms. If such a scenario does not materialize during the next two to four years, the window for such transactions in the industry will likely be

QUANTITATIVE MARKETABILITY DISCOUNT MODEL (QMDM)
Conclusion of the Analysis
C Corporation
Mature Company with Potential for Near-term Sale

Enterprise Level DCF Assumptions	Shareholder Level DCF (QMDM) Inputs	Model Inputs	
1. Forecast Period	1. Range of Expected Holding Periods (Years)	Low	8
		High	10
2. Projected Interim Cash Flows (during forecast period)	2a. Expected Distribution / Dividend Yield	Yield	5.0%
	2b. Expected Growth in Distribution / Div. Yield	Growth	7.5%
	2c. Timing (Mid-Year or End of Year)	Timing	E
3. Projected Terminal Value (at end of forecast period)	3a. Growth in Value over Holding Period	G_V	7.5%
	3b. Premium or Discount to Marketable Value	Prem/Disc.	0.0%
4. Discount Rate	4. Range of Required Holding Period Returns	Low	20.0%
		High	22.0%
		Base Value (Marketable Minority Interest)	$1.00

Average Indicated Discounts for Selected Holding Periods (Mid-Point Return +/– 1%)

Average of 2–4 Year HP	19%	Average of 5–10 Year HP	36%
Average of 5–7 Year HP	32%	Average of 10–15 Year HP	48%
Average of 8–10 Year HP	41%	Average of 15–20 Year HP	55%
Average of 10–20 Year HP	51%		
		Concluded Marketability Discount	25%

Required Holding Period Return (Annual %)	Assumed Holding Periods in Years													
	1	2	3	4	5	6	7	8	9	10	15	20	25	30
					Implied Marketability Discounts									
17.0%	4%	7%	11%	14%	16%	19%	21%	23%	25%	27%	34%	39%	42%	44%
18.0%	5%	9%	13%	16%	20%	22%	25%	28%	30%	32%	39%	44%	47%	49%
19.0%	5%	10%	15%	19%	23%	26%	29%	31%	34%	36%	44%	49%	52%	54%
20.0%	6%	12%	17%	21%	25%	29%	32%	35%	38%	40%	48%	53%	56%	58%
21.0%	7%	13%	19%	24%	28%	32%	35%	39%	41%	44%	52%	57%	60%	61%
22.0%	8%	15%	21%	26%	31%	35%	38%	42%	45%	47%	56%	60%	63%	64%
23.0%	9%	16%	23%	28%	33%	38%	41%	45%	48%	50%	59%	63%	65%	67%
24.0%	9%	17%	24%	30%	36%	40%	44%	47%	50%	53%	62%	66%	68%	69%
25.0%	10%	19%	26%	32%	38%	43%	47%	50%	53%	56%	64%	68%	70%	71%

PV = 100%

EXHIBIT 9.10 QMDM Results: Example #5

closed until the next industry peak. The required holding period return is increased to 21% to account for this unusual uncertainty regarding the expected holding period.

Based on this particular situation, the appraiser elects to consider two distinct holding periods. The first, two to four years from the valuation date, assumes a near-term sale of the business. The second, of eight to ten years, is the likely outcome if the opportunity for a near-term sale during the current industry peak is missed and the controlling shareholder decides to wait until the next cycle. The appraiser recognizes that either one or the other of the two scenarios will likely occur, but there is a reasonable probability of either.

The shorter holding period yields a range of marketability discounts of 12% to 26%. Within that range, the appraiser concluded that 15% was the appropriate marketability discount, thinking that if a sale occurs, it might occur during the initial portion of the holding period. The longer holding period yields a range of marketability discounts of 35% to 47%. Within that range, the appraiser concluded that the appropriate discount was 40%. The question is, of course, how to reconcile these two disparate conclusions.

The appraiser in this situation must perform the same assessment investors do when considering investments that will result in one of two radically different outcomes. Balancing the majority shareholder's stated commitment to a near-term sale against the challenge of consummating such a sale on reasonably favorable terms, the appraiser deems the shorter holding period to be somewhat more likely than the longer holding period, concluding that a 25% marketability discount is appropriate.

In this case, the appraiser attempted to simulate the (hypothetical) negotiations of hypothetical willing buyers and sellers. The seller obviously desires a lower discount and a higher price, while the buyer wants a higher discount and lower price. The reconciling element in the discussion would have to be a probability assessment of expected returns under both specified scenarios. The best tool for evaluating this hypothetical discussion is the pro forma return analysis found in the *QMDM Companion*, which is shown as Exhibit 9.11.

The hypothetical seller argues for a 15% discount (higher price), consistent with the shorter holding period. The hypothetical buyer, on the other hand, says that this is too much to pay. There is no premium return relative to the required return range of 20% to 22% for taking on the potential for a much longer holding period than two to four years (as seen by the highlighted but unshaded area in Exhibit 9.10 at an assumed 15% marketability discount).

The hypothetical buyer then argues for a 35% to 40% marketability discount because of the risk of the longer holding period. The hypothetical

RETURNS EXPECTED TO BE REALIZED OVER VARIOUS HOLDING PERIODS GIVEN MARKETABILITY DISCOUNT SELECTED

2.50% *Selected Discount Increment*

Discount Applied	Subsequent Holding Period in Years													
	1	2	3	4	5	6	7	8	9	10	15	20	25	30
15.0%	32%	*22%*	*19%*	*18%*	17%	16%	16%	15%	15%	15%	14%	14%	14%	14%
17.5%	36%	24%	20%	18%	17%	17%	16%	16%	15%	15%	15%	14%	14%	14%
20.0%	41%	26%	22%	19%	18%	17%	17%	16%	16%	16%	15%	14%	14%	14%
22.5%	45%	28%	23%	20%	19%	18%	17%	17%	16%	16%	15%	15%	14%	14%
25.0%	50%	**30%**	**24%**	**22%**	20%	19%	18%	17%	17%	**17%**	**16%**	15%	15%	15%
27.5%	55%	33%	26%	23%	21%	20%	19%	18%	17%	17%	16%	15%	15%	15%
30.0%	61%	35%	27%	24%	22%	20%	19%	19%	18%	18%	16%	16%	15%	15%
32.5%	67%	38%	29%	25%	23%	21%	20%	19%	19%	18%	17%	16%	16%	15%
35.0%	73%	*40%*	*31%*	*26%*	24%	22%	21%	20%	19%	19%	17%	16%	16%	16%

EXHIBIT 9.11 Analysis of Potential Realized Returns

seller counters by saying that there would be too great a premium return in the event of a near-term sale, and very little penalty to return for the longer holding period. See the highlighted but unshaded portion with an assumed marketability discount of 35%, which would yield returns of 31% to 40% if a sale occurred in two or three years.

The appraiser concluded that hypothetical willing buyers and sellers would consummate a transacation at a marketability discount of 25%.

Absent use of a shareholder level discounted cash flow model, it would be very difficult to consistently or credibly address a fact pattern such as this while developing a marketability discount.

Summary of the Examples

The five examples illustrate markedly different investments in minority interests of private business enterprises. The concluded discounts are summarized in Exhibit 9.12.

Example Description	Concluded Discount
1. An unleveraged family limited partnership holding land	65%
2. An unleveraged family limited partnership holding commercial real estate, providing high distributions	15%
3. A leveraged family limited partnership holding commercial real estate	25%
4. A rapidly growing C corporation paying no dividends	27%
5. A mature C corporation with potential for near-term sale	25%
Average Concluded Discount	**31%**

EXHIBIT 9.12 Summary of QMDM Condensed Examples

While the average discount for the five examples of 31% is within the commonly cited benchmark range, application of that benchmark to any of the particular examples could lead to a discount that is too high or too low by a material amount. It should be clear from the wide range of potential investment situations illustrated by the five examples that a shareholder level discounted cash flow method within the income approach is an appropriate valuation method. The QMDM provides a consistent framework for application of this method.

THE UNIFORM STANDARDS OF PROFESSIONAL APPRAISAL PRACTICE AND THE QMDM

The *Uniform Standards of Professional Appraisal Practice* (USPAP) are updated each year by the Appraisal Standards Board of The Appraisal Foundation.[2] Because of the widespread recognition and acceptance of USPAP, business appraisers should be familiar with the standards generally, the business appraisal standards specifically, and how changes in USPAP can influence valuation practice.

USPAP 2006 contains two provisions that relate specifically to the valuation of illiquid minority interests of businesses.

Standards Rule 9-4(c) states:

> *An appraiser must, when necessary for credible assignment results, analyze the effect on value, if any, of buy-sell and option agreements, investment letter stock restrictions, restrictive corporate charter or partnership agreement clauses, and similar features or factors that may influence value.*

Standards Rule 9-4(d) states:

> *An appraiser must, when necessary for credible assignment results, analyze the effect on value, if any, of the extent to which the interest appraised contains elements of ownership control and is marketable and/or liquid.*

These changes are important for business appraisers because they place *additional requirements* on appraisers not previously in the standards, and they are quite specific in nature.

---

[2] *Uniform Standards of Professional Appraisal Practice 2006* (Washington, D.C., Appraisal Standards Board, Appraisal Foundation, 2006).

The first portion of each clause is the same: "An appraiser must, when necessary for credible assignment results, analyze the effect on value, if any …" To the extent that the listed conditions exist, they have the potential of affecting the value of the interest being appraised. Appraisers cannot adequately fulfill these requirements by simply stating, "In my judgment, there is no effect on value." The standards call for *analyzing* the effect on value.

The question is, how can appraisers analyze the effect on value of buy-sell agreements, restrictive agreements, and marketability or control? Fortunately, *USPAP 2006* provides a comment, which is a binding portion of the standard, immediately following SR 9-4(d):

> Comment: An appraiser must analyze factors such as holding period, interim benefits, and the difficulty and cost of marketing the subject interest.

> *Equity interests in a business enterprise are not necessarily worth the pro rata share of the business enterprise interest value as a whole.* Also, *the value of the business enterprise is not necessarily a direct mathematical extension of the value of the fractional interests.* The degree of control, marketability and/or liquidity or lack thereof depends on a broad variety of facts and circumstances that must be analyzed when applicable. [The italicized portion was found in USPAP 2005—all else is new in USPAP 2006]

We now examine the new requirements of *USPAP 2006* in light of the Quantitative Marketability Discount Model. We should be clear at the outset. The drafters of the 2006 revisions to USPAP are not endorsing the QMDM or any other quantitative rate of return model for developing marketability discounts. However, their appeal to common sense factors affecting the value of nonmarketable business interests is entirely consistent with use of the QMDM.

The comment cited three factors that must be analyzed in the context of SR 9-4(d), including holding period, interim benefits, and the difficulty and cost of marketing the subject interest. In addition, SR 9-4(c) requires analysis of buy-sell and option agreements, investment letter stock restrictions, restrictive corporate charter or partnership agreement clauses, and similar features or factors (or generally, restrictions on transfer). We now look at each of these elements in the context of the QMDM.

- *Holding period.* The holding period corresponds to the expected holding period assumption of the QMDM. Investors in nonmarketable investments are keenly interested in when they will be able to sell their investments and realize their returns. Investors accept the fact that they cannot know the precise duration of the prospective holding period with any certainty, but their investment decisions are based on a range of reasonable holding periods in the context of their informed judgment. A portion of Exhibit 9.5 is reproduced as Exhibit 9.13 to illustrate "the effect on value, if any," of the expected holding period.

The effect on value of changes in the expected holding period is clear. Given the QMDM assumptions reflected in the top portion of the Exhibit, we see that as the expected holding period is increased, the marketability discount increases, which decreases value. Qualitative comparisons do not accommodate this type of analysis.

- *Interim benefits.* Interim benefits are the expected distributions / dividends of the QMDM. In the Exhibit, benefits equal to a 4.0% C corporation equivalent dividend yield are forecast to grow at a rate of 6.0% per year. This forecasted stream of benefits comprises the "interim benefits" discussed in *USPAP 2006*. Can we "analyze the impact on value, if any," of the interim benefits? Under the preceding assumptions, the calculated marketability discount for an eight-year expected holding period and a 21.0% required holding period return is 34%, which correlates closely with the concluded 35% marketability discount in the Exhibit.

Enterprise Level DCF Assumptions	Shareholder Level DCF (QMDM) Inputs	Model Inputs	
1. Forecast Period	1. Range of Expected Holding Periods (Years)	Low	5
		High	10
2. Projected Interim Cash Flows (during forecast period)	2a. Expected Distribution / Dividend Yield	Yield	4.0%
	2b. Expected Growth in Distribution / Div. Yield	Growth	6.0%
	2c. Timing (Mid-Year or End of Year)	Timing	M
3. Projected Terminal Value (at end of forecast period)	3a. Growth in Value over Holding Period	G_V	10.0%
	3b. Premium or Discount to Marketable Value	Prem/Disc.	0.0%
4. Discount Rate	4. Range of Required Holding Period Returns	Low	20.0%
		High	22.0%
		Base Value (Marketable Minority Interest)	$1.00

Concluded Marketability Discount		35%

					Assumed Holding Periods in Years									
		1	2	3	4	5	6	7	8	9	10	15	20	25	30
						Implied Marketability Discounts									
Required Holding Period Return (Annual %)	17.0%	2%	5%	7%	9%	11%	13%	15%	17%	19%	21%	30%	37%	43%	47%
	18.0%	3%	6%	9%	12%	15%	17%	20%	22%	24%	27%	36%	43%	49%	53%
	19.0%	4%	8%	11%	15%	18%	21%	24%	26%	29%	31%	42%	49%	54%	58%
	20.0%	5%	9%	13%	17%	21%	24%	27%	30%	33%	36%	46%	54%	59%	62%
	21.0%	5%	11%	15%	20%	24%	27%	31%	34%	37%	40%	51%	58%	63%	65%
	22.0%	6%	12%	17%	22%	26%	31%	34%	38%	41%	44%	55%	61%	66%	68%
	23.0%	7%	13%	19%	24%	29%	33%	37%	41%	44%	47%	58%	65%	68%	71%
	24.0%	8%	15%	21%	27%	32%	36%	40%	44%	47%	50%	61%	67%	71%	73%
	25.0%	8%	16%	23%	29%	34%	39%	43%	47%	50%	53%	64%	70%	73%	74%

PV = 100%

EXHIBIT 9.13   Analysis of Holding Period Effect

If all assumptions remain the same except that the expected dividend yield is reduced to zero, the calculated marketability discount for eight years and a 21.0% expected holding period rises to 53%. This would be equivalent to assuming that agency costs consume all potential dividends to the illiquid interest. On the other hand, if there are no agency costs, the dividend yield could be increased to 6.0%, and the corresponding marketability discount would be 25%. This type of analysis cannot be performed on the basis of qualitative comparisons.

▪ *Difficulty and cost of marketing the subject interest.* There is greater risk associated with owning an illiquid investment than an otherwise comparable liquid one. Higher expected return is the investment reward for accepting incremental risk. The required holding period return of the QMDM is developed with explicit consideration for the difficulty and cost of marketing subject interests. Exhibit 9.3 is reproduced here for illustration purposes.

The investor-specific premiums listed on Lines 9–12 clearly address the "difficulty and cost of marketing the subject interest." These include uncertainties of the expected holding period, information acquisition cost premium, holding period monitoring costs, and an adjustment for the large size of the interest (which limits marketability). Together, these elements add 3.0% to 4.5% of incremental holding period risk to the required return. Absent these considerations, the required return range

QUANTITATIVE MARKETABILITY DISCOUNT MODEL (QMDM)
QMDM ASSUMPTION #4
Required Holding Period Return (Shareholder-Level Discount Rate)
  (Using the Adjusted Capital Asset Pricing Model)

			Estimated Range		
	Components of the Required Holding Period Return		Lower	Higher	Source/Brief Rationale
1	Long-Term Government Bond Yield-to-Maturity		5.50%	5.50%	
2	Ibbotson Common Stock Premium	6.00%			
3	x Market Beta	1.00			
4	= Beta Adjusted Common Stock Premium	6.00%			As developed in text
5	+ Small Cap Stock Premium	3.00%			
6	+ Specific Company Risk	2.00%			
7	= Total Equity Premium		11.00%	11.00%	
8	Base Holding Period Required Return		16.50%	16.50%	<> Base equity discount rate
	Investor-Specific Risk Premium(s) for This Investment				
9	+ Uncertainties of Expected Holding Period		1.00%	2.00%	Per Text
10	+ Information Acquisition Cost Premium		1.00%	1.00%	Per Text
11	+ Premium for Expected Holding Period Monitoring Costs		0.50%	0.50%	Per Text
12	+ Adjustment for Large Size of the Interest		0.50%	1.00%	Per Text
13	+ Rights of First Refusal Limiting Transferability (ROFR)		0.50%	1.00%	Per Text
14	Total Investor-Specific Risk Premium for This Entity		3.50%	5.50%	Sum of above
15	Estimated Range of Required Holding Period Returns		20.00%	22.00%	Enterprise discount rate plus shareholder risks
16	Rounded Range		20.00%	22.00%	To Nearest 0.5%
17	Mid-Point of Estimated Required Holding Period Return Range			21.0%	Assumption #4 of the QMDM

EXHIBIT 9.3 Calculation of Required Holding Period Return

would be 17.0% to 17.5%. The increase in the required return resulting from the investor-specific premiums has a material and measurable impact on value. Qualitative comparisons do not allow for this type of analysis.

■ *Restrictions on transfer (SR 9-4(c))*. A variety of elements which we place into the general category of restrictions on transfer are discussed in SR 9-4(c). Restrictions on transfer tend to increase the risk of investing in illiquid investments relative to illiquid investments without such restrictions. At Line 13 in the Exhibit, we added a premium of 0.50% to 1.00% because a right of first refusal agreement limited the transferability of the subject interest. The increase in required return resulting from consideration of the right of first refusal has a material and measurable impact on value. Qualitative comparisons do not provide a framework for this type of analysis.

The QMDM is an ideal tool to assist appraisers in meeting the new analytical requirements found in *USPAP 2006*. Once again, neither the Appraisal Standards Board nor the Appraisal Foundation have endorsed the QMDM or any other model for conducting the new, required analysis of Standards Rules 9-4(c) and 9-4(d). However, it is difficult to see how this new analytical requirement can be met absent the QMDM or similar tools.

CHAPTER 10

Application of the Integrated Theory to Tax Pass-Through Entities

INTRODUCTION

The appropriate valuation treatment of S corporations and other tax pass-through entities is one of the most durable valuation controversies facing business appraisers. The input of the Tax Court has not been helpful in reaching an economically sensible consensus on the issue.[1] In this chapter, we apply the disciplined approach of the Integrated Theory to the valuation of S corporations and other tax pass-through entities at both the enterprise and shareholder levels of value.[2]

Exhibit 10.1 summarizes the results of applying the Integrated Theory to the valuation of S corporations at each level of value.

Application of the Integrated Theory suggests that the appropriate valuation treatment at the enterprise level differs from that at the shareholder level.

- *Enterprise Levels.* At the enterprise levels, an S corporation has the same value as an *otherwise identical* C corporation.[3] In other words,

---

[1] We have analyzed the Tax Court rulings regarding the valuation of S corporations in three highly publicized cases (*Gross*, *Heck*, and *Adams*) in other venues. We do not rehearse those analyses here, but rather proceed to describe the appropriate valuation treatment of S corporations at the enterprise and shareholder levels of value. In litigation, the valuation expert's duty is to present defensible, well-reasoned valuation evidence to the Court, not simply parrot previous decisions that may have been based on limited or faulty valuation evidence presented at trial.

[2] For the remainder of this chapter, references to S corporations also apply to other tax pass-through entities.

[3] We will discuss what is meant by *otherwise identical* shortly. Misunderstandings related to this concept contribute to confusion in the debate regarding the relative values of S and C corporations.

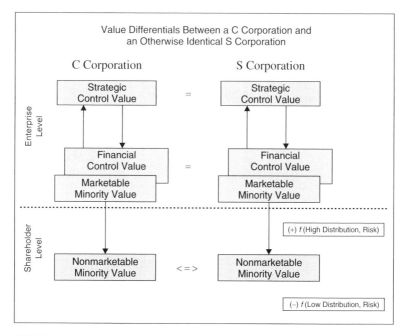

EXHIBIT 10.1 Relationship between C Corporation and S Corporation Values at Each Level of Value

the S corporation election confers no particular benefit to the value of the enterprise. The operating cash flows are identical, so there is no compelling economic rationale to suggest that the value of the two enterprises should not also be identical.

- *Shareholder Level.* At the shareholder level, a particular minority interest may have a different value than that same interest in an otherwise identical C corporation. As we will demonstrate, the S corporation election ultimately confers a tax benefit on the shareholders rather than the enterprise. The tax benefit is manifest in different shareholder cash flows. It is these shareholder cash flow differences, appropriately considered in the context of their risk, timing, and duration, which generates potential differences in value.

The Nature of the S Corporation Benefit

The benefit of S corporation status is easily summarized: the election eliminates the dreaded double taxation of C corporation earnings that are distributed to shareholders. Earnings are taxed one time at the level of the

C corporation and again upon distribution to shareholders. The valuation controversy stems from confusion regarding whether the tax benefit derived from the elimination of the second level of taxation for an S corporation accrues to the enterprise or the shareholders. Unfortunately, the mechanics of the tax pass-through contribute to this confusion.

The S corporation election replaces the corporate income tax with a personal shareholder tax burden on S corporation income passed through to the individual shareholders. The elimination of the corporate income tax leads some observers to the erroneous conclusion that the benefit of the election by necessity accrues to the enterprise. The S corporation's income continues to be fully taxable; the legal obligation simply transfers from the S corporation to the individual shareholders. The economic obligation, however, remains with the enterprise. The real benefit of the S corporation election is the elimination of personal tax on economic distributions to shareholders. Thus, the S corporation benefit accrues to the shareholders rather than the enterprise.

A brief example will clarify. In the example, we assume that the effective corporate and personal income tax rates are identical. The small differences observed in many tax jurisdictions are interesting, but do not blunt the force of the argument. In Exhibit 10.2 we consider *otherwise identical* C and S corporations under three different distribution scenarios.

We make the following observations with respect to Exhibit 10.2:

- Taxes are paid on the taxable corporate income in each scenario, regardless of distribution policy. While the *legal obligation* to pay the tax falls to the S corporation shareholders individually, the *economic obligation* remains with the enterprise, as distributions sufficient to pay the personal tax obligation are practically assured. The rare instances in which insufficient distributions are made are best viewed as additional reinvestment of the undistributed corporate tax obligation into the enterprise.

- Corporate earnings are fully taxed in each scenario, but economic distributions to shareholders are not. We use the term "economic distributions" to refer to all shareholder distributions beyond the level needed to fund the personal taxes due on corporate earnings. Economic distributions to C corporation shareholders are taxed at the dividend income rate of 15%, while the same distributions to S corporation shareholders are not taxed.

- The fact that taxes are paid on the taxable corporate income suggests that, for any given level of economic distribution, the retained earnings available to the C and S corporations for reinvestment are identical. Therefore, the S corporation election does not confer any benefit on the enterprise.

EXHIBIT 10.2 Analysis of Economic Distributions

		0% Economic Payout		50% Economic Payout		100% Economic Payout	
		C Corp	S Corp	C Corp	S Corp	C Corp	S Corp
Taxable Corporate Income		$100.00	$100.00	$100.00	$100.00	$100.00	$100.00
Corporate Tax on Corporate Earnings	40.0%	($40.00)	$0.00	($40.00)	$0.00	($40.00)	$0.00
Shareholder Tax on Corporate Earnings	40.0%	$0.00	($40.00)	$0.00	($40.00)	$0.00	($40.00)
Net Income Available for Economic Distributions		$60.00	$60.00	$60.00	$60.00	$60.00	$60.00
Economic Payout Ratio		0.0%	0.0%	50.0%	50.0%	100.0%	100.0%
Economic Distribution to Shareholders (Pre-tax)		$0.00	$0.00	$30.00	$30.00	$60.00	$60.00
Shareholder Tax on Economic Distribution (%)		15.0%	0.0%	15.0%	0.0%	15.0%	0.0%
Shareholder Tax on Economic Distribution ($)		$0.00	$0.00	$4.50	$0.00	$9.00	$0.00
Economic Distribution to Shareholders (After-tax)		$0.00	$0.00	$25.50	$30.00	$51.00	$60.00
Shareholder Level Benefit of S Corporation Election			$0.00		$4.50		$9.00
Retained Corporate Earnings		$60.00	$60.00	$30.00	$30.00	$0.00	$0.00
Enterprise Level Benefit of S Corporation Election		$0.00	$0.00	$0.00	$0.00	$0.00	$0.00

- The tax-free nature of economic distributions to S corporation share-holders gives rise to a potential S corporation tax benefit at the shareholder level. The magnitude of the cash flow benefit increases with the portion of available earnings distributed to shareholders. In the case of no economic distributions, there is no cash flow benefit related to the S corporation election. The valuation impact of the tax benefit is contingent upon the accompanying shareholder risks and the expected duration of the shareholder benefits.
- Finally, the magnitude of the shareholder level cash flow benefit is directly related to the prevailing dividend income tax rate avoided by the S corporation election. The shareholder level tax benefit is greater under a tax regime in which dividends are taxed at the higher ordinary income tax rates.[4]

The Enterprise Level Value of S Corporations

In this section, we apply the conceptual framework of the Integrated Theory to analysis of the S corporation tax benefit presented in Exhibit 10.2 to demonstrate that, at the enterprise levels, the value of an S corporation is equal to that of an otherwise identical C corporation.

Exhibit 3 reproduces Exhibit 3.6 from Chapter 3.

For the value of an S corporation to be different at the enterprise level from an *otherwise identical* C corporation, there must be a difference in

	Conceptual Math	Relationships	Value Implications
Strategic Control Value	$$\dfrac{CF_{e(c, s)}}{R_s - [G_{mm} + G_s]}$$	$CF_{e(c, s)} \geq CF_{e(c, f)}$ $G_s \geq 0$ $R_s \leq R_{mm}$	$V_{e(c, s)} \geq V_{e(c, f)}$
Financial Control Value	$$\dfrac{CF_{e(c, f)}}{R_f - [G_{mm} + G_f]}$$	$CF_{e(c, f)} \geq CF_{e(mm)}$ $G_f \geq 0$ $R_f = R_{mm}(+/- \text{ a little})$	$V_{e(c, f)} \geq V_{mm}$
Marketable Minority Value	$$\dfrac{CF_{e(mm)}}{R_{mm} - G_{mm}}$$	$G_v = R_{mm} - \text{Div Yld}$	V_{mm} is the benchmark for the other levels

EXHIBIT 10.3   Conceptual Math of the Enterprise Levels of Value

---

[4]As was the case prior to 2003.

at least one of the three inputs to the Gordon Model: cash flow (denoted as CF), risk (as manifest in the discount rate, R), or growth in cash flows (denoted as G).

1. *Cash Flow.* The transfer of the legal obligation to pay taxes on the corporate earnings of the S corporation from the corporation itself to the individual shareholders has led some appraisers to the improper conclusion that the enterprise cash flows of an S corporation are substantially greater than those of an otherwise identical C corporation. However, as we demonstrated in Exhibit 10.2, the economic obligation to pay taxes on the corporate earnings of the S corporation does not transfer to the individual shareholders. In other words, the enterprise cash flows are unchanged, and there is no S corporation tax benefit at the enterprise level.[5]

2. *Risk.* The relevant risk at the enterprise level relates to the business risk of the enterprise. These risks generally encompass areas such as revenue volatility and the prospects for margin compression, susceptibility to competition, the effects of regulation, dependence on suppliers or key managers, and sensitivity to economic and market conditions, among others. The S corporation election has no effect on these or any of the other myriad business risks typically considered in the enterprise discount rate.

   Appraisers and courts are occasionally distracted in the development of enterprise discount rates for S corporations by a desire to match the tax characteristics of the discount rate to that of the cash flow stream. In other words, some advocate converting S corporation enterprise discount rates to a pre-tax basis to discount the pre-tax corporate earnings. While this is an admirable goal, it is ultimately misguided, given an understanding that the economic obligation for the tax on corporate earnings remains with the S corporation. Rather than embarking on the potentially perilous path of converting discount rates to a pre-tax basis, it is preferable to simply apply appropriate discount rates developed using traditional methods to the earnings of the S corporation after deduction of the corporate tax obligation.[6]

---

[5] We continue to assume equivalence between effective corporate and personal tax rates.

[6] For our part, while recognizing that reasonable conclusions can be the algebraic result of applying pre-tax discount rates to pre-tax earnings, we harbor a nagging suspicion that such discount rates are devoid of any real economic meaning. As a result, we think the much safer course for appraisers is to rely on after-tax discount rates whenever possible.

3. *Growth.* It is sometimes suggested that the transfer of the legal obligation for taxes on corporate earnings away from the S corporation permits the S corporation to retain more earnings for reinvestment, thereby fueling greater growth in cash flows. This misconception is also corrected by a proper understanding of the economic obligation for taxes on corporate earnings. As illustrated in Exhibit 10.2, after considering the economic obligation for taxes on corporate earnings, the S corporation has the same amount of retained earnings available for reinvestment as its C corporation counterpart.[7] As a result, there is no reason for assuming a growth differential between S and C corporations at the enterprise level.

Disciplined application of the Integrated Theory allows us to demonstrate that, at the enterprise levels of value, there are no differences in cash flow, risk, or growth between otherwise identical S and C corporations. We conclude, therefore, that there is no economic basis for asserting that, by virtue of having made the S election, the electing enterprise is more (or less) valuable than it was on a pre-election basis.

Other Observations Regarding Relative Value at the Enterprise Level

The conceptual framework of the Integrated Theory is necessarily quantitative. In this section we summarize other qualitative observations which reinforce our conclusion that the enterprise value of an S corporation is no different than that of an otherwise comparable C corporation.

First, we observe that, with the exception of very small corporations owned primarily by individuals, the most likely acquirers of S corporations are either C corporations or groups of shareholders who are ineligible to own shares of an S corporation. In other words, the S corporation tax benefit—even if perceived to reside with the enterprise—cannot be transferred to the most likely acquirers of the enterprise. If the S election increased enterprise value, one would expect S corporation acquirers to have a comparative advantage relative to C corporation buyers. Such advantage is not apparent in the marketplace. The consistent experience of investment bankers at Capital and elsewhere suggests that buyers pay no more for S corporations than for otherwise equivalent C corporations.

Second, treating the S corporation as a "tax-free" enterprise assumes that the tax benefits conferred upon S corporation shareholders will persist

---

[7]Shareholders of S corporations who reinvest all after-tax income will benefit from the build-up in the basis of their investments. We discuss the issue of basis later.

indefinitely. We have demonstrated that the magnitude of the shareholder tax benefit is a function of the level of economic shareholder distributions and the tax rate on dividend income avoided by the S corporation election. Buyers are well aware that tax rates can and do change and therefore do not capitalize such benefits into perpetuity even if incorrectly assumed to reside with the enterprise.

Third, if the S corporation election materially increased the value of the enterprise, appraisers must then recognize that most C corporations have the option to make the S election. In other words, if the enterprise level S corporation value premium were as substantial as sometimes suggested, one would expect to see a great deal of financial engineering to allow large (even publicly traded) C corporations to convert to S corporation status in order to unlock the S corporation value premium. This simply has not happened.

Finally, some observe that the net proceeds to S corporation shareholders from a sale of the enterprise may be greater than the net proceeds to the sellers of an otherwise comparable C corporation.[8] For one, the S corporation election can facilitate asset sales by eliminating embedded gains issues, and many acquirers prefer to consummate asset, rather than stock purchases. In addition, to the extent S corporation earnings are retained, the basis of the S corporation shareholders in the stock increases, minimizing capital gains realized upon eventual sale of the underlying stock.

However, we caution appraisers and courts not to confuse value (based on the capitalization of expected enterprise cash flows) with proceeds (the negotiated value of the enterprise, adjusted for the corporate and personal liabilities and expenses arising from the transaction).

We have demonstrated that the capitalizable enterprise cash flows for an S corporation are the same as those of a comparable C corporation. The transactional expenses and liabilities that create the wedge between value and proceeds may, however, differ for S and C corporations.

- As previously mentioned, the S corporation shareholder's basis increases as corporate earnings are retained, leading to a smaller capital gain tax

---

[8] Readers are referred to a debate on this issue in the *Business Valuation Review*:

- Johnson, Owen T., "Letter to the Editor," *Business Valuation Review*, December 2001, p. 56.
- Burke, Brian H., "Letter to the Editor," *Business Valuation Review*, March 2002, p. 44.
- Johnson, Owen T., "Letter to the Editor and Response to Mr. Burke's Letter," *Business Valuation Review*, March 2002, pp. 44–45. (Mr. Johnson was a senior vice president at Mercer Capital at the time of the exchange.)

burden upon eventual sale of the stock. Alternatively, an S corporation may be able to extract a higher price from an acquirer seeking an asset transaction, and endure fewer tax disadvantages than the typical C corporation asset sale. In either case, the net proceeds to the selling shareholders of the S corporation are greater than they would be for an otherwise comparable C corporation.

- No lunch is free, however, particularly with respect to the sale of S corporation assets. When an S corporation engages in an asset sale, its shareholders retain the corporation and the accompanying residual or "tail" liability. The tail liability encompasses the unknown liabilities accruing from business operations prior to the transaction. Buyers naturally desire to avoid inheriting this liability, while sellers naturally desire to pass it along to the buyer.[9] As a result, S corporation shareholders that negotiate a higher price by acquiescing to an asset sale see their effective proceeds reduced by the expected present value of the unknown tail liability.

Accordingly, the net proceeds from sale of an S corporation may be less than, equal to, or greater than those received from sale of an otherwise identical C corporation. Differences in net proceeds do not, however, affect the value of the enterprise. Further, an S corporation that yields greater proceeds from an asset sale than a similar C corporation's stock sale is not *otherwise identical*. The asset sale occurs only because the S corporation has fewer liabilities (embedded capital gains) than does the C corporation.

The Shareholder Level Value of S Corporations

Earlier in this chapter, we demonstrated that the potential tax benefit associated with the S corporation election actually accrues to the shareholders, rather than the enterprise itself. As a result, the value of the enterprise is unaffected by the S corporation election. In this section, we illustrate how to determine the effect on value, if any, of the potential S corporation tax benefits at the shareholder level of value.

We are occasionally credited with developing a model to value the S corporation benefit.[10] While we appreciate the credit, we have not

---

[9]In fact, for many buyers, the desire to purchase assets rather than stock is driven more by the fear of accepting the (unknown) tail liability of a corporation than by the tax benefits from writing up asset values and increasing depreciation expenses.

[10]Fannon, Nancy, "Valuation of Pass-Through Entities," *Financial Valuation: Application and Models: Second Edition* (James R. Hitchner, John Wiley & Sons, Inc., 2006).

	Conceptual Math	Relationships	Value Implications
Marketable Minority Value	$\dfrac{CF_{e(mm)}}{R_{mm} - G_{mm}}$	$G_v = R_{mm} - \text{Div Yld}$	V_{mm} is the benchmark for the other levels
Nonmarketable Minority Value	$\dfrac{CF_{sh}}{R_{hp} - G_v}$	$CF_{sh} \leq CF_{e(mm)}$ $G_v \leq R_{mm} - \text{Div Yld}$ $R_{hp} \geq R_{mm}$	$V_{sh} \leq V_{mm}$

EXHIBIT 10.4 Conceptual Math of the Marketable Minority and Nonmarketable Minority Levels of Value

done so. Rather, we advocate valuing nonmarketable minority interests in S corporations using the very same shareholder level discounted cash flow approach we apply to such interests in C corporations. We find that the relevant shareholder tax benefits of the S corporation election can be reliably incorporated into the value of the subject interest using the Quantitative Marketability Discount Model.

Consulting the conceptual framework of the Integrated Theory (Exhibit 10.4), we observe that any difference in value between a subject minority interest in an S corporation and a similar interest in an otherwise comparable C corporation must be attributable to a difference in interim shareholder cash flows (CF_{sh}), risks over the expected holding period (manifest in R_{hp}), or growth in value over the expected holding period (G_v).

S Corporation Considerations for the QMDM Inputs

There are four broad classes of QMDM inputs. In the following sections, we describe the specific considerations required when applying the QMDM to a subject interest in an S corporation. In order to facilitate comparability and understanding, we mirror this example of developing a marketability discount for an S corporation after the detailed example developed for a C corporation in Chapter 9. The C corporation had a marketable minority value of $10 million based on net earnings of $1.0 million, a discount rate of 16%, and expected growth of 6.0% ($1.0 million/(16% − 10%) = $10 million). The corporation paid a dividend equal to 40% of its earnings, providing a 4.0% expected yield for investors, providing a first year dividend of $400 thousand. The expected holding period was five to ten years, and the required holding period return was 21.0% (with a range of 20% to 22%). The concluded marketability discount was 35%.

Forecast Period   The first input to a shareholder level discounted cash flow model is the expected holding period during which the subject interest is anticipated to remain nonmarketable. With respect to differences between S and C corporation interests, we expect situations in which there is a difference in the expected holding periods to be rare. For this example we have assumed an expected holding period of five to ten years. This is identical to the expected holding period used in Exhibit 9.4.

It is interesting to note that the holding period assumption does have a material impact on the effect of the S corporation tax benefit on the value of the subject interest, though. Properly conceived as a shareholder benefit, the potential tax savings to the shareholder arising from the S election are relevant only during the expected holding period, rather than into perpetuity. Perpetuity calculations of the shareholder tax benefit for investments with limited expected holding periods are, for this reason, incorrect. The QMDM captures this distinction.

Projected Interim Cash Flows   The second input to the shareholder level discounted cash flow model is a projection of interim shareholder distributions. As illustrated in Exhibit 10.2, the economic distributions to S corporation shareholders are not taxable, in contrast to identical distributions to C corporation shareholders. As a result, the S election has a direct and quantifiable effect on the interim cash flows (reflected in the distribution yield and distribution growth inputs to the QMDM).

In applying the QMDM, we account for the favorable tax attributes of S corporation economic distributions by expressing the distribution yield on a C corporation equivalent basis. In other words, the net economic distribution after all taxes have been paid is grossed up to reflect the pro forma dividend from a C corporation that would yield the same after-tax distribution.

Based on the preceding discussion in this chapter, we are assuming that an S corporation otherwise identical to this C corporation would have a marketable minority value of $10 million. The S corporation would distribute 40% of after-tax earnings to its shareholders, and would retain $1.0 million after having done so.

In order to maintain equivalency between the C corporation and the S corporation to the extent possible, we assume that the S corporation will distribute 40% of its pre-tax earnings to fund the corporate tax liability passed through to the shareholders (see Lines 1–4 in Exhibit 10.5).

We assume a 64% aggregate distribution payout ratio, inclusive of shareholder-level taxes, to provide for a $0.40 dividend to shareholders after those taxes (Lines 6–9). This leaves the S corporation with $0.60 of retained earnings ($1.667 − $1.067 = $0.60), just like the C corporation

QUANTITATIVE MARKETABILITY DISCOUNT MODEL (QMDM)
QMDM ASSUMPTION #2a
C Corporation Equivalent Yield for Tax Pass-Through Entity

	C CORPORATION EQUIVALENT DIVIDEND YIELD FOR TAX PASS-THROUGH ENTITIES		Inputs / Calculations	
1	Expected Pre-Tax Earnings of Pass-Through Entity		$1.67	*Per Share, appraiser's estimate*
2	Personal Federal Ordinary Income Tax Rate	35.0%		
3	Personal State Ordinary Income Tax Rate	7.7%		*Blended Federal/State Rate*
4	Blended Marginal Tax Rate		40.0%	*Federal Rate × (1 – State Rate) + State Rate*
5	**Pass-Through Taxes**		$0.667	*Line 1 × Line 4*
6	**Expected Total Distribution Payout Percentage**	64.0%		*Appraiser's estimate of annual distribution payout*
7	Expected Total Distributions		$1.067	*Line 1 times Line 6*
8	– Pass-Through Taxes on Pre-Tax Earnings		($0.667)	*From Line 3 above*
9	= After-Tax Dividend		$0.400	
10	After-Tax Dividend		$0.400	*From Line 9 above*
11	÷ Blended Tax Rate on C Corp Dividends	15.0%	85.0%	*Federal/State corporate marginal rate (1 – personal blended tax rate)*
12	= C Corporation Equivalent Dividend		$0.470	*After-Tax dividend ÷ Blended Tax Rate on Dividends*
13	C Corporation Equivalent Dividend		$0.470	*From Line 12 above*
14	÷ Marketable Minority Interest Value	÷	$10.00	*Per Share, appraisers estimate (Exhibit x)*
15	**Implied Ongoing Dividend Yield — C Corporation Basis**	**=**	4.70%	*C Corporation Equivalent Basis, Rounded*

EXHIBIT 10.5   C Corporation Equivalent Dividend Yield for a Tax Pass-Through Entity

after paying a dividend of 40% of net earnings. We now "gross-up" the after-tax S corporation dividend to its C corporation equivalent (Lines 10–12). Assuming a blended personal tax rate on dividends of 15%, the $0.40 dividend translates into a $0.47 C corporation equivalent dividend. Given the marketable minority value of $10 (per share), the C corporation equivalent yield is 4.7%. This compares to the 4.0% yield for the otherwise identical C corporation in Chapter 9.

A $0.40 economic distribution from an S corporation is superior to a $0.40 dividend from a C corporation. All else equal, the tax-free nature of S corporation economic distributions would lead to a higher value for a given subject minority interest, relative to a similar interest in a comparable C corporation.

Projected Terminal Value (Growth in Value)   Within the QMDM, the projected terminal value of the subject interest at the end of the expected holding period is determined by applying the expected growth in value to the marketable minority value of the subject interest at the valuation date. We have previously shown that the growth prospects of the enterprise are unaffected by the S corporation election. Accordingly, we do not expect any difference in the expected growth in value assumption to contribute to a difference in the value of minority interests in S and C corporations.

In a previous section of this chapter, we ascribed the potentially lower capital gain obligation upon the eventual sale of the interest to the net proceeds from sale of the enterprise, rather than the value of the enterprise. Some logic can be applied when considering the value of a specific minority interest. However, appraisers that wish to incorporate the benefit of increasing basis from undistributed earnings may do so by estimating the benefit specifically and reducing the concluded marketability discount as a result (as demonstrated in the following example).

Because our example S corporation retains precisely the same amount as the example C corporation, the expected growth in value of 6.0% assumed in Chapter 9 is also assumed for the S corporation.

Discount Rate   The final element of the shareholder level discounted cash flow model is an appropriate discount rate to determine the present value of the projected interim cash flows and terminal value. In the QMDM, we call this discount rate the required holding period return (R_{hp}).

The required holding period return is the sum of the enterprise discount rate and incremental holding period premiums (HPP) accounting for shareholder risks borne during the expected holding period. The salient question in the valuation of minority interests in S corporations, then, is whether the risks of the holding period are different for S corporation shareholders than their C corporation counterparts. We suggest that, in many cases, minority shareholders in S corporations face greater risks than those in C corporations, and therefore would assume larger holding period premiums.

For example, S corporation shareholders face the risk that the tax benefits from the S corporation election, which are assumed to persist throughout the expected holding period, may be lost, either through revocation of the S corporation election or through a legislative change in the dividend income tax rate. In addition, because of the arithmetic required to restate S corporation distributions to a C corporation equivalent basis, the anticipated S corporation interim cash flows are more sensitive to changes in the level of enterprise earnings and economic distribution payout ratios. Finally, while shareholders are unlikely to allow such practices to persist, the legal obligation to pay taxes on corporate earnings regardless of whether sufficient distributions to fund the tax payments are received is real. The prospect of such an outcome occurring even once likely supports some additional return premium. Exhibit 10.6 derives the required holding period return for the example S corporation.

The build-up of the required holding period return is identical to that found Exhibit 9.3 for the C corporation with one exception. At Line 14, we add an increment of return (0.50%) to account for the potential for adverse cash flow that exists in nearly every tax pass-through entity, even if such an outcome is unlikely. Compared to the 21.0% required holding period

QUANTITATIVE MARKETABILITY DISCOUNT MODEL (QMDM)
QMDM ASSUMPTION #4
Required Holding Period Return (Shareholder-Level Discount Rate)
(Using the Adjusted Capital Asset Pricing Model)
S Corporation Minority Interest

	Components of the Required Holding Period Return	Estimated Range Lower	Estimated Range Higher	Source/Brief Rationale
1	Long-Term Government Bond Yield-to-Maturity	5.50%	5.50%	
2	Ibbotson Common Stock Premium	6.00%		
3	x Market Beta	1.00		
4	= Beta Adjusted Common Stock Premium	6.00%		As developed in text
5	+ Small Cap Stock Premium	3.00%		
6	+ Specific Company Risk	2.00%		
7	= Total Equity Premium		11.00%	11.00%	
8	**Base Holding Period Required Return**	16.50%	16.50%	<> Base equity discount rate
	Investor-Specific Risk Premium(s) for This Investment:			
9	+ Uncertainties of Expected Holding Period	1.00%	2.00%	Per Text
10	+ Information Acquisition Cost Premium	1.00%	1.00%	Per Text
11	+ Premium for Expected Holding Period Monitoring Costs	0.50%	0.50%	Per Text
12	+ Adjustment for Large Size of the Interest	0.50%	1.00%	Per Text
13	+ Rights of First Refusal Limiting Transferability (ROFR)	0.50%	1.00%	Per Text
14	**+ Potential for Adverse Cash Flow**	0.50%	0.50%	New Risk
15	**Total Investor-Specific Risk Premium for This Entity**	4.00%	6.00%	Sum of above
16	**Estimated Range of Required Holding Period Returns**	20.50%	22.50%	Enterprise discount rate plus shareholder risks
17	**Rounded Range**	20.50%	22.50%	To Nearest 0.5%
18	**Mid-Point of Estimated Required Holding Period Return Range**		21.5%	Assumption #4 of the QMDM

EXHIBIT 10.6 Calculation of Required Holding Period Return for Example S Corporation

return midpoint for the C corporation, the corresponding return for the S corporation is 21.5%.

As with any other discounted cash flow model, the QMDM is sensitive to the selected discount rate. To the extent the discount rate applicable to an S corporation shareholder interest exceeds that applicable to an otherwise comparable C corporation shareholder interest, the value of the S corporation interest will be lower.

Synthesis The value differential at the shareholder level between a subject S corporation interest and a corresponding interest in a C corporation is a function of the level of economic distributions (CF_{sh}) and shareholder risks during the expected holding period (as manifest in R_{hp}). The potential for higher economic distributions suggests that S corporation interests will be worth more, all else equal, than their C corporation counterparts. In contrast, the incremental holding period risks suggest, all else equal, that the S corporation interest will be worth less than the corresponding C corporation interest. The balance of these two competing considerations determines the value differential in each particular circumstance.

EXHIBIT 10.7

$$V_{sh(S)} = \frac{CF_s}{R_{(HP+SP)} - G_v} \;>=<\; \frac{CF_c}{R_{hp} - G_v} = V_{sh(c)}$$

Exhibit 10.7 summarizes the effect of these competing considerations on the value of a minority interest in an S corporation ($V_{sh(S)}$), relative to a minority interest in a C corporation ($V_{sh(C)}$).

At this point, we need to determine the value of the S corporation interest relative to the corresponding C corporation interest. Exhibit 10.8 summarizes the basic QMDM analysis for the S corporation.

In Exhibit 9.4, the appraiser concluded that the appropriate marketability discount was 35%. The calculated discounts for a 21.0% required return were 31%, 34%, and 37% for holding periods of seven, eight, and nine years. The corresponding discounts for a 21.5% required return are 30%, 33%, and 35% for the S corporation in 10.8. At this point, there is little differentiation between the two. The higher expected cash flows from S corporation ownership have been substantially mitigated by the higher expected risks.

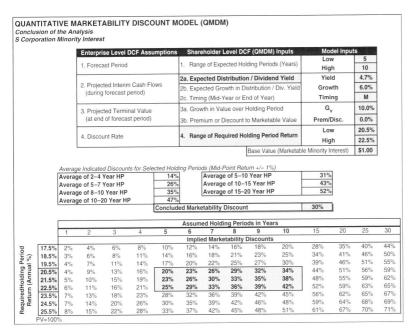

EXHIBIT 10.8 QMDM Results: S Corporation Interest

S Corporation Tax Basis Build-up										
Analysis of Benefit of Tax Savings Upon Sale					Expected Holding Period Range					
Years of Forecast	1	2	3	4	5	6	7	8	9	10
1. Pre-Tax Earnings Growing @ **6.0%**	$0.167	$0.177	$0.187	$0.199	$0.210	$0.223	$0.236	$0.251	$0.266	$0.282
Distribution Payout % **64.0%**	($0.11)	($0.11)	($0.12)	($0.13)	($0.13)	($0.14)	($0.15)	($0.16)	($0.17)	($0.18)
Retained Earnings	$0.06	$0.06	$0.07	$0.07	$0.08	$0.08	$0.09	$0.09	$0.10	$0.10
Cumulative Retained Earnings (Basis Build-Up)	$0.06	$0.12	$0.19	$0.26	$0.34	$0.42	$0.50	$0.59	$0.69	$0.79
Capital Gains Tax Savings at **15.0%**	$0.01	$0.02	$0.03	$0.04	$0.05	$0.06	$0.08	$0.09	$0.10	$0.12
Present Value Factors **21.5%**	0.823	0.677	0.558	0.459	0.378	0.311	0.256	0.211	0.173	0.143
Cumulative PV of Basis Shelter at Each Year	$0.01	$0.01	$0.02	$0.02	$0.02	$0.02	$0.02	$0.02	$0.02	$0.02
Potential Adjustment to Marketability Discount	−0.7%	−1.3%	−1.6%	−1.8%	−1.9%	−2.0%	−1.9%	−1.9%	−1.8%	−1.7%

Average Shelter for Expected Holding Period	**$0.019**	Relative to $1.00 of Marketable Minority Value
Average Potential Adjustment to Marketability Discount	**−1.9%**	Relative to otherwise concluded Marketability Discount

EXHIBIT 10.9   Analysis of S Corporation Basis Build-Up

However, we have not yet considered all of the expected cash flows from S corporation ownership. Given that this S corporation is retaining significant earnings, the tax bases of its shareholders will be increasing pro rata over the expected holding period. The benefit of the basis build-up is quantifiable, as shown in 10.9.

The table summarizes the annual retained earnings and the cumulative basis build-up. At the end of each period, the portion of the implied capital gain sheltered from taxes is calculated based on an assumed capital gains rate of 15% from the preceding example. The present value factors using the required holding period return of 21.5% are then calculated, and the present values of the cumulative basis shelter is then calculated for each potential holding period. In this case, the present value of the basis shelter is $0.019 relative to $1.00 of marketable minority value, suggesting a reduction of the marketability discount of about 2%.

Some analysts would consider a lower discount rate applicable to the tax shield, and in some jurisdictions, the blended capital gains rate exceeds 15%. Varying the discount rate down to as low as 8% and raising the capital gains rate to as much as 20% raises the calculated value of the tax shield to as much as $0.05 or $0.06. The Integrated Theory states that the value of an illiquid interest is the present value of its expected cash flows discounted to the present at an appropriate discount rate. By considering the benefit of the tax shield from basis build-up, we have considered all of the cash flows attributable to the interest.

In this case, the analyst took the benefit of the tax shield into consideration, together with all the other elements of his analysis, and concluded that the appropriate marketability discount for the S corporation interest was 30%. Recall that the concluded marketability discount for the otherwise identical C corporation was 35%. In this case, the S corporation interest was worth more than the C corporation interest. As the preceding discussion makes clear, that result was not a foregone conclusion, but was dependent on the facts and circumstances of the examples.

We have presented this example in a fashion to be able to see the impact of the S election on the value of a minority interest relative to an otherwise identical C corporation interest. In practice, appraisers value interests of tax pass-through entities based on the facts and circumstances surrounding each engagement. The QMDM provides an excellent tool for capturing the benefits and risks of the S election from the viewpoint of minority shareholders and incorporating those factors directly into the development of appraisal conclusions.

CONCLUSION

Are S corporations worth more than C corporations? Using the conceptual framework of the Integrated Theory, this question need not be so vexing for appraisers. We reproduce Exhibit 10.1 to summarize our conclusions

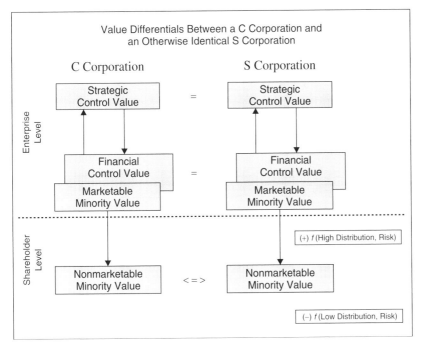

EXHIBIT 10.1 Relationship between C Corporation and S Corporation Values at Each Level of Value

regarding the valuation of S corporations at the enterprise and shareholder levels of value.

At the enterprise levels of value, there is no basis for a difference in value between S corporations and C corporations, as the potential tax benefit of the S corporation election inures to the individual shareholders rather than the enterprise. Because there is no difference in enterprise cash flows, risk, or growth prospects, there is no difference in enterprise value.

At the shareholder level of value, two conflicting factors interact to determine whether the subject minority interest in an S corporation is worth more or less than the corresponding interest in a C corporation. The potential for higher economic distributions to the S corporation shareholders suggests that the S corporation interest is worth more, while the incremental risks borne by S corporation shareholders suggests that the C corporation interest is worth more.

The resolution of the S corporation value conundrum is simpler than many assume—a focus on cash flow, risk, and growth. Professor Gordon was on to something.

Index